W9-DAP-719

TRUTH AND CONVICTION

LAW AND SOCIETY SERIES
W. Wesley Pue, General Editor

L. JANE McMILLAN

TRUTH
and Conviction

Donald Marshall Jr.
and the Mi'kmaw Quest for Justice

UBC Press • Vancouver • Toronto

© UBC Press 2018

All rights reserved. No part of this publication may be reproduced,
stored in a retrieval system, or transmitted, in any form or by any means,
without prior written permission of the publisher, or, in Canada, in the
case of photocopying or other reprographic copying, a licence from
Access Copyright, www.accesscopyright.ca.

27 26 25 24 23 22 21 20 19   5 4 3 2

Printed in Canada on FSC-certified ancient-forest-free paper
(100% post-consumer recycled) that is processed chlorine- and acid-free.

Cataloguing data is available from Library and Archives Canada.

ISBN 978-0-7748-3748-4 (hardcover)
ISBN 978-0-7748-3750-7 (epdf)
ISBN 978-0-7748-3751-4 (epub)
ISBN 978-0-7748-3752-1 (Kindle)

Canadä

UBC Press gratefully acknowledges the financial support
for our publishing program of the Government of Canada
(through the Canada Book Fund), the Canada Council for the Arts,
and the British Columbia Arts Council.

This book has been published with the help of a grant from the Canadian
Federation for the Humanities and Social Sciences, through the Awards
to Scholarly Publications Program, using funds provided by the Social
Sciences and Humanities Research Council of Canada, and with the help
of the University of British Columbia through the K.D. Srivastava Fund.

Printed and bound in Canada by Friesens
Set in DIN and Devanagari by Artegraphica Design Co. Ltd.
Copy editor: Lesley Erickson
Proofreader: Judith Earnshaw
Indexer: Judy Dunlop
Cartographer: Eric Leinberger

UBC Press
The University of British Columbia
2029 West Mall
Vancouver, BC V6T 1Z2
www.ubcpress.ca

In memory of J.R.

DONALD MARSHALL JUNIOR

Iapjiw Mikmwite'lmulten
We will always remember

CONTENTS

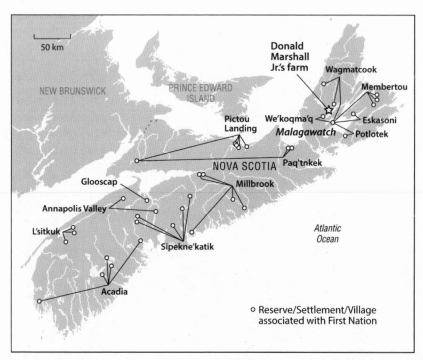

This map shows Mi'kmaw communities in Nova Scotia. The lines connecting the dots represent the current satellite lands of each community. Band lands that are adjacent to communities are not represented. All Cape Breton Bands share Malagawatch.

Membertou is Donald Marshall Jr.'s birth community. The star between Wagmatcook and We'koqma'q indicates the location of his farm. Malagawatch is where he went eel fishing and is also the location of the Grand Chief Donald Marshall Senior Aboriginal Youth Camp. The Donald Marshall Centre for Justice and Reconciliation is located in Wagmatcook.

TRUTH AND CONVICTION

Kepmite'tmnej | The Mi'kmaw Honour Song

Kepmite'tmnej ta'n teli l'nuwulti'kw
Let us greatly respect our being L'nu
Ni'kma'jtut mawita'nej
My people let us gather
Kepmite'tmnej ta'n wettapeksulti'k
Let us greatly respect our native roots
Ni'kma'jtut apoqnm atultinej
My people, let us help one another
Apoqnmatultinej ta'n Kisu'lkw teli ika'luksi'kw
Let us help one another as the Creator
wla wskitqamu way-yah-hey-yoh
intended when he put us on the earth.

Way-yoh-way-hi-yah
Way-yoh-way-yoh-way-hi-yah
Way-yoh-way-hi-yah
Way-yoh-way-hi-yah
Way-yoh-way-hi-yah
Way-yoh-way-hi-yah
Way-yoh-way-hi-yah-hay-yoh
[*VOCABLES*]

– George Paul, Metepenagiag First Nation[1]

INTRODUCTION

Donald Marshall's story is not just a cautionary tale about the criminal justice system ... and how it can and must be improved; it is also a story of grit and integrity, of not giving up, of not losing all hope. It is a story of strength and spirit, of personal and cultural endurance, of the ultimate triumph of truth over lies. It is a story Canadians should commit to memory.

– Justice Anne Derrick, "Foreword," Bill Swan's *Real Justice: Convicted for Being Mi'kmaq: The Story of Donald Marshall Jr.*

IT WAS LATE AUGUST 1991, the summer after the Kanesatake Resistance or Oka Crisis, when my mother and I set out from southern Ontario to Halifax, Nova Scotia, where I would begin my studies in marine biology. One evening, at a motel in Quebec, we settled in front of the TV to watch the single English-language station, the CBC. We ached through the darkness of a movie called *Justice Denied,* the true story of the wrongful conviction of Donald Marshall Jr. We learned that the seventeen year old had been arrested in 1971, convicted of murder, and given a life sentence. He had spent eleven years in prison for a murder he did not commit, and his wrongful prosecution had stemmed, in large part, from systemic racism in the Canadian justice system. He had been an Indigenous man in the wrong place at the wrong time and the target of police tunnel vision.[2] He had been denied a fair trial, and his ultimate acquittal in 1983 had been tainted by the same racism that had infected his prosecution.

The film recounted his prison life – days marked by riots, physical violence, inmate deaths, and substance abuse, by an escape, recapture, and numerous trips to segregation. Through it all, Donald Marshall steadfastly maintained his innocence, but he was trapped in a system that would not release him unless he confessed and showed remorse. But how can you show remorse for something you didn't do?

Donald Marshall Sr. had died on August 25, and the CBC was broadcasting *Justice Denied* to commemorate his life and passing. The news footage that followed the movie showed the grand chief's stately funeral. Members of the Grand Council and chiefs of the Mi'kmaw Nation wore regalia, amulets, and special status sashes. They walked alongside the Marshall family, who carried Donald Marshall Sr. – father, grandfather, godfather, uncle, husband. Warriors drummed and sang honour songs. The Knights of Columbus donned feathered caps and cloaks. The diversity of the participants signified the diplomatic duties of the grand chief and the many connections he had forged while navigating the social boundaries between First Nations and settler society.[3] Hundreds of community members filed through the streets of Membertou, Cape Breton Island, to honour the late chief and his family. Even though I was a stranger to Nova Scotia and the Mi'kmaq, the procession captivated me and grounded Donald Marshall Jr.'s wrongful conviction in the realities of kinship and nationhood.

Three weeks after viewing *Justice Denied*, I was listening to the blues musician Jeff Healey at the Misty Moon, a large cabaret-style venue for live acts in downtown Halifax. I met Donald that night. Following Mi'kmaw culture, in which it is customary to drop the diminutive once your namesake has died, he introduced himself as "J.R." rather than "Junior." We fell in love, and we were together for the next thirteen years. When we met, Donald had been out of prison for almost ten years, and it had been a year and a half since the royal commission into Donald's case – the Marshall Inquiry – had documented the forensic errors and entrenched racism underlying his wrongful conviction. The commission's report had become the driving force and justification for judicial reform in Nova Scotia, and the Mi'kmaw Nation had adopted its eighty-two recommendations to legitimate their claims to self-determination and reinvigorate their legal traditions.

At the time, Donald was starting to weave together the full nightmare of his wrongful conviction, and as I learned more, any faith I had in the Canadian justice system evaporated. I came to realize that the rage-infused racism – the rawness of discrimination – was far more widespread than I had ever imagined. It was ugly. It was violent. It was inhumane. I saw only a surface smear at first, one I did not understand. Soon, I was immersed in it.

The consequences of the failure of justice cannot be underestimated. Donald Marshall's wrongful conviction for murder shaped Mi'kmaw relations with the government of Nova Scotia and with Canadian society in general, and it permeated Mi'kmaw legal consciousness. The case demonstrated that Mi'kmaw mistrust was justified, that their demands for the right to control their own justice processes were vindicated. Beyond Mi'kma'ki, Donald Marshall became a well-known symbol of injustice to Indigenous people across the country and around the world.

The violence done to Donald and the Mi'kmaw Nation became poignantly apparent the year after we met, in 1992, when Donald and I attended the annual ceremony of St. Anne's Mission in Potlotek, a spiritual gathering to honour the Mi'kmaw patron saint and to celebrate the Grand Council's endurance and its role as the nation's governing body. Rather than ascending to the title and position of grand chief, Donald climbed the stage and transferred the symbols of Mi'kmaw leadership to another man.

That same year, we moved from Halifax to Cape Breton Island, to Donald's home, known as "Junior's farm," situated along the Bras D'Or Lake between two First Nations communities. I met Donald's large extended family, his incredibly vibrant mother, brothers, sisters, nieces, nephews, cousins, aunts, uncles, and friends. They generously welcomed me into their lives and are my loved ones today. On my first visit to the We'koqma'q Mi'kmaw community, I drank homebrew and ate moose meat pie with the gentlest of giants, big-hearted men and women who were living their traditions, warriors defending their rights and, far too often, just trying to survive. Increasingly absorbed in Mi'kmaw culture, I transferred universities and switched from marine biology to anthropology.

Donald and I also began to fish eels commercially. That is how we made our living. We were charged, in 1993, with catching and selling eels out of season, using improper gear, and doing it all without a licence. The case went all the way to the Supreme Court of Canada and proved to be as significant to the Mi'kmaw Nation as the royal commission. The court released its landmark decision in 1999, upholding fishing and hunting rights that the Crown and the Mi'kmaq had enshrined in the Peace and Friendship

Treaties of 1760–61. The judgment represented the Supreme Court's modern reaffirmation of the authority of treaties, the rights negotiated in good faith by the Indigenous parties to these fundamental agreements, and the Crown's duty to honour the promises it had made centuries ago. The decision revived recognition of First Nations sovereignty and self-governance and helped inspire the doctrine of reconciliation, the national project of Canada's twenty-first century.

Beyond being "Junior's Jane," I became an ally in the fight for Mi'kmaw rights. My proximity to discrimination concentrated my indignation. I spent years sitting at the kitchen table listening to Donald recount the horrors of his wrongful conviction. As the fishing case made its way through the courts, and as Donald's celebrity grew, people came to know me, trust me, and tell me their stories. Over time, Mi'kmaw teachers, with deep patience and generosity, shared their stories and revealed the conceits and treacheries of colonialism. They inspired me to fight against the systemic and daily oppressions of Indigenous peoples, to unsettle my ignorance and privilege.

Often lauded as a hero, as a champion of the underdog, Donald lived his life in the public gaze. He became a symbol of Indigenous resilience in the face of systemic racism. I spent many months with Donald in courts of law and in strategy meetings to help implement the recommendations of the Marshall Inquiry. Our work on Indigenous justice issues took us across the country. We witnessed something positive emerge out of events that were deeply painful. Donald's life and our shared experience showed the potential of applying Indigenous law to countercultural genocide.

But I saw first-hand the long-term emotional and physical effects of Donald's battle with a racialized justice system. His health took a particularly bad turn in 2002 when he required a double lung transplant to extend his life. We relocated to Toronto, where he underwent a life-saving surgery on May 5, 2003. He lived for six more years. At the time of his death, on August 6, 2009, we were no longer partners, but we remained the best of friends. At his funeral, we sang the Mi'kmaw Honour Song, "Kepmite'tmnej," as he was drummed into the ground, back to the earth.

DONALD MARSHALL'S LEGACY was acknowledged on Treaty Day, October 1, 2002, when the Mi'kmaw Nation and the Province of Nova Scotia joined together to commemorate the 250th anniversary of the signing of the 1752 Peace and Friendship Treaty.[4] Alex Denny, a grand captain of the Grand Council, spoke at the ceremony:

> The Mi'kmaw know who they are, and it is the Mi'kmaw that must not forget. A person that comes to mind is Donald Marshall Junior. Junior is without a doubt a figure that has marked our history with victories. Victory from a justice system that was blinded by racism. Victory in the form of reaffirmation of our fundamental rights as laid out by our forefathers in the treaty of 1760–61. As long as I have known Junior, not once have I seen a young man so dedicated to ensuring that we, the Mi'kmaw, do not forget the hundreds of years of pain and suffering encountered yet stay true the words penned between the Mi'kmaw Nation and the Crown.

At that time in my life, the connections between Donald's trials, tribulations, and triumphs and the resilience and revitalization of Mi'kmaw law and legal consciousness had started to come into focus. And they became clearer as I immersed myself in my studies and dedicated myself to helping bring about reconciliation through public education and dialogue. I completed a PhD in anthropology in 2003, the same year Donald underwent transplant surgery. I spent three years teaching law and society at York University and then returned to Nova Scotia to take up the Canada Research Chair in Indigenous Peoples and Sustainable Communities at St. Francis Xavier University, in the heart of Mi'kma'ki. I've since worked with Mi'kmaw bands, political organizations, justice programs, and service providers as an advocate, principal investigator, proposal writer, policy framer, research coordinator, program evaluator, participant, and board member. In the early 2000s, criminologist Don Clairmont and I managed the forensic evaluations of the Mi'kmaq Justice Institute, one of the most promising but short-lived programs to emerge from the Marshall Inquiry recommendations. Between 2013 and 2016, I also conducted an extensive community-focused review of the implementation of the Marshall Inquiry recommendations for the Mi'kmaq–Nova Scotia–Canada Tripartite Forum.

Looking back, I realized that Donald's personal experiences had proved to be important historical moments that spurred cultural productivity in Mi'kma'ki. By locking Donald up for a crime he didn't commit and then convicting him for exercising his treaty rights, the Canadian justice system – and, by extension, the larger settler society – had threatened valued components of Mi'kmaw culture, law, and rights. However terrible the price, Donald's experiences with the Canadian criminal justice system have fostered significant changes in the way Mi'kmaq understand and express their legal identities and cultural practices. The Marshall Inquiry and the Marshall decision gave the Mi'kmaq what they needed to justify their demands for decolonization, for their own justice system based on their own laws. This book retraces the steps of Donald's personal journey and the Mi'kmaw quest for justice. It brings to light the obstacles that the Mi'kmaq encountered as they went head to head with the provincial and federal governments and with justice officials in their pursuit of community-based, culturally oriented, and decolonizing justice programs. It's a story of colonial oppression, resistance, and resilience, presented in the hope that it will help arrest five hundred years of cultural genocide by fostering a fuller awareness among Canadians and others of the consequences of imposing a foreign system of justice on Indigenous communities.

As an applied anthropologist, I'm interested in Indigenous law and legal principles. What impact did colonization have on those principles? And what are the challenges of revitalizing and institutionalizing Indigenous law in Canada today? Most importantly, will a pluralized legal system (that is, a system that allows for the application of multiple systems within one geographic region, nation, or population) help counter cultural genocide and improve access to justice for Indigenous people? The events that followed the wrongful conviction of Donald Marshall and the effect they had on Mi'kmaw legal consciousness suggest that it will.

At its simplest, *legal consciousness* refers to what people do and say about law, and legal consciousness changes over time. How do people participate in the law and interpret the law? Do they think it's fair, or do they think it should be amended? Does everyone agree, or are certain expressions of legal consciousness contested? How do people express their beliefs, and what form does their acquiescence or resistance take? The experiences of individuals such as Donald Marshall (individuals who belong to groups dominated by settler society) and expressions of Mi'kmaw legal consciousness tell us what is working and what isn't working; they tell us which legal and extralegal methods of social control are valued and which are reviled. They reveal openings where the revitalization of Indigenous legal principles could put First Nations such as the Mi'kmaq on the pathway to self-determination.

Truth and Conviction opens with a retelling of Donald's story of wrongful conviction and imprisonment based on the stories he shared with me and other sources. It's important to relive these events because reconciliation, as defined by the Truth and Reconciliation Commission of Canada (which released its calls to action and final report in 2015), is a "process of healing relationships that requires public truth sharing, apology, and commemoration that acknowledge and redress past harms." Accounts of the royal commission and its recommendations are followed by an examination of Mi'kmaw hopes and dreams, in the form of an exploration of the legal traditions (*L'nuwey Tplutaqn*) they hope to revitalize. The challenges of launching Mi'kmaw justice initiatives such as the Mi'kmaq Justice Institute and implementing the commission's eighty-two recommendations helped revitalize Mi'kmaw law even as they revealed seismic fault lines in our justice system, including a deeply rooted lack of political will and capacity when it comes to redressing historical wrongs. The provincial and federal governments responded to Mi'kmaw enthusiasm and innovations with a disappointing focus on administrative fixes.

Donald's search for a livelihood following his release, our charges and his conviction for illegal fishing, and the repercussions of the Supreme Court's Marshall decision set the stage for telling the parallel story of Mi'kmaw attempts to implement their treaty rights on their own terms and manage their own legal affairs through traditional processes such as sentencing and justice circles. In 2000, Donald participated in the first justice circle to deal with a breach of federal fishing regulations. Six years later, he participated in a healing circle (this time as the wrongdoer) after being charged with uttering threats and dangerous driving. Descriptions of these two events reveal the promise of restorative justice in Indigenous communities.

The story, at least in this book, ends with a portrait of Mi'kmaw legal consciousness today, based on the research I conducted on behalf of the Mi'kmaw Nation for the twenty-fifth anniversary review of the implementation of the Marshall Inquiry recommendations. That research also assessed the potential of the Truth and Reconciliation Commission, particularly its calls to change the justice landscape for Indigenous peoples.

With few exceptions, advocates of legal reform, regardless of whether they are Indigenous or non-Indigenous, believe that the revitalization of traditional justice principles will help correct systemic racism in our justice system. But what are "traditional" justice practices? If we adopt an ethnographic approach to decolonizing justice, as I do, then we must accept that Indigenous cultures are not, nor have they ever been, static and homogenous. They have been caught up in conflicts and power struggles both internal and external that have produced multiple expressions of legal consciousness since the beginning of time and often within the same nation or group, depending on how they experienced colonialism. Who, today, gets to decide what is or isn't traditional? This is a complex and highly contested question, and Indigenous justice is a complex and politically charged area of inquiry. In Nova Scotia, the legal experiences of the Mi'kmaq have been shaped by broad cultural contexts such as oral traditions and cosmology, by colonization and discriminatory legislation, by treaty and residential school litigation, and by the wrongful prosecution of Donald Marshall Jr.

Arresting five hundred years of cultural genocide depends on a fuller awareness of the consequences of imposing a foreign system of justice on Indigenous communities. By educating ourselves – all Canadians – on the principles and cultural values of Indigenous legal traditions and customary law, we can generate an affirmative approach to social equity, dispute management, and the overrepresentation of Indigenous peoples in the criminal justice system.

1

Meki o'pla'lusnaq | A Great Wrong
The Wrongful Conviction

DONALD MARSHALL JR. met Sandford or "Sandy" Seale, the black youth he would be accused and convicted of murdering, by chance just before midnight on the evening of May 28, 1971, in Wentworth Park in Sydney, Nova Scotia. The two boys were both seventeen years old, and they knew each other, but not well. Seale was heading home after trying to get into a sold-out dance at St. Joseph's Parish. Donald was looking for friends in the park to party with after work. He had been paid but had not yet cashed his cheque.

The youths encountered two men. The older of the two, Roy Ebsary, called them over and asked for a cigarette. He wore a long, dark cloak and claimed to be a priest from Manitoba. The two men said they were looking for bootleggers and women. Following a brief exchange in which one man said, "We don't like niggers or Indians," Ebsary became enraged, pulled a knife from his cloak, stabbed Seale in the abdomen, and screamed, "This is for you, black man."[1] Ebsary then turned on Donald and slashed his arm with the knife. Donald ran for help while Ebsary and the second man, Jimmy MacNeil, ran to Ebsary's home, which was located nearby. Seale lay wounded on the ground.

As he ran from the park, Donald encountered Maynard Chant. He told him and a couple walking by about the stabbing. A former RCMP officer overheard the conversation and called the police. Donald and Chant returned to the park to tend to Seale. By then, others in the park had discovered Seale and asked Donald to call for help. He went to a nearby home, explained the situation, and showed the residents his wounded arm. The homeowner called an ambulance and the police. Donald waved down the police as they approached. He gave one of the officers, Constable Dean, descriptions of Ebsary and MacNeil. Constable Dean passed the information on to his partner, Constable Walsh, and then took Donald to the hospital. An ambulance took Seale to Emergency, where he underwent surgery.

Meanwhile, Chant hitchhiked to his home, forty kilometres away in Louisburg. His first ride dropped him near the St. Joseph Parish dance, which had just ended. The Sydney City Police were breaking up drunken fights, and when they saw Chant's bloodied shirt, they picked him up. Once they heard he had been in the park where the stabbing had taken place, they took him to the hospital for questioning. But Officer MacDonald, who was in charge of the investigation and stationed at the hospital, didn't bother to take a statement on the grounds that Chant had not been in the park at the time of the stabbing.

After being stitched up by the doctor, Donald was told he could go home. On the way out, he saw Chant speaking with a detective. Another officer asked Donald to go with him to the lobby, where two suspects were being held. Marshall confirmed that they were not the two men who had confronted the boys in the park. Two other officers, Constables Mroz and Walsh, armed with Marshall's description, searched the park for the suspects. Other officers joined in the search but found nothing. Chant was sent to the police station to wait for his father to pick him up, and the police drove Donald to his home in Membertou. News of the stabbing had spread quickly, and Marshall again told the story of meeting Ebsary and MacNeil in the park. Later that night, he and his cousin rode their bikes to the scene of the crime to search for evidence. They found no sign of the knife, Roy Ebsary, or Jimmy MacNeil.

At the request John MacIntyre, the sergeant of detectives, Donald agreed to spend the next day at the police station. He hoped to identify Ebsary and MacNeil if they were brought in. There were no leads, no weapon, and no other eyewitnesses. Sandy Seale died from his injuries that same day, May 29, at 8 p.m. It was now a murder investigation, and MacIntyre took charge.

On Sunday, May 30, MacIntyre asked Donald to view a lineup of possible suspects. Six of the seven men were young, even though Donald had described the man who stabbed Seale as older. The murderer was not among them. MacIntyre asked Donald to stay close to the station in case he was needed, but in reality MacIntyre had already informed the RCMP (the provincial police force in Nova Scotia) that Donald was a suspect. The RCMP, in turn, telexed headquarters, in Halifax, identifying Donald as the prime suspect, even though MacIntyre had yet to interview or take a statement from a single witness, including the only eyewitness – Donald Marshall.

JOHN MACINTYRE WAS an old-school cop: power and a badge. He was a large man, fiercely independent and ambitious, and he had received no law enforcement training before joining the Sydney City Police. Assigned to the investigative branch in 1950, he made detective sergeant in 1955 and sergeant of detectives in 1966.

Donald Marshall Jr. was well known to MacIntyre and the Sydney City Police and had become a special target of MacIntyre's wrath. MacIntyre disliked Donald, and the feeling of mistrust was mutual. Donald and his buddies often amused themselves by hanging out in parks and by going to dances, where they drank, fought, and generally got up to no good. The cops had chased them back to the reserve on numerous occasions, and Donald, by the time he was sixteen, had served several short stints in county jail for liquor offences. Unlike Roy Ebsary, however, who had a reputation for violence and had been convicted on a weapons charge involving a knife, Donald had no record for violent behaviour. But Donald, unlike Ebsary, was constantly under surveillance, and MacIntyre had come to believe that Donald and his friends had vandalized his family's headstones at Holy Cross Cemetery.

Donald, or Junior, as he was known to his friends, was born on September 13, 1953. He was the eldest son of thirteen children and connected to large extended families on both his mother's and father's sides. His father, Donald Marshall Sr., was the grand chief of the Mi'kmaw Nation. As grand chief, he travelled frequently within the seven traditional districts of the Mi'kmaw Nation in Atlantic Canada, carrying out his customary cultural, spiritual, and political roles. Well regarded by some people in settler communities, Grand Chief Marshall operated a relatively successful drywall business, had ties to the Knights of Columbus, and played in bowling and baseball leagues. Junior's mother, Caroline Googoo, from We'koqma'q, was a dedicated homemaker, devout Catholic, and skilled basket weaver. She worked as a cleaner at the hospital in Sydney and in the homes of its wealthy residents. Donald grew up in a loving, hardworking, Mi'kmaw-speaking home.

At the time of his birth, the Sydney Reserve was composed mostly of small plywood shacks that could be accessed only by a single dirt road. Over time, small, overcrowded homes replaced the shacks, but there were few basic amenities – no sidewalks or streetlights. Some households lacked electricity and water.[2] Even though the reserve was renamed Membertou (Mawpiltu in Mi'kmaw) after the leader of the Mi'kmaw Nation in the sixteenth and seventeenth centuries, a great warrior and *puoinaq* (spiritually powerful healer), the reserve was poor beyond any standard. The people who lived there were isolated socially, culturally, and physically from mainstream Nova Scotia society. Mandatory curfews and laws prohibiting Indigenous peoples from voting, purchasing liquor, or playing pool kept people at home and on the reserve. It wasn't until the 1960s that Membertou residents began frequenting city bars and attending local dances.

In the early 1970s, when Donald was a teenager, only 350 people lived on the reserve. Small tuck shops sold tobacco and candy but not much else. And there were few employment opportunities either in Membertou or in Sydney, a city of thirty thousand. Shopping, going to a movie, or buying a bottle of wine took on different meanings for Mi'kmaq who had to travel to the city and then navigate the overt racism of the people who lived there.[3] Racial slurs based on stereotypes marked exchanges between the Mi'kmaq and working-class townsfolk.

Sydney City Police officers reinforced the divisions. Many Mi'kmaq experienced intense surveillance, coercive force, racial profiling, and physical abuse at their hands. A resident of Membertou recalled his encounters with the police during the 1970s: "They always told us to get back to [the] reservation. When we went to dances, for example, they did not say it politely either. They would say, 'Get back to your reserves, you goddamn Indians.'"[4]

Relations were hostile during Donald's adolescence in the 1960s and '70s, decades when townsfolk and the police continued to view Mi'kmaq as a dangerous, lawless underclass.[5] The police conducted what the locals called "roundups" on the reserve. They picked up adults with unpaid fines, most frequently resulting from charges of causing disturbance, and took them to the county jail. Mi'kmaw youth sometimes made a game of tormenting the police, often resulting in chases. There was an expectation of violence, of being caught. When there was trouble between a settler white and a Mi'kmaw, it was the Mi'kmaw who got the blame. The white person went home; the Mi'kmaw went to jail.

While Donald had frequent run-ins with the police, Sandy Seale was a promising athlete from a prominent black family that was friendly with MacIntyre. Seale's death devastated Donald, but he was cautioned by friends not to attend the funeral, as the killer was still at large. He went, instead, to the funeral home to pay his respects. Seale's brother John shook hands with Donald, and they both expressed their hope that the killer would soon be found.

DONALD MARSHALL JR. was charged with Sanford Seale's murder on June 4, 1971. He was only seventeen years old, and he was not granted bail. Years later, the public inquiry into the police investigation and arrest would show that MacIntyre's investigation had focused on pressuring three youths – Maynard Chant, John Pratico, and Patricia Harriss – into giving false statements to incriminate Donald. Chant was only fourteen years old and on probation. The second witness, John Pratico, was a mentally unstable sixteen year old who would later be diagnosed as a self-aggrandizing fantasist. Neither had been in the park at the time of the stabbings.

Donald Marshall is led by police after being arrested for the murder of Sandy Seale.
The Canadian Press/Cape Breton Post

The police made no effort to corroborate Donald's account, and they dismissed any evidence that did. When legitimate witnesses came forward on their own initiative, MacIntyre ignored evidence of Donald's innocence because it contradicted his inculpatory storyline. When two men came forward independently and described seeing Ebsary and MacNeil in the park, their statements were dismissed as irrelevant and not added to the police file. Other than the false accounts of Chant and Pratico, there was no other evidence directly connecting Donald to the crime. It was enough for the police.

The third critical witness, Patricia Harriss, spoke to the police in mid-June, a few weeks after Donald's arrest. Harriss was fourteen and in grade 7. She told the police that she had spoken to Donald Marshall Jr. near the park on May 28, the night of the murder. She said Marshall had been in the company of two men whose descriptions matched those of Ebsary and MacNeil. She did not mention seeing Sandy Seale. Before signing her statement, one that clearly confirmed much of Donald's account, MacIntyre took over the questioning, which lasted for several hours. No parent was present. Harriss felt alone and under duress. Exhausted from the ordeal, she signed a statement at 1:20 a.m. on June 18 placing Donald and Seale together at the time of the murder. The statement omitted any mention of the two other men.

When Harriss later told her mother about the false statement and the circumstances of its coercion, her mother retained a lawyer. The lawyer simply advised them to go to court and tell the truth. In court, however, Harriss felt she had no choice but to maintain the fabricated portions of the story that had satisfied the police.

DONALD'S PRELIMINARY INQUIRY took place over two days on July 5 and July 28, 1971. The Crown prosecutor, Donald C. MacNeil, was a man whom the Nova Scotia Human Rights Commission had censured for comments made in open court about "lawlessness among Indians and the need to teach them respect for the law."[6] Maynard Chant, John Pratico, and Patricia Harriss all lied on the stand. Donald was committed to trial by jury in the Nova Scotia Supreme Court and taken back to jail.

Less than three months later, on November 2, 1971, Donald was arraigned before Justice Dubinsky and a jury. At the time, residents of Membertou Reserve were systematically excluded from jury duty because the rolls included only those who owned property. Reserve land was held by the Crown and set aside for the use and benefit of treaty nations. The jury that tried and ultimately convicted Donald – ostensibly a jury of his peers – was composed of twelve persons, all white, all men.

Donald suffered other disadvantages. His first language was Mi'kmaw, but the trial was conducted in English. Moreover, as a result of his socialization and upbringing, he did not understand or share Canadian society's culturally coded expectations of courtroom decorum. He did not have access to the rules of behaviour or knowledge of Western norms prescribing appropriate conduct. Clearly intimidated, he appeared unengaged in the courtroom. However, from his perspective, he was showing deference by keeping his head down and avoiding eye contact throughout the proceedings. Donald had no experience in criminal court, trusted his lawyers, and remained silent on their advice. He was shy, soft-spoken, afraid and, most importantly, innocent of the crime with which he had been charged. He understood that he had been set up, but he had a naive and ultimately misplaced faith that the legal process would vindicate him.

When John Pratico, one of MacIntyre's key youth witnesses, took the stand, he claimed that he had seen Donald stab Sandy Seale in the park. Pratico had been drunk on the night of the murder and was released from a psychiatric institution just nine days before he took the stand. While Maynard Chant was testifying, Pratico met Donald's father in the court-house hallway and told the grand chief that his son had not killed Sandy Seale. When Marshall Sr. asked Donald's defence counsel, Simon Khattar and Moe Rosenblum, to come out of the courtroom, Pratico repeated his claim. Khattar got a sheriff to witness the recant, and the sheriff sent for the Crown prosecutor and MacIntyre. Pratico admitted in front of all these people that he had, in fact, not seen Donald stab Sandy Seale. Everyone advised Pratico to tell the truth, but the Crown prosecutor cautioned him about the penalties for perjury. Rather than believing Pratico, the police and the Crown prosecutor assumed that Donald's Mi'kmaw friends had coerced Pratico into changing his testimony.[7] Indeed, prior to the trial, Tom Christmas, Donald's close friend, had been charged with obstruction of justice for confronting Pratico about his lies and urging him to tell the truth. Christmas was subsequently sentenced to two years for breaking and entering. He was not called as a witness.[8] The Crown prosecutor, in his investigation, should have interviewed the witnesses who had given con-tradictory statements and disclosed the inconsistent statements to the court, but he did not.

Back in court, Justice Dubinsky's interpretation of the Canada Evidence Act, particularly section 11, "cross-examination as to previous oral state-ments," prevented the court from thoroughly examining Pratico's dramatic about-face.[9] Although, the law allows generous scope in cross-examining witnesses in order to reveal inconsistencies in their testimonies, neither the defence nor the prosecution had an opportunity to explore the reasons for Pratico's conflicting statements. When the Crown tried to introduce evi-dence of what Pratico had said outside the courtroom, the trial judge refused to permit it, and the Crown did not insist, chalking up the recant to witness intimidation. In cross-examination, when the defence raised his statement, the Crown objected. The judge denied a thorough cross-examination of the recant and silenced Pratico's truth.[10]

Justice Dubinsky also directed the jurors to accept the credibility of the Crown witnesses because, he asked, What motive could they have for blaming Donald if he was innocent? He improperly allowed a reference to a tattoo on Donald's arm that read "I hate cops," and he permitted Sandy Seale's parents to be called as witnesses. The trial judge's accumulative errors were so fundamental that a new trial should have been the inevitable result of any appeal, but both the Crown and defence failed to raise them. In the absence of these objections, and given that Practico's statement outside the courtroom was not entered into evidence, Donald was convicted of non-capital murder and sentenced to life in prison.

Crown Prosecutor MacNeil commended the city of Sydney's police for their "long hours of hard work, day and night" to bring the case to court. He described the efforts of the Detective Division as "brilliant."[11]

WHEN HE HEARD the verdict, Jimmy MacNeil, Roy Ebsary's companion in the park that fateful night, was overcome by guilt. He came forward ten days later and told the police that he had witnessed Roy Ebsary murder Sandy Seale. Although his statement corroborated Donald's, the police made no effort to determine if MacNeil was telling the truth. While Donald awaited transfer to the federal penitentiary to serve his life sentence, MacIntyre interviewed Jimmy MacNeil; Roy Ebsary; Mary Ebsary, Roy Ebsary's common-law wife; and Greg, their son. But he did not interview Ebsary's daughter, Donna, who had watched her father wash blood off a knife in the kitchen sink on the night of the murder. Neither MacIntyre nor the Crown brought Donald in to identify Ebsary, even though he was still close by at the local county jail, nor did they search Ebsary's house for the murder weapon.

Sydney City Police and the Department of the Attorney General asked the RCMP to examine Jimmy MacNeil's allegations, but the RCMP failed to investigate the declaration thoroughly and discounted the claim. Inspector

Alan Marshall did not conduct interviews with anyone – not with Donald, Jimmy MacNeil, trial witnesses, or members of the Mi'kmaw community. He did not even speak to Roy Ebsary. Instead, he relied only on sources directed to him by MacIntyre, who, having got his conviction, had a vested interest in controlling the case. Without thoroughly reviewing the case, Inspector Marshall concluded that Donald Marshall had stabbed Sandy Seale.

The miscarriages of justice continued. The police failed to disclose to anyone outside of law enforcement that Jimmy MacNeil had come forward with new and potentially important information. When Donald's lawyer, Moe Rosenblum, launched an appeal, he didn't know that Jimmy MacNeil had identified Roy Ebsary as the murderer and that the RCMP had reinvestigated the case, nor was this information disclosed to the inexperienced Halifax Crown counsel handling the appeal. On September 8, 1972, the Nova Scotia Supreme Court dismissed the appeal, and Donald's world was collapsed into a prison cell with no key.

Three years later, Donna Ebsary summoned the courage to come forward and tell the police that she had seen her father washing blood from a knife on the night of the murder. By then, MacIntyre was chief of police and officially off the case. The new sergeant of detectives, William Urquhart, a man who had worked with MacIntyre on the original investigation, chose not to take a statement from her. From the perspective of the police, the case was closed.

2

Melgwisgat | Nightmare
Prison and Freedom

DONALD WAS TRANSFERRED from the county jail in Sydney to Dorchester Penitentiary in New Brunswick, far away from his family. He became inmate number 1997. Receiving a life sentence was like being told he had a terminal illness.[1] The maximum-security prison was a horror show. Years later and in countless conversations, Donald described to me the mania of the place – the noise, the stench, the violence, the drugs, the gang rapes, and the constant fear. Trust was not part of prison life. It was fatal for inmates to let their guard down. They ate alone in their cells. One of his worst memories was the feeling of utter violation he had experienced when wardens repeatedly strip searched him and told him to bend over and spread.

Donald's family visited when they could. But the grand chief and his wife depleted their savings and had to borrow from others to make the long journey. The dry-walling business suffered, as did the family in numerous ways. Crank calls forced them to change their telephone number, which further damaged the business. Donald's father persevered in his duties as grand chief, but he had difficulty facing his people because they thought his son was a murderer. The stigma was overwhelming. Donald, the eldest

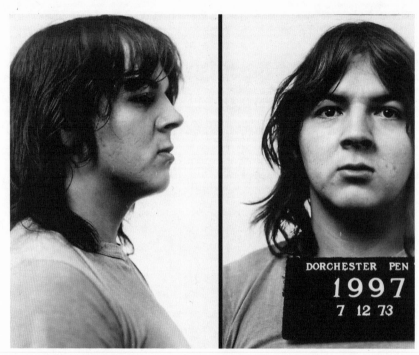

Donald Marshall was known as prisoner 1997 at Dorchester Penitentiary in 1973.

boy, watched from behind bars his younger brothers and sisters grow up – another layer of torture for the close-knit family.

Donald spent the next decade being transferred between Dorchester Penitentiary and Springhill Institution, a medium-security facility in Nova Scotia. Every intake process required another assertion of innocence. But his time at Springhill was less isolating, and the facility was closer to home. Dorchester, in contrast, housed dangerous criminals, and violent attacks among inmates happened often. He toughened up. A full-scale riot broke out while Donald was inside. The outbreak scarred him and contributed to post-traumatic stress and flashbacks that plagued him throughout his life.

Donald passed the years by doing his best to cope with paralyzing boredom. He trained to become a plumber and bonded with his instructor, Arnold Estrabrooks. He played sports, ran a canteen, kept a pet bird, went to school, tried to get his case reheard, applied for escorted and unescorted passes, and worked with the Indian Brotherhood to advocate for prisoners' rights. Selected by his peers, he served various roles on the executive of the Brotherhood for eight years. The Brotherhood organized social gatherings and events during family visits. The inmates were awarded a grant from Indian Affairs to make and sell arts and crafts, and Donald supported other cultural practices in prison.

Beyond these activities, Donald sometimes wrote poetry:

TAKE MY HAND

The sky turns dark and the stars appear;
It's time for me to think of the one I love.
As I sit here with no one to hold my hand;
My heart gets weak as I fight to hold back the tears that rush down my face.
And I ask God to set me free, so I can be with the one I love.
But it seems my prayers never reach that great man above;
Someday I only hope these prayers of mine will be answered;
So someone may soon take my hand and lead me
Forever, away from these Prison walls.

JUNIOR MARSHALL
Dorchester Pen.[2]

Over the years, Donald wrote hundreds of letters to family, friends, girlfriends, and pen pals. An early letter, written from Dorchester on Christmas Eve 1973, expresses his sense of loneliness and isolation:

Hi Kid, Just a few lines to say that I want to go home. Gee, I hope you don't get mad at me because I wrote. I'm writing to you because I'm homesick and lonely, so I want to hear from some of my friends, that's if I have any left … it's pretty boring in here but I guess I'll have to take it until I get my new trial which is supposed to come up in February. I think if I can't beat it this time, I wouldn't know what to do. String myself. Ha … Well I got to go to church pretty soon. Mid-night mass that is. Hey man, I hope you don't turn me down because I wanna hear from you and it took me six months to get your address little friend. P.S. Don't be like my other friends ok – write to me.[3]

Donald took up extensive correspondence with a woman named Hazel, whose ministry provided spiritual and emotional counselling for inmates. They wrote to each other for years. His letters tell of his harrowing experiences, worries for his family, desire for revenge, dreams of freedom, and his exhaustion at having his declarations of innocence unheeded.

January 14, 1979

Dear Hazel,

Sorry for not writing sooner but I'm just getting settled down. I had a few problems with my caseworker but the little talk I had with him helped me. I really don't know what they want from me. I am trying my best to get out of here but I can't see an opening yet. No, I didn't have a visit at xmas because of the weather … I got warned today about hockey. I've been into a few fights and they don't like it. I thought it over and I'll try and play better okay … I've been thinking about my murder case. It really bothers me knowing that I was put in here and being forgotten by the people that put me in here. It really hurts to know something like that. Maybe I am stubborn but there isn't a man around that will put me down again. It hurts so much. If they were interested I would have been out long ago. I got this far without them and I think I could do it on my own. Well how's everything with you? Good I hope. I don't have much more to say so I'll tip my rose to a close. Until I hear from you. So you take care and I'll be thinking of you.

Love Friend Always, Junior.[4]

February 27, 1980

Dear Hazel,

Sorry for not writing but things haven't been going my way the last couple of months. But I'll have it sorted out soon. I was transferred to Dorchester 3 weeks ago and I should be heading back to Springhill Monday. I have to wait for an answer from the Transfer

Board. I was already up on one and they wanna send me back. The reason for sending me up here was because a few people didn't want me in Springhill. They said I'm getting away with too much and I know everything that goes on in the place. Man, I've been there almost 6 years. I gotta know some things. They figure I am getting out soon and they are getting in the way to keep me in prison. Well I've been taking it pretty cool so that doesn't give them too much to throw at my face when I get back. People are so deadly; it scares me because I hate being hurt. They don't understand all they wanna do is play with a guy's mind. The only way a guy avoids it is just to laugh. If he doesn't he is a fool to fall in their stupid trap. I fell in it before! I'm just going to sit back and see what they are up to … A guy got stabbed here today. This place is some wild. I'm glad I am going back [to Springhill] …

Love Friend Jr.

March 29, 1981

Dear Hazel,

Just received your letter and it was nice hearing from you. I'm doing pretty good and I'll be heading back to Springhill in 3 or 4 weeks. My father was up to visit me; I called for him because I don't want them to worry about me. As this place isn't a playhouse. Three guys already got stabbed since I've been back. A guy has to watch himself in here and I am trying my best to do that. Well it was an experience coming back here because it gives me more strength to realize prison isn't the life for anyone. Hey kid, don't worry about me losing my good feelings and attitudes. I feel a lot better than I did before. I know it is up to me to do the climbing Hazel and thanks for reminding me. That's just what I will do. I only have 13 months for parole. That's just like climbing because I start out with 120 months … I'm going to stay pretty low when I get back to Springhill. I'm not gonna give them any rope to hang me again. I got a good chance on getting out next year so I'll work hard for it. I promise you that because you are the one that really helped me. Thanks for letting me know that I've been faithful to you. Is Bolivia overseas? I'll miss you but you keep in touch okay. Well I'll let you go now. So take care and write soon. Here is a poem I wrote for you and it's hard to find someone like you!

Love Friend Junior.

Miraculously, Donald learned to survive. The experience haunted him for the rest of his life. Throughout his incarceration, he adamantly maintained his innocence, but his steadfast unwillingness to confess to a crime he did not commit cost him parole eligibility because he could not prove that he had been rehabilitated. He learned that case workers view indications of remorse, in the form of acknowledgment of responsibility, as the first step towards rehabilitation and renunciation of the offending criminal conduct. They view those who maintain their innocence as more dangerous, as being of greater risk to the community and prone to recidivism. If he were paid a dollar for every time they called him a liar, he would have been very rich.

In their reports, his case workers expressed their frustration with his failure to come to terms with his crime and put it down to a moral failing on his part. His requests for passes and parole were consistently and soul crushingly denied. The pass procedure relied on community assessments to determine an inmate's fitness for release. In Donald's case, "the community" included members of the Sydney City Police – John MacIntyre and William Urquhart. Both men unswervingly gave negative appraisals, claiming Marshall was "highly likely" to reoffend. They did not grant him permission to attend his grandmother's funeral. Seeing that his good behaviour would not be rewarded, Donald went through rough periods of drug use and fighting, and he was punished with numerous long stretches in solitary confinement, in the segregation unit known as "the hole."

Donald was eventually permitted to attend two supervised wilderness survival camps for offenders. The first camp went without incident, and Donald welcomed the break from the confinement of prison cells. It had been years since he could watch a sunrise outside and bathe in privacy. Near the end of the second outing, feeling trapped in the system and without hope that his innocence would ever set him free, he decided to escape. When the vehicle carrying the inmates stopped for gas and coffee on its way back to prison, he made a run for it while the guard filled the tank. The news bulletin read: "RCMP in Truro, Nova Scotia, say 26 year old Donald Marshall, a convicted murderer, escaped custody at Alma near New Glasgow when he overpowered guards and sprinted into the woods. Marshall was being returned from Musquodoboit Harbour when the escape occurred. The RCMP says Marshall was considered dangerous."[5] There was no dramatic overpowering of the guard – Donald simply slipped into the woods when no one was looking.

Donald enjoyed three days of freedom with a girlfriend, who let his mother know he was safe. His mother, not wanting the police to kill Donald when they tried to capture him, notified the RCMP of his whereabouts. The police surrounded the residence and confronted him with their weapons drawn. He offered no resistance and was returned to Springhill and placed in solitary confinement. The following month, he was sentenced to four months, consecutive to his life term, for being unlawfully at large. His presentence report described him as a good worker who alternated between serving exemplary time and experiencing setbacks: "Marshall has really not accepted his guilt for his offence and claims now this recent incident was a means to get his day in court."[6]

Donald demanded that his case be reviewed so he could prove his innocence. His efforts were fruitless. He applied for another leave of absence and was again denied. He was transferred back to Dorchester, where a guard had just been killed and the prison was in chaos. Despite promises of early parole if he confessed, Donald maintained his innocence. When he was eligible for full parole in 1981, he tried to get transferred to a farm camp. When that failed, he tried to get transferred back to Springhill, but his former case workers declined the request, saying he needed to "deal with his murderous side." Depression suffocated him.

Then the stars aligned. During a visit with his girlfriend, Shelly Sarson, and her brother Mitchell, Donald was asked if he knew a man named Roy Ebsary. Shelly's brother had lived at Ebsary's house while he was going to school, and Ebsary had admitted to him that he had "killed a black guy and stabbed an Indian in the park in 1971."[7] Donald now had the name and location of Sandy Seale's murderer.

Donald immediately called Membertou for help. The first person he reached was Roy Gould, who had been chief when Donald was wrongly convicted. Gould, a strong ally, had been advocating on Donald's behalf for over a decade and was then director of communications for *Micmac News*. Gould told Danny Paul of the Union of Nova Scotia Indians to go to the police and give a statement. Inspector Urquhart took the statement and turned it over to the Crown Prosecutor's Office. The union retained thirty-one-year-old Stephen Aronson to be Donald's lawyer. Thankfully, Aronson stepped up to the plate as a lawyer of last resort, surmounted his concerns that Mitchell Sarson and Donald Marshall had colluded, and gave everything he had personally and professionally to the burden of reversing a ten-year-old conviction.

Meanwhile, when Donald applied for an unescorted pass to go home for Christmas, Chief MacIntyre once again strongly opposed the request on the grounds that Donald was at high risk to reoffend. Donald spent his tenth Christmas behind bars.

In January, Donald wrote to Roy Ebsary and asked him to come forward with information regarding the murder of Sandy Seale. After meeting with Donald, reviewing the trial materials, and ascertaining the basis of conviction and assessing the likelihood of parole, Aronson sent MacIntyre a letter asking him to reopen the investigation. MacIntyre asked the RCMP to investigate the new allegations. Harry Wheaton and Jim Carroll of the General Investigation Section began an inspection of the case. Maynard Chant gave a statement that he had lied and had not been in the park when Seale was stabbed. Ebsary phoned Wheaton and confessed to the stabbing. Analysis of physical evidence recovered from Ebsary's home revealed that fibres on one of the knives matched the jackets worn by Donald Marshall and Sandy Seale on May 28, 1971.

Wheaton and Carroll interviewed Donald at Dorchester Penitentiary on February 18 and March 9, 1982. They were less skeptical of his innocence but still sought an explanation for his involvement, implying that he had likely done something nefarious in the park that night. The officers told Donald that if he was to have any hope of getting out of prison, he had to tell them a story they could believe. Knowing full well that the prison system required admitting guilt to something, even if untrue, Donald complied and gave them a story that he thought would corroborate Ebsary's version of events, which he knew (from Mitchell Sarson) involved him and Sandy Seale trying to rob Ebsary. They took a written statement from Donald.

In his report of March 12, 1982, Wheaton stated that he had discovered that Maynard Chant, John Pratico, and Patricia Harriss had lied under pressure from the Sydney City Police. Wheaton concluded, "After reviewing this case, I feel that Marshall is innocent of the offence and that we presently have enough evidence to support a *prima facie* case against Ebsary for the murder of Seale." An official from the Nova Scotia Department of the Attorney General prevented the RCMP from investigating the actions of John MacIntyre and William Urquhart.

After eleven years in penitentiaries – isolated from his family, his culture, and his community – Donald's tenacious efforts to prove himself innocent had finally paid off. On March 30, 1982, with the unwavering help of Stephen Aronson, Donald Marshall Jr. was released from Dorchester Penitentiary on day parole to Carleton Centre in Halifax, Nova Scotia. At the centre, which was a community correctional facility, Donald met Jack Stewart, who helped inmates transition into regular society. While in prison, Donald's sole focus had been on getting someone to believe his innocence; he never accepted his life sentence and had done none of the exit planning. According to Stewart, "He came out more ill-prepared than any other lifer I've taken out … It was frustrating … It was scary."[8] To help with the transition, Donald was allowed to participate in Indigenous baseball tournaments. He was a highly skilled left-handed pitcher who could have played A-level ball. Donald was also permitted to attend St. Anne's Mission in Chapel Island. More than anything, Donald simply wanted his innocence publicly affirmed so he could get on with his life and experience all that he had been denied for eleven years. But he was not yet free.

WHILE ON PAROLE and still an inmate at Carleton Centre, steps were taken towards an acquittal. Stephen Aronson informed the federal justice minister of the day, Jean Chrétien, of his intention to apply for relief and seek an acquittal. A pardon, he argued, would be wholly insufficient in this case and might give the impression that his client was being forgiven for committing a criminal act. Upon review of the RCMP's investigation, the case was referred to the Nova Scotia Court of Appeal on June 16, 1982, and a special reference was held under section 617b (today, section 690b) of the Criminal Code.

With Stephen Aronson as his counsel, Donald faced a five-judge panel headed by MacKeigan, a man who had defended Justice Dubinsky's erroneous handling of the original case. MacKeigan refused to hear evidence of the police bullying that had led to the perjured testimonies of the three witnesses, John Pratico, Maynard Chant, and Patricia Harriss. Complicating matters further, one of the other panel members, Justice Leonard Pace, had been the attorney general of Nova Scotia during the first trial, a blatant conflict of interest.

The court addressed only one question: Had Donald Marshall Jr. been guilty or innocent of the charges against him? The court had no interest in acknowledging a catastrophic failure of the Canadian justice system. Rather, Donald was put in a position where he had to prove his own innocence. No one could talk about who, or what, had been responsible for his wrongful conviction. Under section 617b, the appeal court judges had three choices: uphold the conviction and send Marshall back to jail, order a retrial, or acquit and set him free. Despite circumstances not being in Donald's favour, both the defence and Crown counsels asked the court to acquit once they heard the evidence. The Crown, however, used Donald's jailhouse statement regarding the robbery, which had been coerced by Wheaton and Carroll, against him. The court quashed Donald's conviction, but the panel blamed Donald for his wrongful conviction. It was the most appalling and heartbreaking exoneration of an innocent man. Donald Marshall, the court stated, had been "the author of his own misfortune," and "any injustices experienced were more apparent than real."[9]

The court's pronouncement reflected a serious and fundamental error. The judges had taken the evidence laid before them (as well as information never admitted into evidence) to convict Donald of a crime – an imagined robbery – to which he had never been charged. Following their review of the evidence, they shamefully put all the emphasis on the claim that Donald Marshall and Sandy Seale had been trying to rob Roy Ebsary on the night of the murder. They also concluded, mistakenly, that Donald had "admittedly" committed perjury when he failed to tell the court that this stabbing had occurred in the course of a robbery – a fiction enabled by the police and prosecution. Had a *voir dire* been held on the involuntary nature of the jailhouse statement, as Stephen Aronson had demanded, it is unlikely it would have been admitted as evidence.[10] The court's suggestion that Donald's "untruthfulness ... contributed in large measure to his conviction" was not sustained by the evidence.[11] In their efforts to limit the damage following a public announcement of the wrongful conviction, the police, the Court of Appeal judges, the Crown, and provincial justice officials had unnecessarily prolonged the suffering of Donald Marshall, his family, and the Mi'kmaw Nation.[12]

The Reference decision impeded Donald's ability to seek compensation for the wrongs perpetrated against him. While some could find no justification for the judgment, others argued that the judges were protecting their own interests, and the interests of the province, by uncritically accepting discriminatory practices as just, in spite of overwhelming evidence to the contrary. Their decision, "fit comfortably with the popular racist stereotypes of *Indians* as liars, thieves and drunks" and absolved those responsible for the miscarriage of justice.[13] The police officers and members of the legal profession responsible for Donald's wrongful conviction were never charged nor held to account for their misconduct, including their failure to disclose evidence. There were no examinations of the trial judge's errors or the perjured witness testimonies. The blame was placed solely on Donald Marshall. Outraged and confused over the court's process, Donald was once again victimized rather than vindicated.

Finally, in May 1983, the Nova Scotia Court of Appeal ruled that Donald Marshall Jr. had been wrongly convicted and entered his acquittal.

Two years later, in 1985, Roy Ebsary, the older white man in the long dark cloak, was convicted of manslaughter in the death of Sandy Seale. Once he was found fit to stand trial, it took three tries to convict him. The initial charge of murder was dismissed because of insufficient evidence, but Ebsary was committed to trial on the reduced charge of manslaughter. He was released on his own recognizance. The first trial resulted in a hung jury. The second trial resulted in a conviction, and he was released until his sentencing hearing. Ebsary was sentenced to five years in a federal penitentiary. Ten months later, the conviction was overturned on appeal and a new trial ordered. The third trial ended in another conviction, and Ebsary was sentenced to three years. The conviction was upheld on appeal, but the sentence was reduced to one year. A further appeal to the Supreme Court of Canada was denied in September 1986.

Donald had to attend Ebsary's trials and relive the trauma of his wrongful conviction. Ebsary's defence counsel, Luke Wintermans, challenged Donald's testimony, arguing that Donald had a direct financial interest in the outcome of the case because of a pending compensation lawsuit.[14] With Felix Cacchione as counsel, Donald had sought compensation for his court costs and wrongful conviction, but the prejudice induced by the Reference court's decision along with conflicts between the province and federal government over fiduciary responsibility for Indigenous persons had complicated the process. The province contended that Donald, as an Indigenous person, was a federal, rather than a provincial, responsibility under the Indian Act. The province also made the case that because Donald had been convicted of a criminal offence in a court with a federally appointed judge and incarcerated in a federal institution, the province should not have to pay for the errors. The federal government rejected the province's position on the grounds that the administration of justice is a provincial responsibility.[15]

In 1984, the province appointed a one-person commission, the Campbell Commission, to examine the issue of compensation. Many doubted the system's ability to take the experience of Indigenous peoples into account when considering the issue. The government's principal objective was to score political points in relation to the compensation issue – score them quickly and pay as little as possible. But it did not fully consider the extent of injuries suffered as a result of the wrongs. In 1984, exhausted from fighting, Donald settled for $270,000. The compensation awarded was restricted solely to Donald's period of confinement without consideration of the factors that had led him to be imprisoned for eleven years. Half went to legal fees.

Donald experienced little relief or vindication. Stephen Aronson and Felix Cacchione, who had represented Donald in several different ways during his acquittal and compensation hearings, reduced their fees as soon as they heard the amount. Aronson left his law practice, financially spent and emotionally bust. Donald and his supporters speculated that the province had been more concerned with wrangling with the federal government over compensation than with a justice system that had failed to protect the innocent from wrongful conviction. Clearly, the injustices done to Donald Marshall and, subsequently, to the Mi'kmaw Nation were becoming a matter of public debate. That the sacrosanct justice system was fallible was unsettling to many. That the province was unwilling to address this problem, directly and openly, heightened suspicions that politicians were in collusion with law enforcement and the judiciary. Despite the province's desire to wash its hands of the case, the public pressured the government to hold an inquiry.

3

Koqwaja'taqn | To Do the Right Thing
The Royal Commission

CALLS FOR AN INQUIRY had begun as soon as Donald was released from prison in March 1982, and by October 1986 the province of Nova Scotia had no more excuses. The RCMP's investigations into Sandy Seale's murder had concluded. The Court of Appeal had determined Marshall's innocence. And Ebsary, having exhausted his appeals, was serving a reduced sentence for manslaughter. In 1983, journalists on CBC's *Sunday Morning* radio program stated openly that Donald Marshall Jr. had been a victim of racism, fabricated evidence, and perjured testimony. John MacIntyre launched a defamation suit against the CBC, but then withdrew the action on the eve of the trial.

Donald's case had exposed fault lines in the criminal justice system and Canadian society, but he was just barely hanging on. That same year, Steven Aronson had initiated a civil action, by way of an originating notice of action, against the City of Sydney and the officers involved in Donald's case (namely, John MacIntyre and William Urquhart) for negligence and malicious prosecution. The notice lapsed in 1984, before it was served, because the possibility of an inquiry was becoming stronger. Felix Cacchione vigorously advocated for an inquiry into his wrongful conviction, but Cacchione was appointed to the bench in June 1986 and could no longer act for him. Donald saw this appointment as part of a conspiracy to disrupt his efforts to get at the truth of his wrongful conviction.

The public began to mobilize against the wall of silence built by the Tory government of Premier John Buchanan. People demanded to know what had gone wrong in Donald Marshall Jr.'s prosecution, and the Opposition used the issue to politically embarrass the government. Mi'kmaw political organizations represented through the Union of Nova Scotia Indians demanded that the province take action to investigate the horrific wrongs committed against one of their own. Aside from Donald's own lawyers, however, the legal community demonstrated no sense of urgency to turn the gaze on themselves.

The impetus for a public review came primarily from the media, Mi'kmaw and black organizations, private citizens, and the federal and provincial Opposition parties. By the time the government consented to a public airing of the case, the scope of the concerns went well beyond the specifics of Donald's wrongful conviction. The provincial government and the Department of the Attorney General were being accused of meddling in the affairs of the criminal justice system to cover up political wrongdoing. And a growing list of alleged scandals involving ministers was fuelling public outrage. The justice system, often taken for granted as being fair, was being portrayed as overtly racist and possibly corrupt. The announcement of a royal commission in October 1986 was an exercise in damage control and public relations.[1]

Convened through a provincial Order-in-Council, pursuant to the Public Inquiries Act, the Royal Commission on the Donald Marshall, Jr., Prosecution was empowered to inquire into the wrongful conviction, report its findings, and make recommendations to the governor-in-council respecting the investigation of the death of Sandy Seale. The scope of the inquiry included the charges laid against Donald Marshall, the prosecution of the case, the conviction and sentencing, and any other related matters that the commissioners consider relevant to the inquiry.

ROYAL COMMISSIONS ARE ad hoc formal public inquiries into a defined issue. The prefix *royal* signifies that the authority for the commission comes from cabinet, acting in the name of the queen. One of the major weaknesses of royal commissions is that the government need not accept or create legislation based on the recommendations, and the commission has no process to implement recommendations. A third party or coordinating agency must convince the government that the recommendations are worthwhile and important. Despite these limitations, royal commissions are invaluable because they can be used to secure information, educate the public, and investigate the judicial or administrative functions of government. They also serve as a forum for voicing grievances and influencing public policy.

The royal commission into Donald Marshall's wrongful conviction had a broad mandate to consider matters the commissioners thought relevant, within reason.[2] The commission could make recommendations within the parameters of its mandate, but its limits prevented interested parties, particularly the Mi'kmaw Nation, from challenging the status quo. The commission could not, for instance, investigate how the colonial relationship between settler governments and the Mi'kmaq (particularly the failure to acknowledge Mi'kmaw treaties and the impact of cultural genocide) had contributed to the wrongful conviction. The commission would focus instead on finding out why Donald Marshall had been wrongly convicted and on determining what actions should be taken to make sure it never happened again. To fulfill their mandate, the commissioners had to determine what really happened on the night of May 28, 1971, and why that truth had not been revealed during the police investigation, the trial, or the appeal. They would also determine whether the compensation process had been fair and reasonable.

The commission advertised in newspapers, inviting interested parties to apply either for full or observer standing. Full standing gave individuals or groups the ability to participate wholly in the hearings, cross-examine witnesses, and make submissions. At least twenty-five lawyers had full standing, as did Donald Marshall Jr.; Sandy's father, Oscar Seale; John MacIntyre; William Urquhart; the estate of Crown prosecutor Donald C. MacNeil; the Department of the Attorney General; the RCMP; specific RCMP officers, including Harry Wheaton and Jim Carroll; the Black United

Front; and the Union of Nova Scotia Indians. Journalists also had to get legal representation to appear before the commissioners.

Hearings began on September 9, 1987, and ended on November 3, 1988. Three high-profile and experienced judges – Chief Justice T. Alexander Hickman of the Newfoundland Supreme Court, Associate Chief Justice Lawrence A. Poitras of the Quebec Superior Court, and the Honorable Mr. Gregory T. Evans, former chief justice of the Ontario Supreme Court – presided. Hickman, the chair, had six years earlier conducted a royal commission into the Ocean Rangers disaster, a public and controversial three-year inquiry into the loss of a drilling rig and its eighty-four-person crew in Newfoundland. In his opening statement, he established the inquiry's scope:

> In order to develop meaningful recommendations all contributing factors must be carefully and critically examined in the context of the current state of the administration of justice in Nova Scotia … We will also examine, among other things, the role of the Attorney General as a member of Cabinet, the relationship of Crown prosecutors with defence counsel and with the police, as well as related matters. In addition … we intend to give consideration to the allegations that minorities of this province are not treated equitably by the justice system. It is our ultimate aim to make recommendations which will ensure that the unfortunate events surrounding Mr. Marshall will not be repeated; to do this we must satisfy ourselves that the present state of the administration of criminal justice in Nova Scotia is sound. We will not avoid a discussion of these issues.[3]

Donald had a powerful legal team representing him – the high-profile duo Clayton Ruby and Marlys Edwardh, from Ontario, as lead, and Anne Derrick, from Halifax, as co-counsel. It was thought that having counsel from outside the local legal community would help the commission drill down to the real problems in Nova Scotia's justice system. At first, the provincial government, which was covering the cost of the inquiry, refused to pay Donald's full legal fees and limited its support to paying his personal counsel during his actual testimony. The commission's counsel, it was believed, would adequately represent him the rest of the time. The commission, however, recommended that public funding cover the costs of legal counsel for parties who had standing but limited resources – Donald Marshall, John MacIntyre, William Urquhart, Oscar Seale, the estate of Donald C. MacNeil, the Union of Nova Scotia Indians, and the Black United Front.

The first phase of the public hearings took place in a church basement in Sydney. Journalists and reporters attended, and television cameras captured much of the proceedings, but they were banned when Donald took the stand. His lawyers argued that the bright lights and cameras would add to his already heightened anxiety brought on by post-incarceration culture shock. The commission focused on events from the time of Sandy Seale's murder to the first RCMP reinvestigation in 1971. Unfortunately, a few key people were unable to participate. During the first months of the inquiry, Inspector Urquhart suffered a heart attack, Justice Dubinsky was in a hospital, and Moe Rosenblum, Donald's lawyer at the original trial, died near the end of October. The second phase took place in Halifax and focused on the events leading up to and following Donald's acquittal. No hearings were held in Mi'kmaw communities.

The commissioners heard from 113 witnesses (only six were Mi'kmaw) and examined 176 evidence exhibits over a total of 93 days, resulting in 16,390 pages of transcript. Despite the outpouring of testimony, no one took responsibility for Donald's wrongful conviction. As the commission progressed, its costs and mandate expanded. The commission ordered independent studies on the question of racial discrimination in the justice system on the grounds that public hearings were inadequate for investigating and assessing such a complex issue. In the end, the inquiry cost an estimated $7 million.[4]

Evidence presented during the first phase included the details of the incident, the police response, the trial process, and the 1971 RCMP review. The first witness was Roy Ebsary, who was questioned about his actions the night he met Sandy Seale and Donald Marshall in Wentworth Park. The press described his testimony as strange, erratic, contradictory, and even flirtatious.[5] The commission concluded that Ebsary had a violent, unpredictable character; was fascinated with knives; and was "capable of stabbing Sandy Seale with little, if any provocation."[6] They also concluded that

Sandy Seale and Donald Marshall had not been attempting to rob Roy Ebsary and Jimmy MacNeil at the time of the murder.

The commissioners found both the police response to the stabbing and MacIntyre's investigation "entirely inadequate, incompetent and unprofessional."[7] The police response, the commission stated, had been negligent, so much so that even the most elementary of police procedures had not been followed. Officers had failed to secure the crime scene, to interview people in the park, and to take statements from Donald Marshall or Maynard Chant. They did not collect evidence from Sandy Seale, they failed to order a forensic autopsy after his death, and they did not systematically search for the suspects in houses in the area. The commissioners concluded that finding the real killer had not been a priority for the police. If Donald Marshall had been white, the investigation would have proceeded differently. The commissioners were "left with the impression that many people in Sydney in 1971 believed Natives were not 'worth' as much as Whites. Since a Native 'troublemaker' would be worth that much less, Marshall's story scarcely merited consideration."[8]

In their sworn testimonies, the police maintained that they had been doing their job, including maintaining racial separation and "discouraging the white girls from fraternizing with the native boys."[9] They felt their job was to rid the town of "Indian" trouble.[10] After Chief John MacIntyre took the stand on December 7–11, 1987, the commission found "that the fact that Marshall was a Native was one of the reasons MacIntyre identified him as a prime suspect" and that "MacIntyre accepted evidence that supported his conclusion and rejected evidence that discounted that conclusion."[11]

Donald hoped that his counsel would reveal the malfeasance and conspiracy behind his wrongful conviction. His supporters hoped someone would be held directly responsible for the corruption and perversion of justice that underpinned it. The commission concluded that MacIntyre, without evidence or an investigation, had held Donald responsible for the crime and linked it to some imagined argument with Seale. Although other police officers attached to the case initially accepted Donald's explanation of events, they did not dare challenge MacIntyre's laser focus on Donald as the prime suspect. He was in charge of the investigation and their superior officer. The commission also discovered that although the RCMP had offered their services, MacIntyre chose to go it alone and failed to pursue any information that corroborated Donald's statement. The commissioners stated, "It is not acceptable for police officers to formulate a theory that has no evidence to support it and some evidence against it, and then to adopt that theory to the exclusion of any others."[12]

The commission also found John Pratico's testimony unreliable and his interactions with MacIntyre inappropriate in the extreme: "It is reprehensible for a police officer to take an unstable and impressionable teenager to a murder scene, review the scene with him and then persuade him to accept suggestions which form the basis for a detailed and incriminating statement."[13] The commissioners found that MacIntyre had denied the three minors (John Pratico, Maynard Chant, and Patricia Harriss) parental supervision, pressured them into giving false statements, and threatened them with detention. MacIntyre had suggested a set of lies to Pratico and Chant to get their statements to read as consistent facts. Harriss testified that she had been told repeatedly that if her story differed from her statement she would go to jail for perjury. The commission concluded, "The pursuit of truth is not the only value held dear by a civilized justice system; so too is freedom from coercion, threats and arbitrary action from those in authority."[14]

Throughout questioning, MacIntyre remained detached and admitted to no wrongdoing. He denied allegations of pressuring and threatening the witnesses and had trouble recollecting events. The commission found him "frequently evasive and on several occasions, simply untruthful."[15] He showed no remorse. When asked whether he now believed Donald had not been involved in the stabbing of Sandy Seale, MacIntyre refused to confirm his innocence. Even when prompted, he wouldn't apologize. His testimony scorched Junior's spirit.

The commission found that both the Crown prosecutor, Donald C. MacNeil, and defence counsel, Simon Khattar and Moe Rosenblum, had failed in their obligations at the original trial, resulting in Donald's wrongful conviction. The Crown had not investigated conflicting statements and should have interviewed every key witness separately prior to trial. Most importantly, the Crown had failed to discharge its obligation to disclose inconsistent statements to the defence. The defence, in turn, had failed to act in Donald's best interests when some teenagers, deducing from newspaper reports that Pratico was lying, contacted them. The defence simply told the teenagers "they were too late."[16] The defence – aware of Chant's, Pratico's, and Harriss's statements – did not request them, nor did they arrange for an independent investigation, seek disclosure of the Crown's case, or interview Crown witnesses. In their response, Khattar and Rosenblum argued that defence counsel in Cape Breton did not make it a practice to seek disclosure of the Crown's evidence. The commission noted that, "Given the reputation for competence they enjoyed in the Cape Breton legal community and the totally inadequate defence they provided to Marshall, the irresistible conclusion is that Marshall's race did influence the defence provided to him."[17]

The miscarriage of justice continued. The commission, basing its decision on a comprehensive opinion provided by Bruce Archibald, a law professor at Dalhousie University, found that the trial judge, Justice Dubinsky, had misinterpreted section 11 of the Canada Evidence Act when he refused to permit a thorough examination of Pratico's declarations of Marshall's innocence, made outside the courtroom to Donald's father, the grand chief, and all parties involved in the case. This significant error and the cumulative effect of incorrect rulings led to Marshall being denied a fair trial. The commissioners concluded that this was "a serious breach of the standard of professional conduct expected and required."[18]

Further incompetence was revealed in the handling of Jimmy MacNeil's voluntary statement, made in 1971 to the Sydney City Police, that he had witnessed Roy Ebsary stab Sandy Seale. The commission revealed that the Crown prosecutor and the attorney general had failed to disclose the new, extremely important evidence to Donald's counsel, which would have resulted in an acquittal. Alan Marshall, the inspector responsible for the RCMP's 1971 review, had also failed to fully investigate the allegation. He hadn't even read the entire file. He instead relied exclusively on what MacIntyre had told him about the case and took MacIntyre's position that Jimmy MacNeil's statement was a "cock-and-bull" story.[19] MacIntyre convinced the inspector that he had the right man. Unlike MacIntyre, Alan Marshall at least admitted to the commission that he had botched the investigation, but his mistakes helped put Donald Marshall in jail for eleven years, for a crime he did not commit.

DURING THE SECOND phase of the inquiry, the commissioners closely examined the RCMP's 1982 reinvestigation of Seale's murder and the special reference to the Court of Appeal. Harry Wheaton and Jim Carroll (the RCMP officers who had thoroughly and professionally reinvestigated the case; uncovered the perjured testimonies of Chant, Pratico, and Harriss; and delivered physical evidence leading to Donald's exoneration) came under fire for the manner in which they had interviewed and coerced a statement from Donald in Dorchester Penitentiary.

Additionally, the commission criticized the RCMP officers for taking too soft an approach in their dealings with the Sydney City Police. Wanting to maintain amicable professional relations between the two forces, they failed to get a search warrant to obtain the Marshall case file from the city police. The investigation was mired in dubious police protocols and procedural mandates, particularly because the matter involved a chief of police. The commission discovered that Wheaton and Carroll had wanted to investigate John MacIntyre's and William Urquhart's actions, but they had been stonewalled by Gordon Gale, the director of criminal law for the Department of the Attorney General. Gale requested that the RCMP confine their investigation to the case files, rather than the Sydney City Police. The patriarchs of the old boy network had drawn together tightly to protect themselves from the public's increasingly critical gaze.

Another key issue under scrutiny at the commission was the setting up and execution of the special reference to the Court of Appeal under section 617b of the Criminal Code. The commission discovered that when the case was first discussed, Donald's lawyer, the federal Department of Justice, and the provincial attorney general had wanted to hold the Reference under section 617c. The chief justice of Nova Scotia, Ian MacKeigan, however, being advised of the forthcoming Reference as a matter of courtesy, had discouraged proceeding in this manner because it would allow for the introduction of new evidence, a full airing of the issues, and appropriate executive action. Under section 617b, by contrast, the Reference would take on the characteristics of a normal appeal.

When it came to the Reference decision, the royal commission made ten critical findings:

- That the Court of Appeal made a serious and fundamental error when it concluded that Donald Marshall Jr. was to blame for his wrongful conviction.
- That the Court selectively used the evidence before it – as well as information that had not been admitted in evidence – in order to reach its conclusions.
- That the Court took it upon itself to "convict" Marshall of a robbery with which he was never charged.
- That the Court was in error when it stated that Marshall "admittedly" committed perjury.
- That the Court did not deal with the significant failure of the Crown to disclose evidence, including the conflicting statements by witnesses, to defence counsel.
- That the Court's suggestion that Marshall's "untruthfulness ... contributed in large measure to his conviction" was not supported by any available evidence and was contrary to evidence before the Court.
- That the Court did not deal with the errors by the trial judge in limiting the cross-examination of Pratico.
- That Mr. Justice Leonard Pace should not have sat as a member of the panel hearing the Reference.
- That the Court's decision amounted to a defence of the criminal justice system at Marshall's expense, notwithstanding overwhelming evidence to the contrary.
- That the Court's gratuitous comments in the last pages of its decision created serious difficulties for Donald Marshall Jr. both in terms of his ability to negotiate compensation for his wrongful conviction and also in terms of public acceptance of his acquittal.[20]

The commission also revealed that Chief Justice MacKeigan had written a private letter to Jean Chrétien, the minister of justice, when he forwarded him the decision. In it, he stated, "We also expressed an opinion on the many factors which led to this miscarriage of justice within the judicial system." His private letter contradicted the Court of Appeal's public declaration that any miscarriage of justice had been "more apparent than real."[21]

The commission also revealed further reasons why Justice Pace should not have sat on the panel. In addition to having been the attorney general in 1971, when Donald's case originally went to trial, he had been scheduled to sit on the appeal arising from the third Ebsary trial. Although another judge ultimately presided over that case, Dana Giovannetti, the lawyer who brought the conflict of interest to the attention of the chief justice, was severely admonished by Justice Pace for raising the issue of bias.[22] Giovannetti testified before the commission that Justice Pace had said in the course of the conversation "that he knew from the time poor old Mr. Ebsary was charged that he could not be guilty."[23]

During the inquiry, the commission's counsel asked the judges of the Court of Appeal to appear and answer questions. The commissioners wanted to know what evidence the court had used to acquit Donald Marshall and yet blame him for his conviction. When the judges refused to testify, subpoenas were issued. The question of the necessity of the judges appearing in response to the subpoenas was contested in court. The Nova Scotia Supreme Court ruled that judges did not have to appear before the commission and had absolute immunity. The commission appealed to the Supreme Court of Canada, which ruled in October 1989 that the commission could not question the judges on these issues. The judiciary continued to be protected, and scrutiny returned to the political operations of the province.

The commission also focused on the role of cabinet and the Department of the Attorney General. When the commission asked a former attorney general of Nova Scotia questions about cabinet discussions of the wrongful conviction, the province took the position that cabinet proceedings were privileged. In response, the commission requested information on the general nature of the discussions in order to maintain the appropriate balance between cabinet secrecy and the proper administration of justice.

The department's stance on the Reference became clear to the commissioners through documents and testimonies. The commission discovered

Editorial cartoon by Bruce MacKinnon in the *Chronicle Herald. Copyright 1990; reprinted with permission*

that Crown prosecutor Frank Edward's factum to the Nova Scotia Court of Appeal had contained the following:

> It is the Respondent's respectful submission that the role of the Court goes much further in this peculiar situation. Here, if the Court does ultimately decide to acquit the Appellant, it is no overstatement to say that the credibility of our criminal justice system may be called into question by a significant portion of the community. It seems reasonable to assume that the public will suspect there is something wrong with the system if a man can be convicted of a murder he did not commit. A minimum level of public confidence in the criminal justice system must be maintained or it simply will not work. For the above reasons, it is respectfully submitted that the Court should make it clear that what happened in this case was

not the fault of the criminal justice system or anyone in it, including the police, the lawyers, the members of the jury or the Court itself.[24]

It also became clear that the deputy attorney general, Gordon Coles, had not investigated the miscarriage of justice in any manner and had staunchly opposed a public inquiry into the matter. When Donald and his lawyers began to scrutinize the behaviour of those responsible for the wrongful conviction, it was found that Coles had not bothered to review the file or keep up on its progress. Gordon Gale testified that he had given permission to release the file to Coles, which Coles denied. Coles had also interfered with the course of justice in the Campbell Commission by trying to limit its investigative scope. He wanted Donald to receive the lowest possible compensation payout. The inquiry found that Coles had abused his power as deputy attorney general. Coles subsequently resigned.

In essence, the commissioners took their limited mandate and, in the face of the obvious displeasure of provincial officials, proceeded to expand it to include a wide range of political and social issues never intended for scrutiny. It was widely felt among the provincial bureaucracy and political players that the Marshall Inquiry had become a "loose cannon."[25] The attorney general's final submission to the inquiry stubbornly maintained the department's "blame the victim" stance. Although the department acknowledged that the checks and balances of the justice system had failed, it denied allegations of corruption, racism, or criminal wrongdoing. Donald Marshall, the department's lawyer insisted, had been at least partly responsible for his life sentence.

ALTHOUGH THE PROVINCE made every effort to control the commission and protect its interests by restricting the inquiry to the failings of the police investigation, the commissioners felt they had to protect their legitimacy and "allay public doubt about the judicial process."[26] To supplement the hearings, the commissioners hired researchers to conduct studies on five key issues: public policy and policing in Nova Scotia; the Mi'kmaq and criminal justice; discrimination against blacks; the office of the attorney general; and prosecuting officers and the administration of justice.

The commission turned a spotlight on injustice in Nova Scotia and Canada, but observers and participants expressed frustration with its limitations. Donald's supporters saw the commission as an opportunity to get at the root causes of systemic discrimination, as an opportunity to seek retribution for the prejudicial treatment of Indigenous peoples within the Canadian justice system. They hoped the inquiry would reveal the racism at play in social interactions controlled by the legal, educational, political, and social standards of the dominant settler society, standards that masked discrimination and excluded Mi'kmaw legal principles. The commission, however, did not explore systemic inequalities in legal processes such as jury selection; the lack of culturally inclusive incarceration procedures; or the overrepresentation of Indigenous peoples in jails and prisons. Donald's treatment in prison and within the parole system were deemed outside the commission's scope. Lawyers for the Correctional Service of Canada, for instance, raised objections to any review of their actions, citing an unpublished agreement with the commission's counsel to restrict all inquiries into areas of federal jurisdiction.[27]

Legal experts criticized the commission for engaging "in a detailed examination of the justice system using the very same instruments and techniques it is examining – truly an exercise in navel gazing."[28] The commission never clarified its methodology for determining the consequences of racism in the criminal justice system. During the first week of sworn testimony, the commissioners ruled that cross-examination of the key witnesses about their attitudes towards "Indians" was improper. This ruling prevented the commission from examining racial perceptions (and the inequalities associated with them) within the consciousness of judges and ordinary Canadians. When lawyers for the Black United Front and the Union of Nova Scotia Indians asked questions to get at patterns of racial bias, the commissioners cut them off. The press nicknamed their section of the room the "leper colony."[29]

The commissioners did not permit questions that probed whether a pattern of "behaviour without intent" existed in the justice system, a pattern that led to discrimination based on colour or race, but they did partially explore the role of political power and class and whether unequal treatment in the justice system was widespread.[30] The commission compared how the RCMP's investigations of the Marshall case had compared with the force's investigation into charges against two Nova Scotia MLAs, Roland Thornhill and Billy Joe MacLean. Although the commission wanted to determine whether politicians and ordinary citizens received equal treatment before the law, they failed to take into consideration that Mi'kmaw persons in Canada are not ordinary citizens. As Indigenous peoples, they are citizens with constitutionally recognized special rights under section 35. The Grand Council, in its submissions to the inquiry, argued that "to achieve equality before and under the law and the right to the equal protection and equal benefit of the law, the Mi'kmaw require substantive equality rather than formal equality."[31]

The highly publicized commission exposed discrimination and socio-economic inequalities in the criminal justice system and in Nova Scotia society. Nova Scotians became aware of the resilience of Mi'kmaw tribal culture in the face of a predominantly white criminal justice system and a settler society that had failed to honour the Peace and Friendship Treaties. Article 8 of the 1752 treaty, of particular concern to the Mi'kmaq who made submissions to the commission, states that Mi'kmaq shall be "tried in His Majesty's Court of Civil Judicature, where the Indians shall have the same benefits, advantages and privileges as any other of His Majesty's subjects."[32] When Viola Robinson, Mi'kmaw lawyer and political activist, made a submission on behalf of the Native Council of Nova Scotia, she called on the citizens of the province to recognize and respect the distinct rights of the Mi'kmaw Nation and emphasized that "the Micmac society of people do have the same benefits, advantages and privileges before the courts." Marie Battiste, a Mi'kmaw educator from the Potolek First Nation, took a similar stance.

Other Mi'kmaw witnesses offered the public glimpses of their experiences and culture. Three witnesses from Membertou – Arty Paul, Tom Christmas, and Roy Gould – described racialized tensions between the police and the community and how culture shapes Mi'kmaw behaviour in the courtroom. They testified that the police were not interested in the truth when they dealt with Mi'kmaw suspects or victims. Paul, Donald's lifelong friend added, "When it comes to solving crimes, Mr. MacIntyre could not solve a jigsaw puzzle."³³ Mi'kmaw witnesses seized the opportunity to demonstrate that different interpretations of legal principles and justice models existed – despite centuries of oppression. In order for Mi'kmaq to experience justice within the settler system, they argued, Mi'kmaw modes of speech, acts of deference, and concepts of guilt and innocence needed to be recognized and accommodated.

The commission conceded that Indigenous peoples have their own non-adversarial dispute-management processes that do not focus on determining innocence or guilt and dispensing punishment. The inquiry validated a community-based approach to justice in which community elders and leaders settle disputes.³⁴ The commission stated:

> The list of Native criticisms of how our judicial process affects them is long. To begin, they argue that it is not relevant to the real lives of Native people. The court is an unfamiliar and intimidating institution, conceptually removed from the indigenous processes of social control based on mediation and restitution. It is usually physically removed as well, making it difficult for Natives to attend ... many have problems comprehending the English language. When you add to those things the reality that all the faces in the justice system are White ... that Natives suffer from stereotyping and other forms of discrimination, you begin to understand why Natives are unhappy with the current system of administering justice.³⁵

When he gave his testimony on June 28, 1988, Donald, who had tenaciously hung on to his language, spoke Mi'kmaw through a translator, Noel Knockwood. He had been denied this right during the original trial. The commissioners noted how the failure to accommodate Mi'kmaw cultural differences had influenced Donald's case:

> Before the Supreme Court and the Appeal Division, the Court asked Marshall on at least 29 occasions to speak up or remove his hand from his face so he could be heard. While Marshall is naturally soft-spoken, the court's numerous interventions probably compounded his discomfort,

and may have seemed to Marshall as evidence that officials were harassing him or were at least hostile to him. The Court, on the other hand may have regarded Marshall's demeanor as a negative factor and that may have influenced the ultimate disposition of the hearings.[36]

If they were paying attention, what Nova Scotians and Canadians bore witness to at the Marshall Inquiry was a profound transformation in Mi'kmaw legal consciousness. Donald's experiences inspired the Mi'kmaq to resist domination and revitalize their own legal principles. Although Mi'kmaq had a voice at the inquiry, the experts rarely turned to community members who were forced to face settler courts for their opinions, and they were largely marginal to the creation of the recommendations.[37]

In November 1988, at the end of the hearings, the commission sponsored a consultative conference to bring together local and national experts on discrimination against Indigenous peoples and blacks in the criminal justice system and the role of the attorney general. Thomas Berger – a former justice of the Supreme Court of British Columbia who led the MacKenzie Valley Pipeline Inquiry, which involved deep consultation with Indigenous communities – chaired the meeting. The goal was to help the commissioners frame the recommendations to best deal with the difficult issues they had uncovered. The list of speakers and invited guests read like a who's who of Indigenous justice scholars, chiefs, lawyers, and members of Indigenous and black organizations. Justices Murray Sinclair and Alvin C. Hamilton, who were conducting the Manitoba Aboriginal Justice Inquiry, were in attendance. Professor Michael Jackson identified the overrepresentation of Indigenous peoples in prisons and the prevalence of social demoralization in Indigenous communities as two of the most egregious effects of colonization and dispossession.[38] The group discussed potential solutions, including legal pluralism and the concept of a separate justice system for Indigenous people, and agreed that a complete unsettling of the Canadian justice system was in order.

4

Ilsutekek | To Make Right
Recommendations and Outcomes

THE ROYAL COMMISSION on the Donald Marshall, Jr., Prosecution released its final report on January 26, 1990. The opening statement of its *Digest of Findings and Recommendations* stated unequivocally:

> The criminal justice system failed Donald Marshall, Jr., at virtually every turn from his arrest and wrongful conviction for murder in 1971 up to, and even beyond, his acquittal by the Court of Appeal in 1983. The tragedy of the failure is compounded by evidence that this miscarriage of justice could – and should – have been prevented, or at least corrected quickly, if those involved in the system had carried out their duties in a professional and or competent manner. That they did not is due, in part at least, to the fact that Donald Marshall, Jr., is a Native.[1]

Donald's lawyer, Anne Derrick, delivered the news. Donald had secluded himself from the press at the Mi'kmaq Native Friendship Centre in Halifax, but when she told him he had been vindicated, she saw visible relief, "It was as though something vast and heavy had been lifted off him. The unexpected had happened and he was in those moments a free man at last."[2]

Donald had little hope, however, that the commission would condemn the individuals and the system that had brought him so much harm.

Donald and his supporters wanted the commission to recommend laying criminal charges against those directly responsible for his wrongful conviction. Donald in particular wanted action taken against the Sydney City Police, especially since he had dropped his civil suit to facilitate the creation of the commission. But it was not to be. The report stated, "It is our view that the function of a public inquiry is not to determine criminal responsibility, but to inform people about the facts of the matter under consideration."[3]

At the end of the day, Donald was dissatisfied and devastated that John MacIntyre had escaped criminal charges. Neither John MacIntyre nor Oscar Seale, Sandy's father, publicly let go of their conviction that Donald was to blame for the death of Sandy Seale. Although greatly encouraged by the nature and tone of the report and its clear absolution of his actions, Donald believed that MacIntyre and the others directly responsible for his wrongful prosecution deserved to be punished. Donald felt that blame throughout the commission had centred on the Crown prosecutor, Donald C. MacNeil, a man who could not answer to the charges because he was dead: "The police chief had a sneaky way of getting around the whole thing by blaming that guy. They should have charged him with perjury."[4]

Donald was pleased, however, that the commission had challenged the sanctity of the justice system and the power of the police by showing them to be products of the society from which they had emerged, rather than impartial authorities. The inquiry led the courts to be more careful in their treatment of Mi'kmaq and blacks, and Donald hoped that Mi'kmaq would eventually gain control over justice in their communities, ultimately reducing the number of people in jail. Justice remained elusive for Donald, but the quest for justice had just begun for the Mi'kmaw Nation.[5] The royal commission concluded:

> Having found that Marshall was denied justice because he is an Indian and that Indians suffer adverse effects from the predominantly White criminal justice system, we need to find ways to change the system. Native Canadians have a right to a justice system that they respect and which has respect for

them, and which dispenses justice in a manner consistent with and sensitive to their history, culture and language ... Natives rely on resolving disputes through mediation and conciliation, methods which emphasize reconciliation rather than laying blame. Those traditional values frequently clash with our adversarial system. That means that if we are going to change the criminal justice system, either in substance or in its delivery, we must take into account the unique historical and cultural background of Native people.[6]

Drawing on research and the hearings, the commission provided evidence of discrimination and prejudice in Nova Scotia's criminal justice system and concluded that Mi'kmaq and blacks experienced unequal treatment before the law. Evidence of deep-seated racism among high-ranking officials in Nova Scotia was brought to light. It was revealed, for instance, that in response to Marshall's request for compensation, Robert Anderson, the director of criminal matters in the attorney general's office, who had since been appointed a judge, had advised Felix Cacchione, Donald's attorney, to not get his "balls in a vice over an Indian." The statement revealed a system of law that does not prize equality, and Anderson admitted at the inquiry that "it sounds like something I might say."[7] It would not have served him socially or politically to challenge local or provincial authorities to defend Indigenous peoples' rights.[8]

Scott Clark, a researcher for the commission, had conducted field-based research into the underlying causes of discrimination in the criminal justice system. He examined the history of settler-colonial relations, and his general findings confirmed the need for community-based justice programs to overcome the adverse effects of Mi'kmaw participation in an ineffective, culturally insensitive, and discriminatory justice system. He connected the overrepresentation of Mi'kmaq in the criminal justice system to the historical consequences of colonization and socioeconomic marginalization. To rectify the situation, Clark – in consultation with representatives from the Union of Nova Scotia Indians, the Grand Council, the Native Council of Nova Scotia, and the Confederacy of Mainland Mi'kmaq – argued that Nova Scotia must recognize the Mi'kmaq's treaty rights to land and resources as well as their constitutionally protected rights. The government needed to accept and help facilitate Mi'kmaw self-governance.[9] Clark's recommendations returned to the public's attention an inherent rights discourse that had been percolating in Mi'kmaw communities since the 1970s. Clark recommended reviews of the criminal justice system, the establishment of a Native justice institute and a tribal justice system, and the erection of provincial courts on reserves.

The commission made eighty-two recommendations, grouped under the headings "Righting the Wrong: Dealing with the Wrongfully Convicted" (1–8), "Visible Minorities and the Criminal Justice System" (9–19), "Nova Scotia Micmac and the Criminal Justice System" (20–30), "Blacks and the Criminal Justice System" (31–34), "Administration of Criminal Justice" (35–45), and "Police and Policing" (46–82). Eleven recommendations dealt directly with the Mi'kmaq, who individually and collectively took them up as the foundation for community-controlled justice and for articulating their dissatisfaction with the provincial and federal governments:

20. Native Criminal Court
21. Native Justice Institute
22. Tripartite Forum on Native Issues
23. Micmac Interpreters
24. Native Court Workers
25. Sittings of Provincial Courts on Reserves
26. Legal Aid Funding
27. Liaison with Bar
28. Native Constables
29. Native Justice Committee
30. Probation and Aftercare

Forty-four of the eighty-two recommendations dealt with police services, particularly cultural incompetency, racial profiling and criminal stereotyping, and the lack of Indigenous police offers.

Recommendation 21, which called for the establishment of a Native justice institute, became the centrepiece of Mi'kmaw justice in the decade following the commission. The commission recommended "that a Native Justice

Institute be established with Provincial and Federal Government funding to do, among other things":

(a) channel and coordinate community needs and concerns into the Native Criminal Court;

(b) undertake research on Native customary law to determine the extent to which it should be incorporated into the criminal and civil law as it applies to Native people;

(c) train court workers and other personnel employed by the Native Criminal Court and the regular courts;

(d) consult with Government on Native justice issues;

(f) work with the Nova Scotia Barristers Society, the Public Legal Education Society and other groups concerned with the legal information needs of Native people; and

(g) monitor the existence of discriminatory treatment against Native people in the criminal justice system.[10]

Once established, the institute would come to symbolize Mi'kmaw survival and the resilience and merit of their own legal traditions.

THE ROYAL COMMISSION exposed that the checks and balances in the criminal justice system, designed to protect the accused, had failed Donald Marshall. At first, the Government of Nova Scotia took the commission and its recommendations to correct systemic faults in the administration of justice seriously.[11] The government made a public apology to Donald on February 7, 1990. In a press release, the attorney general, Tom McInnis, stated, "On behalf of the Province of Nova Scotia, I offer a sincere and heartfelt apology to Donald Marshall Jr., his mother, his father and his entire family."

It was the first official response by the province.

McInnis said the province accepted the commission's recommendations in their entirety, and he asked the chief justice for a judicial inquiry into the conduct of the five provincial appeal court judges who had acquitted

Donald but held him ultimately responsible for his wrongful conviction. Donald's lawyer Anne Derrick and law professor Archie Kaiser had worked tirelessly to bring Donald justice and repair his self-worth. They sought sanctions against the panel of judges who had heard the Reference in order to thoroughly reveal and correct the damage done to the administration of justice, and they clearly laid out their goal in their detailed submissions.

The Canadian Judicial Council examined the matter. The investigating committee, chaired by Chief Justice Allan McEachren, who would one year later preside over the *Delgamuukw* case in British Columbia, concluded, "While we cannot condone or excuse the severity of the Reference Court's condemnation of Donald Marshall Jr., and in particular its extraordinary observation that any miscarriage of justice was 'more apparent than real,' we do not find that the comments can lead to the conclusion that the judges cannot execute their office with the impartiality, integrity and independence the public rightly expects from the judiciary. We therefore do not recommend their removal from office."[12] The restoration of justice was more apparent than real.

To implement the commission's recommendations, the province made the Department of the Solicitor General (which had been re-established as the department responsible for policing and corrections, separating these services from the Department of the Attorney General) responsible for recommendations relating to the administration of criminal justice, particularly those concerning the police and policing. The former director of the Department of the Solicitor General recalls working hard to "tick off all of the boxes" of the recommendations to improve systemic problems in police and correctional services.[13] When the Department of the Solicitor General was abolished in 1993, its functions were assumed by the newly named Department of Justice.

One of the most transformative outcomes of the Marshall Inquiry in terms of criminal law procedure was recommendation 39, which urged the Department of the Attorney General in Nova Scotia to ask the federal government to amend the Criminal Code to provide for a comprehensive regime of disclosure, one that would ensure that exculpatory evidence is disclosed fully and in a timely manner. Influenced by the Marshall Inquiry, the Supreme Court of Canada, in *R v Stinchcombe*, concluded in 1991 that the Crown bore a constitutional duty to disclose all fruits of an investigation, provided they are not irrelevant to the case or subject to the Crown's right to withhold privileged information or time the release of particular items. Failure to disclose, the court argued, undermines the accused's right to make full answer and defence. The court drew directly upon the Marshall commission report and its recommendation: "Anything less than complete disclosure by the Crown falls short of decency and fair play."[14]

Following recommendation 35, chapter 21, section 1, of the Public Prosecutions Act established an independent director of public prosecutions and the Public Prosecution Service in 1990, the first statutorily based independent prosecution service in Canada. Prior to the commission, prosecutions in Nova Scotia were a function of the Department of the Attorney General. There was little transparency, and the attorney general got directly involved in individual prosecutions. By contrast, the Crown attorneys of the Public Prosecution Service conduct prosecutions independently of the attorney general. The governments of Canada and Quebec adopted this model. When handling a case, Crown attorneys must exclude the alleged offender's race, sex, national origin, or political associations from consideration when they determine whether the public interest will be best served by a prosecution. They must also follow a detailed policy on disclosure to guarantee the accused's constitutional rights to a fair trial and full defence. This was the first time in Canadian history that a recommendation from an inquiry into a wrongful conviction was translated into legislation.

The inquiry also led to other changes at the federal level. Since 1975, Justice Canada and the solicitor general had sponsored conferences, commissions, and reports on Indigenous peoples' relationship with settler justice, and since the 1980s, the Law Reform Commission of Canada had advocated for diversion programs and restorative justice as alternatives to adversarial prosecution. In keeping with the widespread view that the criminal justice system did not work well for Indigenous peoples, there was a proliferation of justice initiatives based on alternative dispute resolution and restorative justice philosophies to address problems of overrepresentation and alienation in the legal system. Over and over, the government set policies to improve the justice system and make it equitable. But during those decades, most experts thought problems stemmed from a disjuncture between the criminal act and the punishment. Solutions focused not on changing the system but rather on helping people become adept at being processed through the system. Numerous government reports reiterated these types of recommendations.[15]

Following the release of the royal commission's report in 1989 and the Aboriginal Justice Inquiry of Manitoba's report in 1991, however, the federal government made broad organizational changes to the administration and delivery of Aboriginal justice. In 1992, the Department of the Solicitor General created the Aboriginal Corrections Policy Unit. Over time, the unit's mandate expanded to include research on the treatment of offenders in selected Indigenous communities and returning to a spiritually centred approach to dealing with offenders, one that would focus on restoring relations and reintegrating wrongdoers. This shift was driven largely by prisoners' demands to practise their own spirituality while incarcerated. In 1982, for instance, the Indian Brotherhood at Kent Prison in British Columbia had launched a human rights complaint, which in turn triggered a nation-wide movement to recognize Indigenous spirituality as a religion and protect Indigenous people's right to freedom of religion while incarcerated. Some, but not all, penal facilities across the country eventually sanctioned spiritual ceremonies. Those institutions that chose to participate allowed sweat lodges and sweet grass or smudging ceremonies, elder counselling, and craft production for Indigenous inmates. Donald advocated for these practices when he was with the Brotherhood.

The federal government also transferred responsibility for First Nations policing from Indian Affairs to the Department of the Solicitor General, and the Aboriginal Justice Directorate came into being. Both were launched as part of the Aboriginal Justice Initiative, which had a mandate to advance Aboriginal justice, improve the response of the conventional justice system, and facilitate greater Aboriginal direction of and innovations in justice.[16]

The Aboriginal Justice Directorate, which had a limited five-year term, funded pilot projects to foster the development of alternative and community-based justice programs. Between 1991 and 1996, it supported over six hundred research projects. Pressure from Indigenous and other interest groups led to the program's extension, as the Aboriginal Justice Strategy, for another five years. It had a yearly operating budget of about $7 million. In a shift from its earlier policies of assimilation, the federal liberal government under Jean Chrétien implemented its 1993 Red Book commitment to prioritize Aboriginal justice reform. Through the Aboriginal Justice Strategy, it moved towards the creation of cost-shared, long-term, viable justice programs and institutions and focused on assisting communities engaged in negotiations or working towards sectoral agreements for justice under the inherent right of self-government. With the return to a federal conservative government in 2003, however, these types of programs suffered a series of lethal financial cuts.

FEDERAL AND PROVINCIAL initiatives were vulnerable to shifting political winds, but the Marshall Inquiry report marked a profound turning point for both Donald Marshall and the Mi'kmaq. The report symbolized the opportunity to regain authority over all aspects of their lives, to counter colonization and to govern themselves. The report dissected the legal processes leading to Donald's wrongful conviction and challenged all facets of the provincial justice system. The case brought to light fundamental problems in policing, courts, and the judiciary in Nova Scotia and raised important questions regarding the legitimacy, authenticity, and efficacy of the Canadian criminal justice system, particularly its treatment of Indigenous peoples. The report made concrete the racism and discrimination many Mi'kmaq experienced, and it validated resistance to settler society's domination. The inquiry, along with other inquiries across the country, heightened awareness that the Mi'kmaq and other Indigenous peoples exist as communities outside settler society and that they have distinct cultural understandings and ways of being that require alternative sets of institutions to accommodate those differences. The report included an abundance of evidence justifying the transfer of control back into Mi'kmaw hands, but it did not argue for a separate justice system.

The Union of Nova Scotia Indians took the lead and formulated a response to the royal commission and its recommendations on behalf of the Mi'kmaw Nation. It acknowledged that the inquiry had "opened new doors," "created new opportunities," and "fostered new hopes of our people's aspirations for self-reliance and self-determination."[17] The union put forward a statement of principles, and it offered an alternative reading of the recommendations by dividing them into two groups: (1) those that deal with improvements to the justice system outside Mi'kmaw communities and (2) those that pertain to the development of a justice system within the Mi'kmaw Nation. Two main threads emerged in Mi'kmaw discourses. The first was a rights discourse centred on treaty, constitutional, and human rights arguments for self-determination, including the right to control their own justice system. The second thread focused on the cultural necessity to control a separate justice system in which disputes could be meaningfully managed using Mi'kmaw legal principles.

Mi'kmaw leaders submitted that "it is all but inevitable that Mi'kmaw will continue to interact with the 'outside' system" and that they were committed to working with both the federal and provincial governments to implement changes to the justice system. They welcomed all efforts to indigenize the system: "An indigenization of the present system will only serve to improve the administration of a non-Mi'kmaw form of justice, law enforcement and incarceration upon the Mi'kmaw."[18] But they cautioned that this approach was not a solution for the Mi'kmaw Nation, who wanted to define and operationalize Mi'kmaw justice on their own terms: "To this day, the Mi'kmaw continue to abide by a system of social control that is unique in their communities. It operates upon different principles of fairness and justice. The key question is not whether it exists but rather how do we harness these Mi'kmaw concepts of justice to design and to develop an acceptable and an effective justice system in Mi'kmaw communities."[19]

Taking the royal commission's recommendations as the foundation for institution building, Mi'kmaw political organizations set out to create programs that would satisfy their nation's diverse needs. The Union of Nova Scotia Indians – along with the Confederacy of Mainland Mi'kmaq, the Native Council of Nova Scotia, the Nova Scotia Native Women's Association, and the Mi'kmaq Native Friendship Centre – took the position that while some of the eighty-two recommendations constituted a starting point, the desired end point would be the implementation of a community-based, Mi'kmaw-owned and -operated justice system. They posited that everyone wanted significant changes to the handling of legal practices and that the majority wanted justice services that better reflected their unique culture and socioeconomic circumstances. Most importantly, they believed that all Mi'kmaw parties wanted to be directly involved in the consultations surrounding program development. They made a united stand against the unilateral imposition of programs by the provincial and federal agencies. The Union of Nova Scotia Indians also planned to move forward on other justice issues as a means of obtaining full implementation of the terms of the 1752 Peace and Friendship Treaty, as confirmed by the Supreme Court of Canada in *James Matthew Simon v The Queen* (1985).[20] The dispute between Nova Scotia and the Mi'kmaw Nation over the existence and extent of these treaty rights was occurring simultaneously with the Marshall Inquiry.

In response to recommendation 22, the Tripartite Forum on Aboriginal Issues was established in March 1991. Modelled on the Ontario Indian Commission, the forum would use mediation to resolve unsettled issues relating to justice between three parties: the Mi'kmaw Nation, the Government of Nova Scotia, and the Government of Canada. Two months after it was created, a subcommittee on justice was set up to generate a community-needs assessment for a court worker program and a study on Aboriginal community justice, particularly the policing requirements for on- and off-reserve Mi'kmaq. Criminologist Don Clairmont's study employed nine researchers who interviewed 622 Mi'kmaw households using a survey instrument, discussion groups, in-depth interviews, and other approaches to get first-person views of and experiences with the police and courts. His three-volume report, titled *Native Justice in Nova Scotia*, published in 1992, guided policy formation and program implementation over the following decade, including the launch of pilot projects in Indigenous policing and restorative justice. The study also recommended that a new organization, Mi'kmaq Legal Services, be established to deliver justice services.

Expectations were high. Mi'kmaq dreamed of an organization that would be the pinnacle of Mi'kmaw justice, a symbol of Mi'kmaw survival, and evidence of the value of Mi'kmaw legal traditions. There would be plenty of meaningful jobs. They believed the organization could help correct historical wrongs by ensuring that no Mi'kmaw person would have to endure the racism and mistreatment experienced not only by Donald Marshall but also by the nation as a whole.

5

L'nuwey Tplutaqan | L'nu Law
Mi'kmaw Legal Principles

THE 1990S WERE A RELENTLESS rollercoaster ride for Donald as he adapted to life outside prison and dealt with intense media scrutiny as he battled the justice system. He found some solace in reconnecting with his relatives and elders at the Mi'kmaq Native Friendship Centre in Halifax. In the safe space of the centre, strong women such as Marie Francis, Ducy Paul, Mary Brooks, the Sylliboy sisters, and his cousins, the Googoos from Sipekne'katik, protected and nurtured him. One of the royal commission's recommendations – reopening the issue of whether he had been adequately compensated for the wrongs done to him – once again put a spotlight on the issue of racism and discrimination in Nova Scotia's justice system and the damage that it had inflicted on Donald and the Mi'kmaw Nation.

Testimony given by Donald's girlfriends Karen Brown and Martha Tudor at the compensation inquiry persuasively detailed the psychological and emotional challenges he had faced upon his release and in light of being blamed for his wrongful conviction.[1] Jack Stewart, who had helped Donald transition to life outside prison, and Felix Cacchione, his former lawyer, spoke of Donald's strong sense of tradition, his desire to work with youth, and how the incarceration had interfered with his ability to take on the hereditary role of grand chief. Everyone testified to Donald's love of fishing.

The commission, headed by the Honourable Gregory T. Evans, concluded that Marshall had not been compensated adequately.[2] A new settlement was brokered that included a down payment, and a locked annuity, disbursed monthly, was set up for Donald and his mother. The compensation inquiry also recommended that the Government of Nova Scotia undertake to provide a sum of up to $50,000 to cover all expenses related to the treatment and rehabilitation of substance misuse. Donald wanted the figures kept private, but they were part of the public record.

Evans wanted to make sure Donald was provided with an income so he could live his life with dignity:

> The Government viewed the $270,000 as compensation for the period of time Donald Marshall Jr. spent in jail. It did not take into consideration any negligence or wrongdoing that may have put him there or kept him there. Notwithstanding that, Marshall was asked to – and did – sign a full release of any and all claims which he might have had against the Crown. The monies paid to Donald Marshall Jr. do not in any way purport to compensate him for the inadequate, incompetent and unprofessional investigations of Sandy Seale's murder by John MacIntyre and the Sydney Police Department; the inadequate representation he received at the hands of his counsel; the failure of the Crown prosecutor to disclose the inconsistent statements of key witnesses; the failure of the Attorney General's Department to disclose their knowledge of Jimmy MacNeil's coming forward in November 1971; and the incompetent reinvestigation by RCMP Inspector Marshall in November 1971 – none of which relates to the period Marshall spent in jail.[3]

Evans also took care to note that Donald had suffered these indignities as an Indigenous person:

> He suffered the loss of his ability to use his language in prison because of the fact that he was Native. He may have lost the opportunity to become

Grand Chief of the Micmac Nation due to his incarceration. The evidence indicates that the Micmac community is very close knit and that Donald Marshall, Jr. would have suffered in the extreme by being wrenched away from the community as a youth.[4]

The inquiry underscored that the wrongful conviction had profound consequences for Mi'kmaw communities and had disrupted Mi'kmaw laws of kinship and leadership.

The years immediately following the royal commission were a time of cultural revitalization but also of setbacks and conflict as Mi'kmaq worked and fought to implement the commission's recommendations. Donald was involved in almost every initiative and on every front. He sat on the board of the Community Legal Issues Facilitator Demonstration Project, or CLIF, a pilot project supported by the Tripartite Forum. Although short-lived, CLIF sought to facilitate the provision of fair and equitable criminal justice services to all Indigenous people in Nova Scotia by providing a mechanism for meaningful communication and exchange. CLIF was largely a conduit for court worker services, public legal education, and cross-cultural sensitivity training, especially with police, judges, and corrections staff.

CLIF shared a common goal with all the pilot projects supported by the Tripartite Forum in these years: returning jurisdiction over justice to the Mi'kmaq and fostering a reinvigoration of Mi'kmaw law. In the aftermath of the royal commission, Mi'kmaw demands for justice grounded in Mi'kmaw legal principles (with their focus on relationships, ceremony, and family and community healing) took on more resonance, and Mi'kmaq wanted community command over decision making and the freedom to design and implement services to suit their needs. The Mi'kmaq had two central goals: (1) to ensure better treatment of their people within the Canadian justice system and (2) to control their own system of justice in order to deal meaningfully with problems in their territories. Mi'kmaw legal consciousness found expression in the nation's support of justice inquiries that championed the expansion of locally controlled, culturally based services and, increasingly, treaty rights implementation. Mi'kmaq envisaged a national network of services ranging from customary law and victim assistance to crime prevention and policing, from public legal education to community-based youth and justice programs focused on healing and managing the complex problems associated with cultural genocide and colonization.

BUT WHAT, EXACTLY, was meant by *Mi'kmaw law* or *Mi'kmaw legal principles*, and had they, as the Mi'kmaq insisted, never gone away? Throughout my fieldwork, I encountered numerous examples of people forgiving one another for incredible wrongs. Murders, assaults, and thefts were resolved by retaliations and the invocation of spiritual sanctions – what comes around goes around – that produced a balancing effect by reorienting relationships away from harm. Mi'kmaw justice is about relationships. After periods of hostility, shaming, and avoidance, people come together to deal with another crisis and resolve their differences through ceremony, telling their side of the story, collective grieving, communal feasting, and letting go. Through this work, people are reminded of the ancestral teachings of the sacred gifts, reflected in the concepts of love, honesty, humility, respect, truth, patience, and wisdom.[5] These gifts unite people in relationships of kindness and peace and in knowledge of how to live together with love.

Much of this healing work occurred outside the gaze and constraints of the Canadian justice system. People often told me that "Natives can't charge other Natives," so cases had to be resolved without outside intervention. The Mi'kmaq believed deeply in the settler justice system's inability to understand and respect their lives and culture. Generations of experience and storytelling had told them not to trust the system or have faith in its ability to help. The system was useful, they told me, only if you were guilty and wanted to escape the community's wrath.

These testimonies – along with legends, oral histories, and missionary accounts – counter colonial interpretations of Mi'kmaw culture as simplistic and without law. Prior to the arrival of explorers and settlers, the Mi'kmaq constituted separate and sovereign peoples subject to their own legal practices. In the aftermath of the Marshall Inquiry, the Mi'kmaq hoped to return to that empowered, decolonized state.

At the centre of Mi'kmaw legal culture lie the underlying principles of *weji-sqalia'tek* (we sprout from the land) and *msit no'kmaq* (all my relations) and the law of honour (*kepmite'tmnej*). One honours relationships with other people, the ancestors, and the lands and waters and their gifts, but one does not own them. One has a responsibility to them, not ownership over them. These principles have connected L'nu, the name Mi'kmaw people call themselves, to one another and to their territory since time immemorial. Mi'kmaq people's relationship to their territories are signified in their place names, which are implanted with cultural meanings and form the basis of collective memories when knowledge and experience of land use are shared across generations. Such connections are important to laws of kinship and responsible harvesting. When Mi'kmaq say a place name, they are quoting ancestral speech and acknowledging a sacred connection that they have a responsibility to honour. Msit no'kmaq is a teaching that connects Mi'kmaq to one another and to the world around them.

Oral history tells us that the Mi'kmaw Nation and political life had three levels – national, district, and local – and the Mi'kmawey Mawio'mi, or Grand Council, represented the nation. Stephen Augustine, a current hereditary chief, states that over time the Mi'kmaq evolved into "seven Mawiomis, each further subdivided into seven districts of the Mi'kmaw Grand Council. That is the origin of Mi'kmaw Aboriginal title and Aboriginal rights today."[6]

The Grand Council was the highest authority of Mi'kmaw political, economic, and spiritual organization. It was composed of a grand chief and a governing executive council, which consisted of a grand *keptin* (captain), a *putus* (knowledge keeper), and a war chief. Alongside the executive were the seven *keptins* (district leaders), people who had risen among the ranks of the local chiefs.[7] Mi'kmaw people believed that Kisu'lkw (the Creator), in order to guide the Mi'kmaq in their domestic relations, endowed a few people of every generation with special knowledge of the six worlds of the woodlands, the sky, the earth, the oceans, and the spirits. Although there is debate about its origins, Mi'kmaw oral tradition tells us that the Grand Council also developed in response to a need for organized interaction with other Indigenous peoples in matters of war and trade and helped frame the Wabanaki Confederacy, an alliance with neighbouring tribes. Over generations, wise people and leaders developed a consensual union of the families, and the collaborative leadership "was selfless, and listened, shared and deliberated widely within family, community and other leaders in making decisions (tplutaqn)."[8] Within Mi'kma'ki, council members dealt with social, ecological, economic, and ceremonial matters. The grand chief was a particularly outstanding individual, imbued with all of the characteristics admired by the Mi'kmaq – generosity, superior intelligence, strong kinship connections, aggressiveness in war, and superior harvesting skills. He was responsible for dispute management within his own district and was called upon to settle problems in other areas of the nation, particularly when local and district chiefs needed assistance to bring about an adequate resolution.

As per the laws of leadership and ceremony, the Grand Council met regularly with advisers, elders, and puoinaq (spiritually powerful healers) and held long discussions to plan and manage the affairs of the nation. In the autumn and the spring, it assembled to help leaders assign harvesting territories to families and individuals – its most important task. The nation's health, military strength, and cosmological balance depended on the proper distribution of resources, as informed by the laws guiding geopolitical collaboration, harvesting and sharing, and place and kinship. In the summer, the Grand Council deliberated on peace and war, treaties of friendship, and treaties for the common good.[9]

At the local level, Mi'kmaw society was clan-based, and Mi'kmaw people lived in extended family units. Each clan was represented by a symbol or extension of itself, usually depicted as an animal or a physical feature of the landscape from which the clan had sprouted. The family heads of each district were responsible for planning the seasonal movements of the people; confirming and reassigning harvesting territories; delegating work to immediate relatives; providing hunting dogs, canoes, provisions, and reserves for expeditions; and reminding people of their responsibility to share and care for one another.

In the spring and summer, families congregated in semi-permanent villages along waterways with abundant fish and seafood. In areas where there were higher concentrations of food, populations tended to be higher, and regardless of the size of the village, resource extraction was cooperative.

Weir fishing, for example, required people to work together to construct and maintain the traps and harvest and process the catch. During the fall and winter, the villages separated into smaller familial groups to hunt.

The larger and more elaborate the kinship group, the more powerful its leader. The position of chief, at any level, was predominantly hereditary, and chiefs were usually men, although women held influence over the leaders' actions in the councils and could request deliberations on particular events or concerns. Lineage mattered. Chiefs and elders recited their genealogies in speeches at marriages and funerals to preserve the histories of the families and communities and their ties to the land, the spirit world, and one another. Recitation of the leader's genealogy reminded people of their kin ties and responsibilities and obligations – activities integral to identity formation and the formation of legal consciousness. The orations included descriptions of important events, acts of courage and generosity, and exceptional hunting and fishing adventures, and perhaps most importantly, they included instructions on what constituted desired qualities for living right in the Mi'kmaw way.

Leaders, as family heads, commonly held their positions for life, unless they lost their community's support or committed a crime, for which they could be deposed. They needed strong oratory skills to convince people to accept their directives on war, alliances, and territorial divisions for hunting and fishing. Leaders were responsible for providing subsistence to all connected to them and did not accumulate individual wealth. The practice of polygyny – one person having multiple mates – allowed leaders to expand their networks of followers and alliances to other groups. The greater the family size, the more gifts and contributions to the leader and the greater the ability to redistribute the goods to a larger number of people. Sharing enabled the leader to gain the respect and loyalty needed to keep followers in times of unpredictability such as disputes, war, or famine. Leaders were responsible for the care of orphans and found homes for them with the best hunters, where they were raised as if they were natural children of the head of the family.

The poorer the leaders appeared, the greater their status, because meagreness was attributed to tremendous generosity and kindheartedness towards others, values highly regarded among the Mi'kmaq. A seventeenth-century Jesuit priest observed that one chief made it a point of honour to be always the worst dressed of his people, and to take care that they all were better clothed than he. He held it as a maxim, as he told me one day, that a ruler and a great heart like his, ought to take more care for others than for himself because good hunter as he was he always obtained easily everything which he needed for his own use, and that as for the rest, if he did not himself live well, he should find his desire in the affection and hearts of his subject. It was as if he wished to say that his treasures and riches were in the hearts and in the affections of his people.[10]

Exceptions to chiefly generosity were rare, but when leaders were not generous, followers could withdraw their support and ally themselves with other families.

Lineage and hereditary status mattered, but there was no guarantee that a chief would keep his leadership position or that his eldest son would succeed him. When a chief believed he was going to die, he would designate a successor. The eldest son began his training at an early age, but if he lacked leadership qualities, and if there were no other male children directly descended from the chief, his sister's eldest son would be considered. If this reckoning process failed to produce a leader, the search expanded to the extended family network.

Within each village, the chief was guided by a council of elders, which consisted of the heads or representatives of the families who had distinguished themselves in the sacred gifts and in hunting, storytelling, healing, material production, or warfare. As a group, the council conferred authority on the chief. Chiefs also relied on puoinaq, who had spiritually imbued abilities and conferred power, status, and prestige on the chief.[11] As spiritual leaders, puoinaq had a special role to play in Mi'kmaw law. Male, female, or two-spirited, they were formidable people whose influence was critical to the community's wider legal consciousness. Their powers were derived from their connections to spiritual and animal worlds through beliefs in animism and anthropomorphism.

Puoinaq were guardians of public welfare, morals, and proper conduct in general. They upheld the laws of ceremony and were likely great healers and storytellers. They were well-respected citizens with superior intelligence, perception, intuition, and judgment. The council and citizens called upon them to conduct sweats, find lost articles, determine the time and place of resource extraction, make predictions about enemy activity, commend or rebuke war designs, and find out if a missing person was dead or alive. Since "it was felt that the infraction of the traditional laws of the nation brought misfortune upon the entire nation," it was puoinaq's responsibility to correct or bring about balance by locating the guilty party through divination and meting out the proper remedy to restore relations.[12] Puoinaq were known to use reflections in containers of water to elicit confessions about wrong-doings from onlookers.

Successful predictions and healings bolstered the puoinaq's personal reputation and the chance of being aligned with powerful chiefs and families. Citizens compensated puoinaq for their services with food, tools, household objects, access to hunting grounds, or other culturally significant materials. These ritual specialists were the earliest Mi'kmaw justice navigators. They were well respected for their efforts to restore balance and help heal relationships using their encyclopedic knowledge of medicinal and spiritual remedies. They encouraged reintegrative conduct that would facilitate the prosperity of the community that depended on them for their survival.

Families and communities also relied on elders for guidance. Elders spoke first at public feasts and advised leaders on *L'nuwey Tplutaqan* (Mi'kmaw legal principles). They were the embodiment of wisdom and were revered for their stories of survival and deep knowledge of the world around them. They made important decisions to ensure their community's cohesiveness. Elders' councils were called on to address conflicts and issues that could not be resolved within families, where the majority of problems were addressed. Their advice was sought in all matters concerning the balancing of environmental, personal, and spiritual relations. The words and opinions of the respected elders carried weight, and all strived to adhere to and abide by their instructions.

Mi'kmaw life and law were family-centred. Families established and reinforced community values. From time immemorial, Mi'kmaw legal principles and consciousness evolved in response to the necessities of survival, subsistence, and getting along. The Mi'kmaq negotiated their survival with the environment through spiritual ceremonies, and they derived their rights from the natural laws of the land to which they belonged.[13] Formal and informal practices were designed to direct relations between members of society to ensure their continued existence. Over time, the core values needed to endure and flourish – sharing, resource stewardship, cooperative governance, reciprocity, and honouring kin – became the cornerstones for law, procedure, and identity.

AS MARITIME PEOPLES, Mi'kmaq had access to great varieties of food, which enhanced their ability to survive in the event of the demise of a particular species. The early Mi'kmaq fished, hunted, and collected, but 90 percent of their food came from the sea. Although there were periods of starvation, they developed a flexible and holistic approach to living off the land and sea that enabled them to live and reproduce their populations for millennia. The principles of *netukulimk* (responsible harvesting) guided Mi'kmaw resource use and management and lay at the heart of Mi'kmaw legal consciousness and *tplutaquan* (law). To practise netukulimk required Mi'kmaq to individually and collectively honour the bounty that Kisu'lkw (the Creator) had provided to the ancestors but to do so in a way that respected the sacredness of the places where one hunts, gathers, and fishes, and acknowledged the ancestral interconnectedness of the spirits that reside there. Prior to harvesting, Mi'kmaq made offerings and prayers, "enacting a reverence for all things of creation imbued with spirit."[14] Netukulimk is about respect, reverence, responsibility, and reciprocity. Its practice and philosophy embrace coexistence, interdependence, and community spirit in a synthesis of past, present, and future. Failure to practise netukulimk could lead to a failed hunt; a poor harvest; spiritual sanctions; or communal sanctions, shunning, or shaming.

Children learned responsible stewardship and how to live on the land and with one another from their elders. Respect for elder knowledge was emphasized through daily activities in the home and through public deference in ceremonies and social gatherings. Adults taught children rules and etiquette in the home, and grandparents and other members of the extended family reinforced them. Elders taught by doing; children learned by trying. Adults interfered only if children were in great danger. In public, children demonstrated deference to elders by walking behind them, not crossing in front of them, listening carefully and without interrupting them, avoiding extended eye contact with them, and waiting to be told when it was their turn to speak. When sharing food, protocols ensured that elders received the first and best portions and that these and all other comforts were delivered to them by the young people.

During everyday family activities and ritualized practices, elders transmitted ancient laws, traditional knowledge, social norms and mores, and core concepts and values (such as love, honesty, humility, respect, truth, patience, and wisdom) orally through histories, anecdotes, and *a'tukwaqan* (stories).[15] The language of these histories, stories, and rituals included several hundred words relating to legal concepts and practices, words such as *injury, loss, security, empowerment, harmony, revenge, shame, forgiveness, banishment, integration,* and *balance.* Law lived in the language, and justice was about relations. Mi'kmaw legal principles were more than the compartmentalization of rules. Kinship patterns; marriage practices; political processes; notions of authority, status, inheritance, and class; and relationships to the land, to the spirit world, to outsiders, and to one another were all guided by ideas about how to live right and how to distinguish oneself as L'nu.

Elders told creation stories about how L'nu sprouted from the land and sea with the help of Kisu'lkw (the Creator) and Kluskap (the first L'nu) to teach children about their ancestral relations. Through these ties, children gained a "time immemorial" connection to their territory. They learned that Kisu'lkw had taught their Mi'kmaw ancestors how to live, hunt, fish, pray, and to name the stars and the constellations, which guided the ancestor spirits in their travels to the other worlds. Kisu'lkw also taught the people to live together with common purpose and respect alongside all other human, plants, and animals.[16] Children learned that Kisu'lkw, as a supernatural being manifested in the form of the sun, could cause misfortune because he controlled the destiny of all peoples and things. Sunrise ceremonies were regularly performed to honour the Creator, seek protection, and ask for power to overcome enemies; for success in hunting and fishing; and for prosperity for future generations. Failure to adhere to protocols in these rituals, the legends warned, could lead to illness or misfortune.

Kluskap legends likewise reinforced the tenet that all life forces are sacred and that the balance between good and bad must be maintained to avoid catastrophe. One of the most important trickster figures in Mi'kmaw legends, Kluskap is a spiritual teacher, a warrior, an adventurer, and a transformer. He created the landscape, animated the spirits within it, and provided the people with the skills for survival and then, after many adventures, he retreated to some far-off land. Legend has it that Kluskap will return. (After the Supreme Court's fishing decision, the Mi'kmaq referred to Donald affectionately as Kluskap.) Kluskap legends relate tales of good and evil (often represented by Kluskap's twin brother), provide explanations for natural wonders such as thunder, rain, and death and embody the laws, morals, and wisdom of the Mi'kmaw Nation. Mi'kmaw cosmology tells us that the Creator taught Kluskap how to live right, and Kluskap in turn instructed the Mi'kmaq, teaching them to speak the language, make tools, harvest respectfully, and get along. Although Kluskap is mischievous, he is ultimately benevolent, the embodiment of Mi'kmaw wisdom. Kluskap legends often focus on the benefits of self-control to manage conflicts or disputes or deal with the problems that ensue when people let their anger, greed, or jealousy take over.

Kluskap legends made clear the consequences of wrongdoing and encouraged the fair treatment of all peoples and caring for the spirits in objects. Children were told that if they did not honour and obey their parents and stay close to home, evil spirits would capture runaways, shrink them, and keep them in birch bark boxes. In one story, Kluskap instructs, "When you use this pipe to make your prayers, do it in a sacred manner and your prayers will be answered. If you use it wrongly, harm will come back on you and your families. Use this pipe wisely. Be careful what you pray for, because you will get exactly what you ask for."[17] When the Mi'kmaq interacted with other groups, smoking the pipe together was a symbol of peace. If people refused to take the tobacco pipe when presented with it, it was a sign that they were not a friend. Mi'kmaw people smoked prior to making important decisions and before undertaking risky tasks. The smoke, a conduit to the ancestors' healing powers, was thought to help build concentration and reveal a path to the best or right way of dealing with problems.

Kluskap stories and other legends also taught listeners how to avoid shame and reproach. Tales recounted how to carry out honourable exploits such as avenging wrongdoing in socially sanctioned manners. Most often, the tales specified the value of *utkunajik* (sharing) – so integral to Mi'kmaw identity and culture – and the consequences of greed. When Mi'kmaq travelled to other families' territories, they extended certain courtesies such as gifts to their hosts in a show of respect, and their hosts had a duty to welcome them for as long as possible and hold feasts in their honour. The concepts of reciprocity and sharing were at the heart of agreements and alliances and guaranteed "dignity in spite of flux."[18] Failure to reciprocate could strain relations and break down social cohesiveness, which was necessary for survival. When that happened, people looked to the teachings within legends for examples of dispute management and how to look beyond revenge to reinstate balance. The stories taught, however, that not all disputes are immediately resolved but may fester over time, producing blood feuds, a pattern that continues in Mi'kmaw society today.

Mi'kmaw children also learned ritualized practices to appease and please the spirit world, to correct mistakes, to explain the unexplainable, and to bring harm to others when balance was disrupted. Celebratory observances of sacred beliefs brought tribal members together for collective and emotionally charged rituals. These important socializing events – ceremonies for the dead and the newborn or ceremonies to mark transitions to adulthood, such as first menses and the first moose harvested – reinforced ideas about identity, status, and how to live right and take up one's responsibilities. Mi'kmaw families gathered together seasonally to recite to one another the names of all those who had been born and died since the last gathering, and they recounted significant happenings – unusual weather, conflicts and disputes, and exceptional fishing and hunting expeditions. Amid competitions, games, and ceremonies, people sought out potential marriage partners, and they built political and familial alliances. Leaders and elders instructed newlyweds by advising them on how to get along without quarrelling and delivered lessons regarding marriage at wedding ceremonies. Puoinaq helped solemnize the unions and gave warnings about the consequences of infidelity or acting as a spy for another tribe.

Feasting protocols, dances, and songs were celebrations of beliefs that imparted lessons and integrated individuals into the group. Sharing was the way of life. For instance, during Wi'kupaltimk, a non-adversarial feasting ceremony, people fed one another with the spiritual food of kindness, forgiveness, and love to repair relations and reduce ostracism. After eating, they gathered in a circle, and a recognized authority figure such as a chief or elder led each person around the circle to exchange peace with the others. Stories and songs likewise imparted how to treat food and the taboos associated with obtaining, preparing, and distributing it. Children learned that wasting food was an offence to the spirit who lived within it, and stories and songs emphasized that every part of the animal, even eel skins, must be used – the original snout-to-tail ethos. What could not be put to use had to be ritually disposed of so as not to offend the spirits and jeopardize future relations.

Dance was a means to invoke power and to embody the spirit of animal, plant, enemy, or lover. Songs were sung for different occasions, ranging from welcome songs, to war chants, to mourning descants. Some songs recounted stories, offered fables with a moral lesson, or warned of the consequences of wrongdoing. Special songs, dances, and feasts honoured those who had successfully avenged themselves. Songs could also be used to test magic powers, medicine, and strength. In war parties, for instance, each canoe would challenge the other to a song duel to see who could last the longest.

In addition to feasting, dancing, and song rituals, Mi'kmaq practised cleansing ceremonies in a sweat lodge tradition: "During sweats ... they chanted songs and told stories to make themselves laugh ... being refreshed they put their robes upon them and then went into their wigwams as composed as ever."[19] Marc Lescarbot, following his expedition to Acadia in the early seventeenth century, suggested that puoinaq participation in the sweat lodge indicated its spiritual significance for healing and renewal:

It is a rite of purification and healing, undertaken both to restore and to maintain bodily health, but undertaken even more generally as a preliminary for participation in religious exercise ... In the Indian's eyes the sweatbath was far more than a simple physical efficacy. It brought him intimately and directly into contact with the Powers which uphold his world, giving universal health and sanity of nature. All the elements, fire, stony earth, water and vaporous air, entered into the ritual healing, which was preceded by chants and prayer and was felt to bring a new birth into the life of that greater community of being in which man's existence is only a participation.[20]

The sweat lodge served as a holistic purification ritual and conduit to the spirit world for those seeking guidance prior to decision making. Spiritually sick wrongdoers could also seek solace and healing in the sweat lodge with the help of puoinaq. Regardless of its many uses, the sweat lodge offered a space for communal counselling and healing for those that entered.

ALTHOUGH MI'KMAW LAW emphasizes balance, life in Mi'kma'ki was not perfectly harmonious. While it may be attractive to think of the past as paradisiacal and peaceful, this was not the case. Disputes broke out between family and community members and among groups when the balance between local tribal communities and their natural resources was disrupted. When an offence was committed, the Mi'kmaq treated it primarily as an offence against relationships and only secondarily as a violation of rules. When problems arose, families intervened to produce solutions, and responsibility for managing wrongdoings remained with the parties involved.

If wrongdoing interfered with the daily operations of the community, spiritual practitioners or puoinaq would be called in to assist, to remove sicknesses thought to have caused the troubles, or to find other causes and propose potential solutions. Persons with authority, such as community leaders or respected elders, might speak to the wrongdoers, teaching them how to fix the situation and to find balance in taking responsibility, a condition or state conceptualized as *apiksiktuaqn* (a mutual forgiveness) or *apiksiktuek* (that which forgives). This state, marked by the reintegration of the wrongdoer into the group, was vitally important for social cohesion, group unity and, ultimately, survival.

Aside from talking it out, there were other formal and informal practices to resolve disputes and restore individuals to the community. These practices were guided by the concept of *ilsutekek* (coming together into a circle to make right; to judge correctly according to the nature of the misdeed or injury), and the goal was *asidolisk* (to create balance or make conditions even). To arrive at asidolisk, everyone involved – wrongdoer, victim, and community – needed to engage in *nijkitekek* (that which heals) to generate holistic awareness of the impact of harms on all involved. Mutual forgiveness and the act of restoring community through cooperation was referred to as *apiksiktatultimk*. Forgiveness could not be demanded; it needed to be arrived at through the processes of coming together, ilsutekek, and talking respectfully until everyone feels peace from understanding, nijkitekek.

As in Western tort law, Mi'kmaw law protected familial and communal rights to territories. Mi'kmaq developed laws of trespass with enforceable sanctions if the laws were breached. It was important that a family not be prevented from carrying out its responsibilities for maintaining "a material and spiritual balance between its own needs and those of the animal population."[21] In order to hunt on another's territory, one had to pay a tribute and follow correct spiritual protocols. If someone hunted on another's territory without permission, the wrongdoer had to hand over the catch or a portion of it. If they failed to do so, the dispute could escalate into a feud, disrupting the sacred balance.

Disputes that stemmed from acts of trespass or murder could be resolved quickly through immediate confrontation, employing *hapenkuituik* (the law of vengeance that states that great offences are to be avenged by the family wronged). Early missionaries noted that Mi'kmaq never forgot an injury and that it was considered a weakness to not avenge a wrong. An individual could be ostracized for not completing an act of revenge because establishing balance and demonstrating bravery were critical. In the case of murder, revenge entailed either killing a member or members of another group or taking members to fill the place of the deceased. Pierre Biard, a French Jesuit missionary, noted:

The Gaspesians have at present no fundamental laws which serve them as regulations. They make up and end all their quarrels and their differences through friends and through arbiters. If it is, however, a question of punishing a criminal who has killed or assassinated some Indians, he is condemned to death without other form of law. "Take care my friend if thou killest, thou shalt be killed." This is often carried out by command of the Elders, who assemble in council upon the subject, and often by the private authority of individuals, without any trial of the case being made, provided that it is evident the criminal has deserved death.[22]

Contrary to what Biard suggests, however, custom and the principle of equivalent retaliation limited acts of vengeance into a sort of "ritualistic revenge."[23] Mi'kmaq had a full range of disputing processes and management strategies, including elder instruction, fistfights, the payment of compensation, feuding, shaming, and corrective rituals.

In the case of revenge between tribes, women performed a dance, urging men to take action. If the men could not carry out the revenge to rebalance relations, the women would take it upon themselves and actively shame the men for their cowardice.[24] For internal disputes, Biard commented:

If the offenses are not between tribes but between compatriots and fellow-citizens, then they fight among themselves for slight offenses, and their way of fighting is like that of women here, they fly for the hairs, holding on to this they struggle and jerk in a terrible fashion, and if they are equally matched, they keep it up one whole day, or even two, without stopping until someone separates them.[25]

Fights were moderated by friends or by authority figures in the community, namely, chiefs, elders and, on some occasions, puoinaq. "Fairness" in this form of dispute management meant an equal matching of foes without the use of weapons and a quick resolution. Chrestien Le Clercq, a Recollect missionary, commented, "All dwell contentedly upon this word habenque-douic 'he did not begin it, he has paid him back: quits and good friends.' But if the guilty one, repenting of his fault, wishes to make peace, he is usually received with satisfaction, offering presents and other suitable atonement."[26]

In some cases, however, fistfights might lead only to a temporary resolution. If the person who lost didn't accept defeat, he could seek to avenge his honour. Individual feuds could easily escalate into family feuds, particularly in tight-knit communities where people tend to take sides and ally themselves with friends and family. Feuding between families could also erupt over competition in harvesting areas or because of bad relations stemming from a marriage refusal, public embarrassment, a perceived affront, greed, or the breakdown of an alliance. These feuds needed to be contained, though, because day-to-day survival was easier when people lived in harmony.

War or peace, however, were never declared without seeking the advice and consent of the leaders and elders. Discussions were held in public forums to assess the risks and rationales. Long orations detailed the circumstances of the offence, and people had the opportunity to question the plans to resolve the harms. After each proposal, the leaders checked in with the audience to gauge their support, which they conveyed by making an exclamation. If there was no consensus, the orations continued until they either rejected the plan or approved it and went to war or made peace.

When conflicts or war came to an end, the restoration of balance was marked by ceremonial peacemaking. Some conflicts ended with the burying of a hatchet.[27] Others, such as treaties of peace between the Mi'kmaq and other groups, were marked with the sharing of a pipe, a formal declaration of peace, gift giving, dancing, and feasting. Spiritual and material offerings and presents signalled that the perpetrator had taken responsibility and atoned for the wrongdoing. Le Clercq observed, "They even make considerable presents to those who punish them severely for their misbehaviour, in order, say they, to remove from the hearts of the former all the bitterness caused by the crime of which they are guilty."[28] He suggested that the wronged could not exonerate the perpetrator until gifts had been extended: "It is forbidden them by the laws and customs of the country to pardon or to forgive any one of their enemies, unless great presents are given on behalf of these to the whole nation, or to those who have been injured."[29]

UNLIKE WESTERN SYSTEMS of law – composed of lawyers, codes, courts, and cops – Mi'kmaw law was not a neutral, rigid, and self-contained system for handling right and wrong. Mi'kmaw laws represented a holistic, dynamic system of values embedded in social relations and transmitted from generation to generation. Mi'kmaw culture and law were sophisticated and allowed the nation to flourish for thousands of years. As Donald's experiences and the Marshall Inquiry revealed, colonial encounters with explorers, disease, missionaries, traders, alcohol, and settlers and with the imposition of Western systems of law, education, and governance upset the balance. Missionaries, residential schools, the breakdown of treaties, settlement on reserve lands, and the imposition of the Indian Act did not benevolently assist in the so-called civilizing mission, as many would have it. Instead, colonization disrupted Mi'kmaw relations with the land and resources; discredited the social powers and ritualistic practices of leaders, puoinaq, and Grand Council members; and broke the ties that bound children to their elders and the ancestors. Criminalized by settlers, Mi'kmaw L'nuwey Tplutaqan was targeted for obliteration by Western structures of law and punishment.

As the French entered their territory in the seventeenth century, the Mi'kmaq acted in accordance with their legal traditions and demanded presents and acknowledgment. They managed to maintain a middle ground, a term coined by historian Richard White to refer to the period when Indigenous peoples and Europeans moved past the point of treating each other as aliens and learned to negotiate with and accommodate each other. But over time, colonial encounters and the introduction of new concepts and Christian ideologies such as sin, punishment, guilt, and absolution had a profound impact on Mi'kmaw behaviour. Shifts in their belief systems altered their legal consciousness. Community-based healing and reparation diminished with the rise of individual self-interest and market economies. French fishers, traders, and settlers introduced diseases and alcohol, which led to rapid population decline and altered the form and context of disputes and dispute resolution in Mi'kmaw communities. Le Clercq noted:

Injuries, quarrels, homicides, murders, parricides, to this day the sad consequences of the trade in brandy; and one sees with grief Indians dying in their drunkenness; strangling themselves, the brother cutting the throat of the sister, the husband breaking the head of his wife, a mother throwing her child into the fire or the river, and fathers cruelly choking little innocent children whom they cherish and love as much as and more than themselves when they are not deprived of their reason. They consider it sport to break and shatter everything in the wigwams and to bawl for hours together, repeating always the same word. They beat themselves and tear themselves to pieces, something which happens never or at least very rarely, when they are sober. Sometimes they rob, ravage and burn the French houses and stores.[30]

Jesuit missionaries compounded the trauma by denouncing puoinaq and by condemning Mi'kmaw practices and laws, particularly the laws of ceremony, as profane, evil, and uncivilized.

Although the Mi'kmaw managed to keep the French on a middle ground, co-existence and adherence to the values of netukulimk (responsible harvesting) and sharing became impossible once control of Acadia, renamed Nova Scotia, passed to the British with the Treaty of Utrecht in 1713. The fur trade expanded, and settlement increased. Some Mi'kmaq spent more time pursuing furs and individual gain than they did ensuring supplies for the winter and their redistribution throughout the community. As they were pushed off their lands, the sacred connections to their territories and each other were upset. Participation in the fur trade and the pressure it placed on resources – combined with rapid population decline and British interference in Mi'kmaw life – disrupted the social organization that underpinned Mi'kmaw laws of geopolitical collaboration and kinship and contributed to a decline in the authority of chiefs. The assignment of hunting territories and decisions concerning the seasonal movements of groups, formerly in the hands of elders and the Grand Council, underwent dramatic changes. A group of middlemen emerged as go-betweens among traders, the military, missionaries, and the Mi'kmaq. People who had not demonstrated the required and desired qualities of leadership were now able to assume new forms of power, status, and privilege.

Mi'kmaq actively resisted the expropriation of their land and interference in their affairs. They signed a chain of treaty agreements with the British between 1725 and 1779, and throughout the process they emphasized that they were the first inhabitants and rightful owners of the land.[31]

But the treaties altered long-standing Mi'kmaw dispute-management techniques. A clause in the 1726 treaty stated: "In case of any misunderstanding, Quarrel or Injury between the English and the Indians, no private Revenge shall be taken, but Application shall be made for redress according to his Majesty's Laws." The British assumed, when the Mi'kmaq signed treaties, that they would submit to a judicial process based on the British rule of law and punishment. To access justice, people would make complaints to the governor, the King's representative and responsible for mediating disputes with the Mi'kmaq. In 1749, Edward Cornwallis, the governor of Nova Scotia and a man known for his brutality, opened a commission that made him, along with a council and an assembly, the lawmaker of the colony. In 1752, when the Crown signed another treaty with the Mi'kmaq, it stipulated that all disputes between Mi'kmaq and British settlers would be tried in "His Majesty's Courts of Civil Judicature."[32]

The Mi'kmaq, however, continued to resist British domination and avoided the British courts. Nearly a hundred years later, in 1823, Judge Thomas Chandler Haliburton noted that Mi'kmaq have "a code of traditionary and customary laws among themselves."[33] Only two cases went before the bench in the 1800s, and they brought about a ban on the sale of liquor to Mi'kmaq and protected their right to hunt porpoise. The Mi'kmaq who turned to the British justice system to protect their lands or interests, however, found little support. Noting that squatters had violated all of the reserves in Nova Scotia except two, H.W. Crawley, an Indian commissioner in Cape Breton in 1849, reported:

> Under present circumstances no adequate protection can be obtained for the Indian property. It would be in vain to seek a verdict from any jury in this Island against the trespassers on the reserves; nor perhaps would a member of the Bar be found willingly and effectually to advocate the cause of the Indians, inasmuch as he would thereby injure his own prospects, by damaging his popularity.[34]

Most British subjects thought Indigenous persons were incapable of giving evidence and swearing oaths in courts of law because they were not "civilized" and Christian. The Mi'kmaq were not allowed to swear oaths to their deities or Kisu'lkw, and the courts made no allowances for their language or oral traditions. Mi'kmaw evidence, if translated at all, was generally reduced to a written English statement that could not be read and verified by the witness. Mi'kmaw people were ordered to put their marks (signatures) on statements, regardless of the accuracy.

The Mi'kmaq were not passive; they did not accept the insufficiencies of the imposed legal system. On the contrary, they resisted in a variety of ways, ranging from avoidance, to refusal to participate in legal cases, to active resistance using petitions. For more than a century, the Mi'kmaq determinedly made petitions to Crown officials in England against British violation of the treaties, which the Mi'kmaq articulated as violations of sacred relationships. Petitions made in 1814, 1841, 1854, and 1860 (and even in 1982) cited numerous infractions of human rights and instances of racial discrimination, theft of property, confiscation of land, and violations of persons. They also noted the extreme poverty and poor health in which the Mi'kmaq lived as a consequence of British colonization. The petitions largely went unanswered.

The Mi'kmaq endured encounters with missionaries, treaty making with the British, dispossession of their lands and resources, and the imposition of policies of "civilization." Eurocentric ideologies justified the necessity – indeed the moral imperative – of Indigenous salvation through subordination and subjugation. These rationales, founded on the self-serving doctrines of church and state, went beyond notions of European superiority, the doctrine of discovery, and *terra nullius*. They also facilitated the denial of Indigenous sovereignty and moral virtue. Stereotypes of Indigenous people as primitive and lawless bolstered the genocidal ideologies of colonial supremacy and the benevolence of "Indian civilization programs." The humanity of Indigenous peoples was, by definition, erased, and the wealth of Indigenous knowledge and the depth of their sacred relations to their territories peremptorily repudiated.

FOLLOWING THE CREATION of Canada in 1867, the operation of justice in Mi'kma'ki changed again. The British North American Act entrusted responsibility for Indigenous peoples and lands to the federal government, but the provinces retained authority over lands and resources within their boundaries. The Canadian government implemented sporadic but violent programs of assimilation, acculturation, and elimination, including residential schools, administration of reservations, systemic surveillance by Indian agents, and the criminalization of cultures and livelihoods. In 1869, Canada passed An Act for the Gradual Enfranchisement of Indians, which gave Parliament the authority to remove decision-making abilities from traditional governing bodies, such as the Grand Council, without their consent. It also banned alcohol use by Indigenous people, unless sanctioned by a "medical man."

The Indian Act of 1876, reflecting the entrenchment of racism in Canadian society, dictated who could or could not be considered an "Indian" and which "Indians" could live together in a band and where they could live. The legislation gave the superintendent-general of Indian affairs the authority to hold and affirm the elections of chiefs and councils and limited their terms to three years. Section 62, "Council and Chiefs," stated "that all life chiefs now living shall continue as such until death or resignation, or until their removal by the Governor for dishonesty, intemperance, immorality, or incompetency."

The Indian Act facilitated a strategy of assimilation through incarceration. Rules dictated how money could be earned and spent. Section 18, "Protection of Reserves," stated that if the rules were broken, the superintendent-general or his deputies could proceed, even if they did not know the offender's name: "It shall not be necessary for him or such officer or person to insert or express the name of the person or Indian summoned, arrested, distrained upon, imprisoned, or otherwise proceeded against therein, except when the name of such person or Indian is truly given to or known by the Superintendent-General." Amendments stated that the lack of a form would not invalidate a conviction. An entire section of the act focused on alcohol consumption, criminalizing behaviour that was accepted among settlers. Only a "minister of religion" could permit the use of intoxicants. Furnishing, manufacturing, hiding, or possessing liquor could be punished with a one- to six-month term in jail, possibly with hard labour and a fine. Constables could lock up anyone found intoxicated without process of law until they were sober; if convicted, the accused could be sentenced to a maximum of one month, with an additional fourteen days if they failed to say where they got the liquor. "Indians" in jail could not receive their share of annuities paid to the band.

In 1880, the Indian Act was amended to allow Indian agents to prohibit the sale of or seize grains, root crops, and other products produced by reserve residents and impose penalties for their purchase. Every Indian commissioner, assistant Indian commissioner, Indian superintendent, Indian inspector, and Indian agent was declared an ex officio justice of the peace. It became illegal for Indigenous peoples to hunt or live near their hunting grounds unless they were members of the local band and had received a licence. Section 3 criminalized spiritual and healing ceremonies and dances.

Four years later, in 1884, the Indian Advancement Act laid out in detail the elections and business structures of band councils. Band councils could make certain bylaws, rules, and regulations that – if approved and confirmed by the superintendent-general – had the force of law on reserve. The scope of bylaws included taxes, health care, the religious denomination of the schools, peace and order at assemblies, the appointment of constables, the repression of intemperance and profligacy, the division of property and common use lands, and the maintenance of buildings, roads, water, and woods. Any fines collected for bylaw infractions were paid to the Indian agent, who acted also as treasurer, for the use of the band.

As the Government of Canada proceeded with the settling of the country, amendments were added to facilitate the removal of Indigenous peoples if they stood in the way of towns, roads, and railways. Although the government was required to consult with all male Mi'kmaq over the age of twenty before surrendering land (the Mi'kmaq in Nova Scotia had a unique legal status in that they were considered one band under the Indian Act), a 1911 amendment of the Indian Act overcame the problem of consultation by empowering the Exchequer Court to dispose of reserves thought to impede the progress of a city. In 1927, under section 141, it became a criminal offence to collect funds for claims suits without the consent of the superintendent-general, who was also at the time given the power to regulate Indigenous access to poolrooms.

In 1929, the government opened the Shubenacadie Indian Residential School. Mi'kmaw, Wolastoqiyik (Maliseet), and Passamaquoddy children from across the Atlantic region were forced to attend one of the most insidious institutions of assimilation. The schools, framed as benevolent establishments of settler society, worked to destroy kinship networks and interrupt the transmission of Indigenous knowledge and cultural practices through vigorous religious proselytism. Over 900 Mi'kmaq attended the school by the time it closed in June 1967.[35] Between 1942 and 1949 the federal government also initiated an aggressive campaign to centralize all Mi'kmaw reserves at two locations – Shubenacadie and Eskasoni. Policy makers would use money from the sale of "allotted" lands to help pay spiralling medical, educational, poverty relief, and administration costs. It would also be easier to monitor and control the population.

Mi'kmaw social pastimes were criminalized during centralization. For example, the Indian agents stationed at Eskasoni outlawed *waltes* (*woltestakun*), a dice game played on a circular wooden bowl with counting sticks, a favourite particularly among elders. An elder from We'koqma'q recalled that the Indian agents "were like the bosses on the reserve." When elders got caught gambling, even when it was just for fun, the Indian agent "fined them twelve dollars each, and that was a lot. And I often wonder where that twelve dollars go. That is why I say the law was strong, very, very strong."[36]

She recalled another instance when her neighbour had to face trial for selling chickens distributed by the agent to feed his family. During the trial, it came out that the chickens had actually been roosters: "If it was chickens that laid eggs, he would be in jail for two or three months ... In those days they would put anybody in jail for little things like that."[37] Increasingly, Mi'kmaq went to jail because they could not afford to pay fines.

When the centralization experiment failed, families – reduced to poverty and despair – returned to their lands. With their livelihoods destroyed, many were reduced to welfare dependency and subjected to further assimilation policies.

Following the horrors of the Holocaust, Canadians woke up to the concept of human rights. In 1951, the Indian Act was revised, perhaps in partial compliance with Canada's obligation as a signatory to the United Nations Universal Declaration of Human Rights. The most oppressive sections of the act pertaining to the bans on ceremony and public expressions of indigeneity were removed, but land was not returned, voting rights remained limited to band council elections, liquor consumption was restricted, residential schools were in full operation, and gender discrimination persisted. Indian Affairs maintained its monopoly of control.

Section 88 of the Indian Act empowered the provinces in the 1950s to take children from their families and foster or adopt them into white households. In 1958, the Department of Indian Affairs also instituted a new policy of "involuntary assimilation," this time by terminating Mi'kmaw special rights and political status.[38] The federal government no longer recognized the Mi'kmaq as one band. Each populated reserve became a separate band, a division of the national consciousness that would have serious repercussions for Mi'kmaw assertions of sovereignty and traditional governance. Elected officials were the only authority recognized by the agents of the Commission of Indian Affairs, thus officially removing political authority of the Grand Council. This loss of authority weakened the laws of leadership and geopolitical collaboration and of kinship and place and triggered conflict and confusion in the Mi'kmaw Nation.

Settler policies and laws had a significant impact on Mi'kmaw legal consciousness. By constructing crime as an individual responsibility, the governance and justice system imposed after Confederation made it possible to blame Indigenous people's problems with the law on their "primitive" tribal identities. Stereotypes of Indigenous people as violent, criminal people in need of greater social control reinforced these settler ideologies and ignored the realities of systemic marginalization and discrimination. Indigenous communities could be painted as dangerous places with dangerous people doing harmful things to one another without consequence.

The traditional recourses to justice for the Mi'kmaq, their L'nuwey Tplutaqan (the laws of place and kinship, leadership and geopolitical collaboration, harvesting and sharing, and ceremony and managing disputes) were criminalized. If people resisted, they were punished, fined, or incarcerated, and their livelihoods were taken away. Over time, the Mi'kmaq stopped talking it out with one another, and non-interference (an indicator of internal colonization) became the norm. Silence represented a profound break from the oral nature of Mi'kmaw dispute management and social order – Mi'kmaq dispensed with the need to talk it out because talking had become too painful and too dangerous. The threat of outside interventions that followed in the wake of the Indian Act combined with the effects of centralization and residential schools impaired the sense of familial and community safety so integral to Indigenous legal principles. But Mi'kmaw reliance on their own customs, although weakened, gained strength in the wake of the Marshall Inquiry.

6

Munsi sapa'l'k | Struggle to Survive
Mi'kmaw Justice Initiatives

WHEN THE MARSHALL INQUIRY report came down, the Mi'kmaw Nation wanted nothing more than a return to L'nuwey Tplutaqan, their own law, and Donald wanted nothing more than to go home and go fishing. In 1992, after a difficult spring in which Donald's sister Donna and her husband, Steven Anthony Gould, were killed in a car accident, we moved to Junior's farm in Aberdeen, just outside of We'koqma'q in Cape Breton. Safe in his home, Donald described for me the innumerable horrors he had endured in prison and as a wrongly convicted person. He was troubled by the experiences, and there was little doubt he suffered from post-traumatic stress disorder. The injustices he suffered never left him but, remarkably, bitterness did not suffocate him, and anger did not consume him. Donald had an incredible capacity for recognizing the humanity of the wronged and the persons who wronged them. To him, this was what apiksiktuaqn (forgiveness) was all about. But he never forgave MacIntrye, and MacIntyre never apologized.

An extraordinarily chivalrous gentleman, Donald always held doors open for others and walked on the curbside. He respected women, and he respected me. I felt protected and valued. Humour was critical to his endurance. Donald loved to tease and make jokes – he tricked many of us on

April Fool's. He was very funny, did great impressions, had all kinds of crazy sayings and songs, and we laughed a lot.

Donald enjoyed simple things like visiting, perfecting his moose meat pies, drinking Keith's, listening to the blues, fixing up the house, training his dogs, gardening, and most of all going fishing. He was a fan of baseball and hockey – the Toronto Blue Jays and the Detroit Red Wings (and sometimes the Leafs) were his teams. His stories of survival, his deep compassion for the downtrodden, and his irreducible faith in Mi'kmaw culture and Indigenous rights were inspiring. With great passion, he instilled the values of being Mi'kmaw to his nieces, nephews, and twenty-two godchildren. When his niece Jocelyn wrote a school project about his wrongful conviction he was particularly moved. He led by example, drawing on the teachings of his father, the late grand chief. Incredibly, despite eleven years of incarceration, one of the most direct forms of institutional assimilation, Donald continued to speak and be Mi'kmaw.

Although he never enjoyed the spotlight, Donald took a leadership role in overcoming discrimination and racism in the criminal justice system and in the Mi'kmaw quest for justice. He received hundreds of calls for help, and he answered every one of them to the best of his ability. He generously shared his stories throughout Nova Scotia, across Canada, and around the world. With terrific determination, he dedicated his life to ensuring that the injustices he had experienced would never happen again to anyone.

Upon his exoneration, Donald became the first of an exclusive group of people who knew what it meant to be innocent behind bars, to be survivors of the justice system. David Milgaard and Rubin "Hurricane" Carter reached out to him with and for support. Donald was particularly moved by Rubin Carter's words: "To be concerned is not enough. True justice will never be achieved until those who have not been injured by an injustice are as outraged as those who have."[1] Something these men held in common after their imprisonment was a great desire to make positive contributions to society, to help others in the same situation and, in so doing, to help heal themselves. Donald participated in the activities of the Association in Defence of the Wrongly Convicted (AIDWYC, now Innocence Canada), which was founded in 1993 by a group of people in Ontario concerned with justice gone wrong. Today, Innocence Canada is a nonprofit organization dedicated

Rubin "Hurricane" Carter, Donald Marshall, Jane McMillan, and Anne Derrick discussing wrongful convictions, Halifax. *Photographed by Archie Kaiser, 1992*

to identifying, advocating for, and exonerating the wrongly convicted and preventing future injustices. It established October 2 as the annual "Wrongful Conviction Day" to unite people around the world in raising awareness about the causes of wrongful convictions and advocating for international criminal justice reform. On this day in 2018 the first Donald Marshall Junior Award was presented posthumously, acknowledging his efforts. It will be given annually to family members supporting their wrongly convicted relatives.

Donald also took a leadership role in Indigenous justice. He participated nationally in the Aboriginal Justice Learning Network, working with Romola Trebilcock and Grandfather William Commanda, and he was a supporter of prisoner's rights. Closer to home, in addition to his involvement in CLIF, he served as a consultant for the Mi'kmaq Young Offenders Project and, later, the Mi'kmaw Legal Support Network. When the Mi'kmaq Justice Institute was finally established in 1996, he sat on its board. His wrongful conviction inspired many Indigenous peoples to pursue legal careers. When the Mi'kmaq started a tribal police force he was happy, and he was proud when his nephew became a member of the RCMP. Throughout it all, he witnessed the trials and triumphs of the Mi'kmaq as they struggled against the rigid stance of "one law for all" in the Canadian system and tried to invigorate their legal principles and return to community-based justice.

DONALD RECEIVED REQUESTS to assist youth in trouble with the law. He devoted his energies to establishing outdoor survival camps because he felt they would go a long way towards crime prevention and cultural revitalization. In the renegotiation of his compensation, Donald and his counsel argued for a derivative claim to set up a trust fund with the Grand Council to establish and operate a camp. Although Commissioner Evans agreed that a camp to retain and strengthen Mi'kmaw culture was needed – and that Donald would be an ideal person to work at such a facility – the request for funding fell outside of the scope of the compensation inquiry.[2] Evans believed "the project could serve as a symbolic bridge between the Native and the White communities to establish pilot projects to assist in eradicating difficulties encountered by Micmacs [sic] in dealing with the justice system."[3]

Despite the setback, Donald pursued his dream because he wanted youth to feel pride in being Mi'kmaq. We contacted Justice Evans again and asked if the funds that had been set aside for Donald's substance misuse rehabilitation could be transferred to a youth camp instead. If Donald decided to go to rehab, the costs would be covered by First Nations and Inuit Health Branch. Justice Evans supported the initiative and informed the Province of Nova Scotia. With CLIF director Dale Sylliboy, we created Grand Chief Donald Marshall Sr. Aboriginal Youth Camp in 1995 and drew upon CLIF's connections with Corrections Canada to garner backing. It was a bittersweet irony that Donald was so willing to work with the Canadian justice system to fulfill his aspirations – anything for the kids. Donald's youth mentorship reflected his inherent chiefly characteristics and the teachings of his father.

For the first two years, we held the camps at the Corrections Canada camp facility in Shelburne, Nova Scotia, and then we moved the project to Malagawatch, sacred and traditional Mi'kmaw territory in Cape Breton, for three years. Over five years, Donald took close to two hundred youth under his wing and taught them to respect their Mi'kmaw identity. They fished for lobster and eels, worked with elders and collected traditional medicines, had sweat lodge ceremonies, made drums, learned Mi'kmaw songs, lived in wigwams, built fires, shared stories, and stayed straight. Our counsellors were volunteers, Aboriginal prisoner liaisons, keepers of traditional knowledge, and staff seconded from Native Alcohol and Drug Abuse Counselling who helped the youth deal with their disputes without resorting to self-harm or violence.

In 1997, Rod Carleton directed a documentary about the camp, *Donald Marshall Youth Camp*, for the Aboriginal Justice Learning Network. Donald dreamed of permanent, year-round camps for kids and their families in Mi'kma'ki. He felt a reinvigoration of the traditional laws of place and kinship, by reconnecting with the sacredness of land and sea, would be the best way to keep kids out of jail and to help families heal together. Donald's vision extended beyond Mi'kma'ki to all Indigenous youth. He hoped to set up cultural exchange programs across the country but was unable to see the project to its conclusion. Although we had put together a grant proposal to build the camp in conjunction with the Mi'kmaq Justice Institute and the Mi'kmaq Young Offenders Project, the institute's instability scuttled the opportunity to secure funds.

AFTER THE INQUIRY, Donald and the Mi'kmaw Nation had high hopes for pilot projects supported by the Tripartite Forum in the 1990s. But the small-scale experiments had mixed results, largely because they had to compete for scarce and limited funds, usually from the same source, and they had too short a life span. Unama'ki Tribal Police Services and the Mi'kmaq Justice Institute were cases in point. The first, a Mi'kmaw regional police force, was established in 1994 to provide policing services throughout Cape Breton Island, the home of five Mi'kmaw communities: Potlotek, Eskasoni, We'koqma'q, Wagmatcook, and Membertou. Since the 1970s, the Mi'kmaq had lobbied for control over how their communities were policed, but the Marshall Inquiry finally ensured that their demands were taken seriously. The main goal of the force was to put policing back in the hands of the Mi'kmaq to enhance safety and secure equal access to justice. The force would also (1) provide professional, effective, and culturally responsive police services, (2) improve safety and security for on-reserve communities, (3) give Mi'kmaq a voice in the administration of justice, and (4) ensure that police services were accountable to Mi'kmaw communities.

Mi'kmaw chiefs viewed control over policing as a catalyst towards self-determination. They envisaged tribal police relying on community-based policing methods to reveal the root causes of crime and then employing Mi'kmaw legal principles to resolve problems, facilitate reconciliation, restore broken relationships, and promote community healing. Tribal police practices would be holistic, community-driven, and re-integrative rather than adversarial. Once the Mi'kmaq Justice Institute was established, Mi'kmaw leaders imagined that the force would work with it to bring wraparound justice services to Mi'kmaw communities.

Members of the Unama'ki Tribal Police force were former RCMP officers who were trained to do their own investigations and file management. One officer recalled that the "autonomy allowed them to police without someone constantly looking over their shoulders."[4] Another noted that officers "embraced the responsibility to help their communities get on a healing path, to find solutions for victims and offenders."[5] As Indigenous community members themselves, they understood the consequences of colonization, how poverty influenced crime, and the importance of kinship networks in resolving conflicts.

Within the first three years of operation, the Unama'ki Tribal Police Services had three different chiefs of police. The job was extremely challenging, and the force took seriously its responsibility to create a unique Indigenous policing model. But chiefs of police met with profound resistance from the government.[6] Insufficient funding for training and salaries and inadequate staffing were just the tip of the iceberg. The force also struggled to gain legitimacy in Mi'kmaw communities. The main police station, located in Eskasoni, was more than a thirty-minute drive from Membertou and forty-five minutes or more from the other Cape Breton reserves. Community members complained about poor response times, the lack of twenty-four-hour services, and a lack of visibility.

In a letter to the Aboriginal Policing Directorate, Unama'ki Tribal Police Services described the challenges they faced:

The Unama'ki Policing Service is committed to providing quality policing, and especially community-based policing philosophy and practice, in all the First Nation communities it serves on Cape Breton Island. This is a significant challenge for our newly created police service since resources are quite strained, community expectations are quite high, and the levels of social problems and conventional crime are very high in our jurisdictions. The base complement is scarcely adequate for policing geographically dispersed communities where the level of conventional crimes and crimes of violence as auditors have shown is at least five times the levels encountered in the RCMP jurisdictions and three times than found in Municipal jurisdictions in Nova Scotia. As in many First Nation communities the demand/expectation for policing is quite high; calls for service have increased 400% since the Unama'ki Policing Service began in December 1994.

Because they trusted the new community-run force over the alternatives, community members were more likely to report crimes. To support this growing confidence, the force needed more officers. Renewed interest in Indigenous legal principles and demands for internal dispute-management processes set the stage for the Mi'kmaq Justice Institute.

IN 1994, THE PROVINCE decided not to fund parallel and competing pilot programs. Unama'ki Tribal Police Services continued to receive funding, but CLIF, Shubenacadie Diversion (a program intended to divert Mi'kmaw offenders away from the courts and towards tribunals in their own communities), and the Aboriginal Court Worker Program were discontinued in favour of an umbrella program or organization, based on the Marshall Inquiry recommendations, named the Mi'kmaq Justice Institute. In addition to righting historical wrongs by returning justice to the community, Mi'kmaw people hoped their institute would bring peace to communities, by reducing poverty and crime, and enhance their legal culture through institutionalized recognition of Mi'kmaw treaties and Indigenous rights. It would also, they hoped, provide desperately needed jobs. Under the leadership of Dan Christmas, the Union of Nova Scotia Indians, and the Native Council of Nova Scotia, the institute had a broad mandate to research, design, and implement community-based, culturally specific justice.

The Tripartite Forum hoped to amalgamate the three programs in three phases over one fiscal year. The Mi'kmaq reviewed the state of justice in their territory, did the math, and generated an organizational chart for the institute to become fully operational. On paper, the amalgamation seemed straightforward, but personality conflicts, power plays, political wrangling between various levels of government, and restrictive funding policies made negotiations and a seamless transition impossible. Even though it appeared that all members of the Tripartite Forum agreed that creating the Mi'kmaq Justice Institute was the best path for realizing Mi'kmaw justice, there was little evidence of good will from the provincial or federal governments to guarantee its success. The bottom line for government representatives was fiscal rather than reconciliatory. The director of Aboriginal Affairs and a solicitor for the Department of Justice indicated that the province's major concern respecting the implementation proposal lay "in its projected costs." They hoped the merger would "obtain efficiencies and cost saving overall." The death knell sounded before the doors opened:

As stated earlier, we do not feel it is appropriate for the Province to dictate the content of the proposal. In fact, the organizational chart contained in your April 6th proposal appears to be an effective long term goal. We suggest, however, that while the organizational chart should be the goal, it may be more appropriate to limit actual positions filled until the need for all of the personnel can be justified. In particular, it may not be immediately necessary to hire the program officers. As well, one clerical staff person may be sufficient until the workload is determined. Assistant justice workers may also not be immediately required, although the cost saving of training all workers as one group rather than at a later date may outweigh the cost of retaining those workers.[7]

The justice minister, Allan Rock, and the premier of Nova Scotia, John Savage, agreed that the federal and provincial commitment to the institute would be $500,000 per year, although the projected annual cost of the program was more than $600,000. The province indicated its contribution would be $250,000 per annum towards the cost of the Aboriginal Court Worker Program, subject to budgetary approval and an equal federal contribution. The federal government, however, would not commit to any long-term or permanent core funding because the Aboriginal Justice Directorate's mandate, from which funds were to be drawn, was set to expire in 1996. Mi'kmaw leaders, who also wanted a customary law program, argued that the governments, if they truly had the will, could find other sources to fund Mi'kmaw justice beyond the court worker program. Without long-term funding, it would be difficult to attract, train, and retain experienced and competent staff, and Mi'kmaw communities were in no position to finance a justice system on their own. They needed to prioritize serious and urgent infrastructure shortages in housing, water, education, employment, and health.

Among Mi'kmaq, the Tripartite Forum became an arena of conflict between competing tribal councils. For about two years, it ceased to be a productive space for implementing the Marshall Inquiry recommendations. To get the Tripartite Forum back on track, the premier of the province announced at a Treaty Day celebration that he would take on responsibility for Indian affairs and that respected politician Joe Ghiz would act as an independent chair for the forum. Once negotiations resumed in 1996, the province argued that the organizational structure of the proposed Mi'kmaq Justice Institute was too broad; it then proceeded to arbitrarily limit the number of staff positions the Mi'kmaq had requested. The province also wanted the Mi'kmaq Justice Institute to defray training costs by using existing federal and provincial programs. The strategy made fiscal sense but failed to take into consideration that government training programs were not grounded in Indigenous legal principles or community realities, a condition that led to the need for an institute in the first place.

Reaching consensus was impossible with so many competing power interests. Mi'kmaw chiefs disagreed with the Native Council of Nova Scotia, the self-governing authority for off-reserve and non-Status Mi'kmaq, over the composition of the institute's board. The chiefs believed the board should be composed of the thirteen chiefs, just like other Mi'kmaw boards and associations. The Native Council held that justice should be independent from politics, but separating justice from leadership was more in tune with Western than Mi'kmaw legal traditions. Historically, adjudication and juridical processes were holistically interconnected under the Grand Council, local chiefs, elders, and families. The provincial government, without being invited, also decided to participate in the debate over the representation of chiefs on the board. The Mi'kmaq perceived this interference as inappropriate and believed it perpetuated divisions among the organizations. Eventually, they came to consensus on a ten-member board, with two alternates who would not be chiefs but rather people nominated and selected because of their background in justice issues.

Over time, Mi'kmaw parties to the Tripartite Forum grew concerned that the federal and provincial governments were failing to support activities that fell outside the narrow program guidelines of the Aboriginal Court Worker Program. Would the Mi'kmaq Justice Institute simply become a glorified court worker program? Frustrated and still stinging from the collapse of CLIF, the executive director of the Native Council wrote the deputy minister for intergovernmental affairs in Nova Scotia and other Tripartite Forum members: "At the end of the day all that we have is a commitment for an off-the-shelf Native Court Worker Program ... I understand that that is the best that Justice Canada is prepared to offer. I am of the opinion that this is not the best for the Mi'kmaw Aboriginal people of Nova Scotia and, in fact, 'by duress,' the parties in Nova Scotia to the Tripartite Forum have to take it or leave it. This is a sad example of the role of the Tripartite Forum to discuss, investigate and negotiate measures that will assist in the resolution of issues of mutual concern."[8]

In the time it took to resolve conflicts over the board structure, the federal funding program lapsed. By the time the Mi'kmawey Jajikimtumkewey (Mi'kmaq Justice Institute) came into being, in November 1996, the budget had been cut from $500,000 to $250,000, and the Marshall Inquiry recommendations were no closer to implementation. The institute was short-staffed and underfunded, but it was Mi'kmaw, at least at the outset. A memorandum of association and bylaws defined the institute's membership, fiscal year and audits, rules and procedures, and powers of the board. In January 1997, the board of commissioners selected an executive director, but the selection process was contentious. Some argued that the director should be from a reserve because the position required intimate awareness of reserve life, its challenges and hardships and the intercommunity relationships that influence formal and informal justice discourses, practices, and legal consciousness. The candidate, they argued, also needed to be Mi'kmaw not only in name but also in beliefs and practices. A supporter of Mi'kmaw sovereignty was preferable to someone compliant with maintaining the settler status quo. Although there were very few Indigenous lawyers in the province at the time, some argued that legal training would be necessary for the position. After much debate, a legally trained, reserve-residing Mi'kmaw woman was hired, and the head office was set up in Membertou. With staff in place, the Mi'kmaq Justice Institute set out to develop a set of concepts to frame Indigenous legal principles in a contemporary context.

IN FEBRUARY 1997, the front-page of the *Micmac Maliseet Nations News*, a monthly news magazine, read "Justice: Mi'kmaw Style." The first paragraph described the establishment of the Mi'kmaq Justice Institute in response to the Marshall Inquiry recommendations and the lengthy, conflict-ridden negotiations. The author continued:

> In spite of government bureaucracy, the Mi'kmaw have established the Mi'kmaq Justice Institute and had mandated it to not only administer justice as it relates to Mi'kmaw people but to further promote new justice arrangements which are culturally relevant. The institute is interested in building partnerships between the criminal justice system and the Mi'kmaw/Aboriginal people. The justice system needs to be accountable to the Mi'kmaw/Aboriginal people. It is time for the Mi'kmaw/Aboriginal community to shape justice policy and deliver a justice initiative from a Mi'kmaw customary law perspective.

The Mi'kmaq Justice Institute would be the carrier agency for all justice initiatives except policing.

At first, the ten-member board of commissioners met regularly and with great enthusiasm to implement the institute's goals, which were agreed upon by the Union of Nova Scotia Indians, the Native Council, the Confederacy of Mainland Mi'kmaq, the Friendship Centre, and the Nova Scotia Native Women's Association. The board included several lawyers, a high-ranking member of the Mi'kmaw Grand Council, Donald Marshall Jr., and people with administrative and political experience who held portfolios in the major Mi'kmaw service agencies.

Donald enjoyed attending the board meetings. The discussions were invigorating and helped restore his sense of purpose. He particularly appreciated spending time with Alex Denny, a true justice warrior who was active in the Union of Nova Scotia Indians, a treaty rights advocate, and grand captain of the Grand Council from 1966 until his death in 2004. Kji Keptin Denny and Donald shared a similar holistic vision of Mi'kmaw justice that valued the roles of kinship, elders, and community togetherness. According to Kji Keptin Denny,

> Justice cannot work independently; it has to work with other groups to get to the roots. Elders told us we have to find out what the genes are. Where does this guy come from? Who were his grandparents? Did they do drugs? Drink? Was he molested? What are the problems? You have to study the entire social system of each and every individual, and we did not have the resources to do that. I always envisaged a Mi'kmaq Justice Institute to run the entire thing. Not only do we run the program but that we have our own court system. Our own court houses on each reserve. Mi'kmaq have never been involved with the justice system other than being charged and sent away.[9]

One of the first things the institute did to fulfill its mandate to engage in community networking and outreach was hold information sessions. The most successful was a one-time national conference that built upon the Royal Commission on Aboriginal Peoples' findings. Held in Membertou in partnership with the Aboriginal Justice Learning Network, the three-day conference brought together Indigenous scholars, leaders, justice officials, and police. It placed special emphasis on elder mediation and healing discourses. The institute used the conference and the royal commission's recommendations to forward its agenda.

An overall shift in justice ideology – from penal to community-based healing and restorative practice – and a reinvigorated Indigenous rights discourse should have helped pave the way for implementing the Marshall Inquiry recommendations. But progress was slow. The first services to come online were the Mi'kmaw translation service and the court worker program. Etui-Nsitmek Translation Services had begun as a separate program in 1995 in response to the Marshall Inquiry recommendations. But interpreters required training, and training cost money. The Unama'ki Training and Education Centre in Eskasoni proposed an intensive certificate program in which Mi'kmaw persons provided instruction on ethics, legal terms, court protocols, sentencing, and trial formats to fluent speakers. The program paid special attention to cultural differences, including notions of time, language distinctions (such as the use of prepositions and the sequences of phrases), and social issues reflected in client behaviour. Indigenous university students were targeted for the training program and were exposed to legal proceedings through practice sessions and meetings with legal personnel. Because there were few university students (and fewer fluent students) at the time, the training was opened to interested community members.

Translator services proved to be popular in Cape Breton, where language retention was high. A provincial court, staffed by non-Indigenous personnel, began sitting in Eskasoni in 1996, as per recommendation 25, and translators were in demand. The court was accessible to community members, who had previously been forced to travel to a provincial court in Sydney, some fifty kilometres away. Those without vehicles or the means to hire a ride had found it too expensive to attend the Sydney court. The relocation of the court immediately decreased the number of bench warrants and remands for failure-to-appear charges. The court originally sat every other Thursday, but the day was switched to Tuesdays to avoid coinciding with social income assistance (or ration) day.

Translator services were requested by court workers off reserve as well. Despite the obvious need for translators, the Mi'kmaq Justice Institute, with no administrative operating budget, soon found itself unable to manage the training and efficient coordination of services with the court dockets. The institute was hard-pressed to pay translators, who had to provide for their families and could not wait for the courts to make payments for the service. Financial insecurity quickly trickled down. Increased trepidation in the translator cohort caused staff retention problems. The training budget was not renewed. Well-trained staff left for better job prospects. The demand for translators remained unanswered.

The court worker program also suffered from bare-bones funding. The Mi'kmaq Justice Institute hired three justice workers and opened offices in Millbrook, Halifax, and Membertou. This was a far cry from the original plan for five full-time and ten part-time workers. The justice worker hired to serve the five Cape Breton bands (and the region's five criminal courts) immediately became overwhelmed with cases. Within the first year of the program, he alone handled more than two hundred cases. People contacted the workers at all hours and sought counsel whenever they met at hockey games, the local store, even funerals. Heavy caseloads made it difficult to facilitate follow-up and aftercare referrals. Justice workers quickly become another cog in the settler justice system. They had no time or opportunity to investigate or implement Mi'kmaw legal traditions, the central goals of the institute. The Canadian justice system benefitted from the court worker program. The case workers' hard work – including counselling, referrals to health and social service agencies, and transportation to and from courts – reduced the number of "failures to appear," which meant fewer delays in court. With these efficiencies, government officials were less interested in supporting efforts to indigenize or build alternatives to the process.

As word spread about the Mi'kmaq Justice Institute, it had to meet new internal demands for information regarding human rights, treaty rights, Aboriginal title, and fishing and hunting guidelines. These requests put a great deal of pressure on the organization, and it did not have the infrastructure or the capacity to handle them. A mandate to deal with any and all Indigenous persons in Nova Scotia also sparked conflicts over access. Since the imposition of the Indian Act, Indigenous peoples had not had control over determining their membership, which significantly affected access to equitable rights-based services. The Native Council complained that it made referrals to the institute that were not followed up. High case-loads forced a priority sequencing that benefited on-reserve Mi'kmaq. Unable to help every Indigenous person, people fell through the gaps.

In March 1997, the Mi'kmaq Justice Institute set up a training program in conjunction with the University College of Cape Breton, in Sydney. As with any new university program, establishing the Mi'kmaw Justice Worker certificate program took a great deal of time and energy. One of its goals was to train workers in both Mi'kmaw law and dispute-resolution processes and in procedures and practices in the Canadian justice system. The institute also hoped to use the training program to establish a First Nations Governance Advisory Service, an agency that would help Mi'kmaw communities develop the infrastructure for governance and self-determination. Mi'kmaw political interests wanted the institute to develop a paralegal research service and band governance projects through an expansion of band bylaws, particularly in the area of fish and wildlife protocols and enforcement. The impetus for the governance part of the program also came from the federal government, which wanted bands to exercise their legislative powers under the Indian Act and enforce bylaws – in other words, cost offloading disguised as self-government.

The program was premature. None of the reserves had fully established bylaws, and tribal police services were still in the preliminary stages. Also, the province was not willing to take responsibility for initiatives that fell under federal jurisdiction. When the question came up of enforcing band bylaws, it became clear that using Mi'kmaw legal principles to administer federally regulated bylaws would be tricky because they were entrenched in the settler legal system.[10] The management of things that should have been straightforward – traffic and dogs – got mired in conflicts over jurisdiction, prosecutorial authority, and cost recovery. Indeed, the focus on Indian Affairs–instigated projects divided and diverted Mi'kmaw attention away from implementing their own justice system.

When the certification and training course launched, it had ten students, including the three court workers hired by the Mi'kmaq Justice Institute. Unfortunately, few people were deemed qualified to teach the Mi'kmaw content of the courses, and the institute's executive director, already working at capacity, had to teach it or risk losing the program. Although the governance course provided justice workers with much-needed holistic training and treaty education, by the time the students finished the course requirements, the Mi'kmaq Justice Institute was in serious financial trouble. It failed to pay tuition to the University College of Cape Breton (now Cape Breton University). Students couldn't receive their certificates, and the institute couldn't offer them jobs. A federal audit, held in June 1997, noted that the institute did not have enough staff and that the executive director was overinvolved in the project and not spending enough time doing administrative work. Neither the federal nor the provincial government heeded these early warnings and failed to provide the institute with the core resources needed to ensure its success.

Bureaucratic red tape and a lack of funds also impeded the institute's ability to absorb an existing program – the Mi'kmaq Young Offenders Project – into the fold. Initially under the administration of the Island Alternative Measures Society, the institute took over the project in June 1997, but it wasn't until June 1998 that the provincial Department of Justice authorized the delivery of the program and the transfer of funds. The program – which had a strong reputation in the settler justice community and its own director, staff, and mediation program – applied Mi'kmaw legal principles and dispute-management methods to cases involving youth in trouble with the law in Cape Breton. A diversion project, it handled alternative measure referrals of first-time offenders who accepted responsibility for their offences. Importantly, the project grounded its services in traditional concepts such as ilsutekek, nijkitekek, wi'kupaltimk, and apiksiktuaqn to guide relations towards reintegration and healing. Over time, these concepts became formalized in justice and healing circles and influenced Mi'kmaw legal consciousness. Seeing the merits of the service in Cape Breton, the project was expanded into mainland communities; however, the expansion occurred without any significant increase in funding or staff. As with the justice worker program, staff had trouble dealing with their caseloads.

Between June and December 1997, the executive director and board members chased money to research Mi'kmaw customary law and band governance alternatives. A final report, submitted in July 1998, recommended utilizing the traditional governing authority of the Grand Council as a potential enforcement or adjudicatory body for offences dealing with resources or treaty rights. The institute took up this challenge by designing a training program in mediation for members of the Mi'kmaw Grand Council, an important step in institutionalizing Indigenous legal sovereignty. The Mi'kmaw employment-training service provided the funds, but the course did not materialize because administrative and other demands from Indian Affairs (for instance, taking on wills and estates) diverted the institute's attention yet again.

ON THE SURFACE, the Mi'kmaq Justice Institute was making positive inroads. In June 1998, it received the Canada Law Day Award and recognition in the form of a salute from the National Strategy on Community Safety and Crime Prevention, presented by the minister of justice, Anne McLellan. Beneath the surface, ongoing tensions over money were exacerbated by the failure of the director to submit financial reports. Community demands for Mi'kmaw justice continued to increase, particularly after the Supreme Court of Canada's 1999 *Gladue* decision. The decision, based on the court's interpretation of section 718.2(e) of the Criminal Code, tried to remedy the Canadian justice system's overreliance on incarceration by directing justices to consider "all available sanctions other than imprisonment that are reasonable in the circumstances for all offenders, with particular attention to the circumstances of aboriginal offenders."[11] Community members wanted sentencing and Mi'kmaw justice circles to be extended to adults as well as youths.

The justice circles held by the Mi'kmaq Youth Offenders Project required participation by community members and enforcement officers. Staff had trouble coordinating preparation time, and over time they discovered that finding, training, and maintaining volunteers was difficult in small communities with high rates of unemployment. At first, they engaged a large and active volunteer group and could rely on the participation of Unama'ki Tribal Police Services. Volunteer participation declined, however, when the institute's financial and structural problems – particularly its lack of funds and focus – began to negatively influence staff morale and service delivery. Inconsistent service delivery contributed to the decline of community support for independent programs.

By February 1999, the participation of the Mi'kmaq Justice Institute's board members had begun to fall off. Poor leadership resulted in irregularly scheduled meetings called on short notice. Those best suited to driving systemic change were overtaxed with heavy workloads. Optimism dwindled as repeated efforts to secure funding failed. As board members quit, replacing them was difficult. Approving a candidate required consensus from the original five Mi'kmaw political interest groups, but the Native Council had pulled out of the Tripartite Forum. In April, the institute's payroll bounced, and its translation services were suspended. By May, staff were laid off, and the justice worker program had ceased operations. Alternative funding was found for the Mi'kmaq Young Offenders Project, but its administration reverted to the Union of Nova Scotia Indians. The Mi'kmaq Justice Institute was forced to close its doors.

To compound the tragedy, Unama'ki Tribal Police Services folded when its five-year funding agreement came to an end. It too suffered from funding deficits and lacked provincial support. The former Mi'kmaw chair of the Tripartite Forum's justice subcommittee, summed up the situation:

You went from 1990, when you had this vision of the Mi'kmaw ... by the time you got to 1999, it was a totally different concept. It was totally foreign. What ended up being administered was the federal vision because the feds were basically the gatekeepers. From the beginning, the feds really felt no responsibility, no commitment, no attachment to the Marshall commission. They totally washed their hands of the commission, and they basically felt it was a provincial problem. The province felt it could not afford to go it alone, and they needed to costshare, and the benchmark was the federal program ... I guess if you had to put the blame on anybody, you would have to put the blame on Justice Canada. Their program requirements are so strict and inflexible that you really could not develop a program with it, and all the province did was basically match what the feds did.[12]

An executive of the Native Council commented:

I look at this MJI as a demonstration project which failed miserably, but why did it fail? It failed because it was never meant to succeed. It did not have its act straight, not by the fault of Aboriginal people. It was a political nightmare, driven by Aboriginal and provincial political interests, and the federal government was just sitting on the sidelines saying, "Let it go." I do not think the community would want to get into another hell like that for two years and have nothing. I do not think Aboriginal people in Nova Scotia, no matter where they live, want that. No one has the right to play with peoples' lives like that. No one has the right to say, "I am going to provide services" and then not provide the services. No one has the right to raise the expectations of an Aboriginal person and say, "We will provide you with court services" and then not provide them. That is tantamount to creating a denial. That is exactly what happened to Donald Marshall. He was denied the process.[13]

All of the programs and projects following the Marshall Inquiry – from CLIF to the young offenders project – had similar goals, but they had different carriers, rules, client criteria, and performance-reporting processes. Problems associated with coordinating a number of programs with diverse objectives and protocols impeded comprehensive, substantive, and sustainable developments. In addition, officials within the settler justice system rarely embraced the ideas of self-determined and restorative justice, and the Mi'kmaq did not have the time to educate police and court services officers about their cultural values and traditions or the history of colonialism and its impacts. Officials consequently failed to refer cases and individuals to Indigenous programs. Numerous policy changes and staff turnover at Corrections Canada, Justice Canada, and the prosecutor's office gradually shifted the Mi'kmaq's focus away from institution building in their own communities to negotiating competency with the other two members of the Tripartite Forum. The core goal of "Mi'kmaw justice as community justice" got lost in the bureaucracy of the settler justice system, chasing pocket change, and the daily grind of completing funding reports. The spirit of grassroots mobilization that helped launch these programs withered as they failed to satisfy the burgeoning legal consciousness of people more oriented towards using Indigenous legal principles and less daunted in challenging Canadian law.

Despite the Marshall Inquiry recommendations, Mi'kmaw people continued to go through the justice system without much support. The province superficially embraced the Marshall recommendations rather than assertively facilitating their implementation. The relationship was complicated further by the government's stance: on the one hand, it would not interfere with the program; on the other, it would not empower Mi'kmaq with the authority and money they needed to achieve their goals. The programs made inroads in the short time they existed, but Mi'kmaq did not have the opportunity to gain the experience required to develop them. An oft-repeated sentiment at the time was that funders "only give you enough to hang yourself, and sometimes not even that."[14] As the doors of the Mi'kmaq Justice Institute closed, however, Mi'kmaw legal consciousness was once again set to explode, at Donald Marshall's instigation, but this time with treaty rights dominating the agenda.

7

Najiwsgeieg | We Go Fishing
In Search of a Livelihood

ASIDE FROM JUSTICE work, Donald loved to fish. He enjoyed the privacy of wandering down the river with his fly rod or on the ice with a jig. It was where he found peace and joy. Taught to fish as a boy, he told fishing stories throughout his life. Down Skye River, Donald skillfully hand-jigged a salmon, dropping it at my feet with a sly smile. I was mesmerized. We feasted.

Having had success as an avid food harvester, Donald wanted to secure an income through an activity he enjoyed, one that allowed him to celebrate his Mi'kmaw identity through a respectful relationship with a culturally significant resource. He wanted to work. He sought the wilderness and the exhilaration that small-scale fishing offered him, far away from the spotlight under which he had lived since his wrongful conviction for murder.

We became eel fishers.

Mi'kmaw eeling is labour-intensive. During our first season, the Bernard brothers from We'koqma'q – Lunch, Chuckie, and Seven – and Uncle Ekkian (Donald's mother's brother) lent us fyke nets and taught us the ropes in Malagawatch.

By the next season, we had earned enough to buy our own. We hauled nets (cone-shaped netting bags mounted on rings with leaders to guide the

First pay day for eel fishers at Malagawatch. *L to R:* Winston Bernard, Seven (Peter) Bernard, Dickie Young, Lunch (Lawrence) Bernard, Donald Marshall Jr., Charles (Junior) Bernard, Jane McMillan, Chuckie Bernard, John Wayne Bernard, Grace Welch, and John John Bernard. *Photographed by Phil Welch, 1992*

fish towards the entrance) by hand, and they were heavy when wet and awkward to set, even in the calmest weather. We fixed the nets in the mud with poles that had been cut and trimmed from the local woods with the help of fishing buddies Albert Doucette and Gordon Julian. It was hard and dirty work, but we liked the adventure. Every time there was a thunderstorm, Donald rubbed his hands together and said, "Lots of eels tomorrow, baby!" He was right.

Initially, we liked the trials of catching eels. Fishing reinvigorated and helped reintegrate Donald. We were part of a communal occupation that gave meaning to our lives, an activity grounded in Mi'kmaw customary practices and the laws of harvesting, an activity in adherence to an ethos of sharing. Eels are a favoured food of Mi'kmaw elders. We distributed the biggest and best eels among the old people, and they always asked us for a feed wherever we were, no matter if it were at a funeral, a wedding, or grocery shopping. Many admired Donald's eel-cleaning skills. When powwows or Treaty Day celebrations required eels for the traditional *katawapul* (eel stew), Donald went out of his way to ensure there was enough, spending hours bent over the sink, wrestling the eels into submission to prepare them for consumption. Eels still wiggle after they are gutted.

Eel fishing is not a prestigious or particularly lucrative fishery. Eels are slimy, and the muddy areas where they are fished typically have a pungent,

Donald Marshall fishing eels for the Membertou powwow with a fyke net near Malagawatch, August, 2008. *Photographed by Keith Christmas*

lingering odour. Like any resource extraction process, fishing is dangerous, and the risk of personal injury is high. Donald was not a strong swimmer, which compounded the danger. The financial risks were also high – the catch was determined by uncontrollable factors such as the weather, uncertain reproduction patterns, and gear malfunctions.

We fished in Cape Breton for another season then moved our nets and boat down to Paq'tnkek Mi'kmaw territory (Pomquet Harbour) on the mainland. We had heard that the eels were big there and running well. We spent several nights a week with Donald's cousin Billy Googoo and his family. They helped us navigate the new waters. Kinship matters.

On a bright August day in 1993 a boat approached us while we were checking our nets. It was unusual to see others fishing in the area. As the boat came closer, we could see it contained Department of Fisheries and Oceans officers, uniformed and armed. The officers pulled alongside our boat and examined its contents. They asked us if there was anything else onboard besides eels. We told them that all bycatch had been released. An officer then asked to see our fishing licences. Donald said he was Mi'kmaw and did not need a licence to fish.

"Everyone needs a licence to fish," the officer replied.

"I don't need a license. I have the 1752 treaty," Donald responded.

They asked for our names and address and took a net as "evidence." We thought it was a misunderstanding because we were new to the area. We felt safe because we were in Mi'kmaw territory, and Donald was protected by his treaty rights, affirmed and recognized by the Supreme Court of Canada in 1985 in *Simon v The Queen* and section 35 of the Constitution Act, 1982. James Matthew Simon had been convicted of possession of a rifle and ammunition but successfully argued that he had a right to hunt as set out in the 1752 Peace and Friendship Treaty. From the Mi'kmaw perspective, the *Simon* decision meant the 1752 treaty was in full force and effect.

We headed back to the reserve and told people what happened. We called the Department of Fisheries and Oceans and asked what was going on. We wanted the $250 net back. They told us we needed permission from the chief to fish in that area. We asked Chief Kerry Prosper, and he said we could continue fishing. We let the department know we had his consent and continued to fish. A few days later, we sold the eels and reset the nets. When we went back to fish two days later, we were outraged to find our nets and boat gone. At no time did it occur to us that eel fishing was licensed or that we did not have a right to sell the eels we caught. At the trial that followed, the statement of facts read:

On August 24, 1993, at around 10 o'clock in the morning, Donald Marshall and Leslie Jane McMillan fished for eels by means of fyke nets, a type of fixed net, from a small outboard motor boat in Pomquet Harbour, County of Antigonish, Nova Scotia. For part of the morning Marshall pulled the nets and emptied the eels into the boat while McMillan operated the outboard motor, and for part of the morning McMillan pulled the nets and emptied the eels into the boat while Marshall ran the outboard motor. Marshall and McMillan transferred the eels from the boat to a holding pen ... Marshall helped weigh and load his eels onto a truck belonging to

South Shore Trading Company, New Brunswick. South Shore is engaged in the purchase and sale of fish. Marshall sold 463 pounds of his eels to South Shore at $1.70 per pound. Marshall did not at any time hold a license within the meaning of S. 4(1)(a) of the Maritime Provinces Fishery Regulations and S. 35(2) of the Fishery Act with respect to fishing for or selling eels from Pomquet Harbour.[1]

THE EEL FISHING CASE, which began in Nova Scotia Provincial Court on October 17, 1994, was public, expensive, and lengthy. The trial was set out as a test case for Mi'kmaw treaty rights, and the chiefs were happy it was Donald who had been charged. The case was sure to get lots of media exposure. The Union of Nova Scotia Indians and the Confederacy of Mainland Mi'kmaq agreed to support our defence and provided us with counsel, something we could never have afforded otherwise. Mi'kmaq resented the government's failure to respect their peoples' economic needs and treaty rights, particularly in the context of the cod-fishing crisis. Following the Supreme Court of Canada's *Sparrow* decision, in 1990, which confirmed that Indigenous peoples have the right to fish for subsistence and ceremonial purposes and that that right superseded all other fisheries, the federal government had implemented the Aboriginal Fisheries Strategy. The strategy was directed at regulating any existing Aboriginal or treaty commercial-fishing rights. Without sufficient consultation regarding Indigenous preferences for participation in commercial fisheries or justifying infringements, the Department of Fisheries and Oceans had instituted a communal fishing-licence program, but Membertou, Donald's home community, and Paq'tnkek, where we were caught fishing, had refused to take part because they did not want to accept any federal jurisdiction limiting the exercise of their treaty rights.

To resist these top-down and culturally unresponsive initiatives, the Union of Nova Scotia Indians and the Confederacy of Mainland Mi'kmaq joined forces in the Aboriginal Title Project. Together, they compiled historical documentation to aid in legal defence work for the protection and implementation of Mi'kmaw treaties and title. They were ready for the fight.

As a non-Indigenous person, I did not enjoy the protection of 35(1), and it was the Crown's position that any treaty rights that may be enjoyed by the other defendants were not transferable to me by virtue of my relationship with Donald.[2] I was not immune from prosecution, but early in the process, charges against me were dropped. Judge Embree, who heard the case in Antigonish Provincial Court, understood it to be an Aboriginal treaty rights test case. In court, the Crown vigorously pursued the charges against Donald, and he was defended with great acuity and perseverance by lead counsels Bruce Wildsmith and Eric Zscheile, with the help of the research team put together by the Mi'kmaw Nation. Many of the legal researchers were new Mi'kmaw lawyers and law students who had benefitted from the Indigenous Blacks and Mi'kmaq Initiative at Dalhousie University, a recommendation of the Marshall Inquiry to improve access to education and expand diversity in the law school, bar, and bench.

Because Donald had admitted to catching and selling eels without a licence and with prohibited nets during a closed time, the only issue at trial was whether he possessed a treaty right to catch and sell fish that exempted him from compliance with the regulations. Conservation was not an issue. The trial lasted more than forty days over an eighteen-month period. Volumes of documents were presented and interpreted by anthropological and historical experts on both sides. The testimony of historians William Wicken and John Reid, for the defence, and Stephen Patterson, for the Crown, took thirty-four days and filled more than four thousand pages of transcripts. Media attention and the stress of the case weighed heavily on Donald, who felt an acute sense of personal responsibility for the trial's outcome.

Instead of arguing Donald's right to catch and sell fish under the 1752 treaty, the defence looked to the Peace and Friendship Treaties of 1760–61 for evidence that the Mi'kmaq had the right to catch and sell fish. The Mi'kmaq had signed five treaty agreements with the British Crown between 1725 and 1779. The British recognized that the Mi'kmaq had a sophisticated and comprehensive governance structure and processes for managing nation-to-nation agreements. The 1725 agreement was a peace and friendship treaty designed to end years of conflict between the British and the Mi'kmaq and their allies to conclude the Indian wars taking place in the northeast. The British planned to use the treaty to incorporate the

Mi'kmaq into the colonial network and assist in their battle against the French. As the Mi'kmaq understood it, the treaty protected their customary livelihoods, their resources, and their sovereign and sacred relationships within their territories. However, although the treaty-making process embodied both cultures, the embodiment was unequal because the writing of the treaty was in English and did not encompass Mi'kmaw understandings of the events or the agreements within the text.

The British promised that their settlements would be lawfully made and that they would not interfere in Mi'kmaw planting, hunting, and fishing grounds. When Edward Cornwallis, the newly appointed governor of Nova Scotia, arrived in 1749 with a flotilla of British ships and 2,547 passengers, however, the promise was not kept. Mi'kmaw families who had lived along Chebucto Bay for centuries were not consulted when the town of Halifax was built. When Mi'kmaq resisted and asserted their sovereignty, a proclamation offered rewards for Mi'kmaw scalps or prisoners. In an attempt to encourage the Mi'kmaq and other tribes in the Atlantic region to live peaceably with the British, the 1725 treaty was renewed in 1749 and 1752 and ratified again in Halifax in 1760 and 1761. The 1760 treaty protected the Mi'kmaq's right to trade the products of their hunting, fishing, and gathering for "necessaries."

Upon hearing the evidence regarding the treaties, the court convicted Donald Marshall on all charges in June 1996. He was given an absolute discharge, and the conviction went to appeal. The Nova Scotia Court of Appeal's decision was even more devastating to the Mi'kmaq because it denied the validity of the 1760–61 treaties. Defence counsel argued that if the Mi'kmaw treaties are read as a chain of treaties, then the trade clause constituted a treaty-protected right to commercial activity. The Crown countered that the treaties did not grant any commercial fishing rights to the Mi'kmaq. Conviction upheld, Donald was granted leave to appeal to the Supreme Court of Canada.

At no time in the court proceedings was Donald given an opportunity to express how it was that he came to be a harvester, how he understood his ability to fish as an inherent right and as an integral part of his Mi'kmaw identity. He did not get a chance to describe how he practised the Mi'kmaw legal principles of responsible harvesting and sharing, which had been passed down for generations. Instead, the trial process narrowed the discourse to the written treaty and events in a selected period of time. The defence was precluded from offering the court a sense of Mi'kmaw history and legal traditions prior to the coming of Europeans. In short, the court authorized a particular, non-Mi'kmaw version of history. The treaty process – meant to protect and guarantee Mi'kmaw liberties and access to resources – has been reevaluated in terms that served the settler society while denying Mi'kmaw sovereignty. Treaty rights, from the Crown's perspective, were to be won or, preferably, lost. The case was not about honouring relationships; it was about adversaries duelling over legitimacy.

THE SUPREME COURT of Canada heard the case and on September 17, 1999, decided in favour of Donald Marshall (five judges in favour, two dissenting). Justice Binnie, writing for the majority, stated:

> When interpreting the treaties the Court of Appeal erred in rejecting the use of extrinsic evidence in the absence of ambiguity. Firstly, even in a modern commercial context, extrinsic evidence is available to show that a written document does not include all of the terms of an agreement. Secondly, extrinsic evidence of the historical and cultural context of a treaty may be received even if the treaty document purports to contain all of the terms and even absent any ambiguity on the face of the treaty. Thirdly, where a treaty was concluded orally and afterwards written up by representatives of the Crown, it would be unconscionable for the Crown to ignore the oral terms while relying on the written ones.
>
> The accused's treaty rights are limited to securing "necessaries" (which should be construed in the modern context as equivalent to a moderate livelihood), and do not extend to the open-ended accumulation of wealth. Thus construed, however, they are treaty rights within the meaning of s.35 of the *Constitution Act, 1982* ... What is contemplated is not a right to trade generally for economic gain, but rather a right to trade for necessaries. The treaty right is a regulated right and can be contained by regulation within its proper limits. Catch limits that could reasonably be expected to produce

a moderate livelihood for individual Mi'kmaw families at present-day standards can be established by regulation and enforced without violating the treaty right. The accused caught and sold the eels to support himself and his wife. His treaty right to fish and trade for sustenance was exercisable only at the discretion of the Minister. Accordingly, the closed season and the imposition of the discretionary licensing system would, if enforced, interfere with the accused's treaty right to fish for trading purposes, and the ban on sales would, if enforced, infringe his right to trade for sustenance. In the absence of any justification of the regulatory prohibitions, the accused is entitled to an acquittal.[3]

The decision reverberated across the country, inspiring Indigenous communities to unite in collective action to secure their rights to resources. The federal government, the Department of Fisheries and Oceans, and non-Aboriginal fishers were not prepared for the decision.

The judgment led to immediate conflict and controversy in the Maritimes, grabbing international headlines and marring the Mi'kmaq's legal victory. Non-Indigenous fishers resisted the Supreme Court's findings on the grounds that they believed they held traditional rights to the waters and were unwilling to share the strained – but lucrative – resources with anyone, especially "Indians." Although Donald was an eel fisher, the Mi'kmaq interpreted the decision to mean that they had access to all ocean resources. The case marked an unprecedented turn in colonial relations: it opened a window to remedy patterns of dependency and subjugation in favour of sustainable community advancement, a return to the principles of netuku-limk (responsible harvesting) through the affirmation of traditional knowledge and treaty and Indigenous rights. It marked a resurgence of practices that respect the sacred interconnectedness with the spirits in all life forms. The values of netukulimk are the centrepiece of the Unama'ki Institute of Natural Resources, which opened in 1999, and frame the harvesting guidelines of the Mi'kmaw Nation.

The eel disappeared from the headlines as the controversy shifted to lobster and who had access to this profitable fishery. Fears that Indigenous people would take to the waters and harvest everything at once were heightened when the Department of Fisheries and Oceans, following its own interpretation of the Supreme Court decision, showed excessive force in restricting Mi'kmaw access to the waters. Video footage of hulking government vessels battering small Mi'kmaw dories to force the occupants overboard into the open ocean and other violent confrontations played out on the nightly news.

The Marshall decision sparked increased surveillance and monitoring for all fishers. Heightened fear and competition strained Indigenous and settler relations, preempting any potential for cooperation and collaboration in fishery access and co-management. Given the fragile state of the fishery, acrimony had increased not only between settler and Indigenous peoples but also within these groups as well. Despite the opinion of the Supreme Court, Mi'kmaw claims to territories, resource management, and equitable access were in practice denied. Media accounts propelled animosity towards Indigenous harvesters by perpetuating negative stereotypes and exaggerating instances of overfishing and the use of illegal gear. When Donald went out in public, he was often accosted and blamed by settlers for disrupting generations of family businesses and taking food out of their children's mouths.

The West Nova Fishermen's Coalition, a powerful lobby group representing non-Indigenous fishers angered at the lack of consultation and the outcome of the case, applied for a rehearing with respect to the federal government's regulatory authority. If granted, the coalition wanted a stay in the judgment until the rehearing was complete. The Supreme Court rejected the application but reiterated the law relating to treaty rights, their regulation, and justifiable infringement by the Crown. This reconsideration was extraordinarily rare. The court stated that Mi'kmaw and Maliseet treaty rights were not unlimited and that the Aboriginal fishery could be regulated for conservation purposes or to serve other important public objectives: "The paramount regulatory objective is conservation and responsibility for it is placed squarely on the minister responsible and not on the aboriginal or non-aboriginal users of the resource. The regulatory authority extends to other compelling and substantial public objectives which may include economic and regional fairness, and recognition of the historical reliance upon, and participation in, the fishery by non-Aboriginal groups."[4]

In negotiating interim agreements, the federal government tried to stem conflicts and license all Indigenous access. But the policies and strategies – aimed at maintaining order and the future of the fisheries – sparked more controversy. Mi'kmaw bands were concerned whether signing agreements would infringe the newly affirmed treaty rights. These were serious and challenging considerations for communities struggling to climb out of poverty and supply adequate housing, education, health services, and employment to their members. Band by band, the terms of the agreements were set out, fuelling tensions that suggested the arrangements would divide and conquer the Mi'kmaq and eliminate the necessity to recognize the Mi'kmaq as a nation. In the immediate post-*Marshall* era, the Mi'kmaw leadership was fractured as coercive individual contribution agreements were put in place for twenty-seven of the thirty-four Indigenous communities that fell under the *Marshall* jurisdiction. Eventually, all but two communities signed agreements.

Commercial fishers were appeased by requirements that demanded Mi'kmaw fishers follow settler industry regulations. Their interest lied in controlling Mi'kmaw participation in the commercial fishery and ultimately dispossessing the Mi'kmaq of their self-determining authority over land and sea. Millions of dollars emanated from the Department of Fisheries and Oceans along with a flood of policies and oversight groups: the Aboriginal Fisheries Strategy, the At-Sea Monitoring Initiative, the Marshall Response Initiative, the Fisheries Management Systems, the Atlantic Integrated Commercial Fisheries Initiative (AICFI), the Aboriginal Aquatic Resource and Oceans Management Program, and the AICFI technical advisory committee.

Under the new regime, all initiatives and programs were framed as voluntary. But access to the commercial fishery was guaranteed only through participation in government-run programs, which had complete control over training, licences, and equipment. For instance, the AICFI was portrayed publicly as a program "to support an integrated, orderly commercial fishery in the Maritimes and Quebec" and to provide the mentoring and training required to support First Nations in building capacity in commercial fisheries, but Indigenous fishers could not access its training or infrastructure dollars unless they operated within and complied with policy regulations. If they wanted to exercise their treaty and Aboriginal rights independently, they still had to comply with federal regulations.

Non-Indigenous peoples also benefitted from these programs. In addition to being well paid for licence buyouts and gear transfers, they received most of the contracts for skippering and first-mate positions and healthy salaries for helping Indigenous communities meet the demands of the new programs. Mi'kmaw communities could not access AICFI funds unless they participated in monitoring programs that required infrastructure support and knowledge translation from outsiders. Eventually, the monitoring system shifted, and although the governance and management enhancement programs improved commercial operations, Mi'kmaq complained that the co-management components were slow to take Indigenous knowledge and traditional ecological knowledge into consideration. They argued that elders needed to be consulted consistently in resource management, design, and implementation, but this rarely happened.

ALTHOUGH THE MARSHALL decision recognized Mi'kmaw and Indigenous rights, the plethora of policies, rules, and regulations imposed on Indigenous fishers in order to "include" them in the commercial fishery effectively marginalized them. For instance, officials with the Department of Fisheries and Oceans doggedly refused to recognize autonomous community-based management plans such as those put forward by the Listuguj, Esgenoopetitj, and other Mik'maw communities that resisted being constrained by what they saw as stop-gap measures and narrow interpretations of their rights. Instead, these communities wanted autonomy over resource management and harvesting decisions, and they wanted control over access, procurement, and the distribution of benefits. This autonomy included jurisdiction over commercial as well as food, social, and ceremony fisheries. The solution to centuries of broken treaty promises, they argued, was an integrated, sustainable fisheries management program informed by Indigenous ecological knowledge and governed by Indigenous legal principles.

To achieve their goals, Mi'kmaq across the Maritimes acknowledged the need to unite to collectively exercise their treaty and Aboriginal rights

Donald Marshall Jr., accompanied by Mi'kmaw Grand Chief Ben Sylliboy and Senator Dan Christmas (right) and his cousin, Chapel Island Chief Lindsay Marshall (left), walking through Sydney, NS, during a peaceful protest over Indigenous fishing rights, October 2000. *The Canadian Press/Andrew Vaughan*

affirmed in section 35 of the Constitution Act, 1982, and recognized by the Supreme Court of Canada. Donald looked to his father's legacy, particularly his leadership in the moose harvests after the *Simon* decision, for guidance. In meetings with chiefs and the Grand Council, he encouraged the nation to unite. He joined in marches and supported warriors in Esgenoopetitj when tensions erupted with fishers. His belief in Mi'kmaw rights and the responsibilities those rights enshrined remained resolute. During a particularly volatile CBC Radio call-in show addressing the question "Is the *Marshall* decision good for the Maritimes?," Donald phoned in pleading for peace and respect on the water. Indigenous peoples across the country were planning their fishing strategies and hosting meetings to share and mobilize their knowledge. Donald participated in many of these cultural exchanges. He fished when he could catch his breath, but the stress of being back in court, the lengthy trial and appeals, and fear of the consequences if the Mi'kmaq lost their case all took their toll on his already fragile health. Frustrated by the negative reactions of Canadian society towards Mi'kmaw commercial fishing rights, he never ate another lobster.

Chiefs and tribal councils held exploratory talks to determine the substance of their treaty rights. In 2002, through band council resolutions, the chiefs in the thirteen Mi'kmaw communities agreed to sign an umbrella agreement to confirm the willingness of the Mi'kmaq and the federal and provincial governments to work together to enter into discussions to define, recognize, and implement Mi'kmaw rights. The parties developed terms of reference for consultation, appointed negotiators, and held deliberations on the Made–in–Nova Scotia Process framework agreement.

In 2004, the Made–in–Nova Scotia Process was retitled Kwilmuk Maw-klusuaqn (We Are Seeking Consensus), or the Mi'kmaq Rights Initiative, and the parties signed a framework agreement in 2007. The agreement outlined negotiation procedures for treaty rights as applied to fish, wildlife, forestry, and land. It took a long time to reach a memorandum of understanding, but the process was based on respectful relations and has since led to productive dialogues on governance and on social, cultural, and economic issues. On Treaty Day 2008, the Assembly of Nova Scotia Mi'kmaq Chiefs signed the Mi'kmaq of Nova Scotia Nationhood Proclamation, signalling their commitment, through the Kwilmu'kw Maw-klusuaqn Mission Office (KMKNO), to develop a cohesive system of governance. The chiefs recognized the need to heighten transparency and accountability if they were going to be effectively and equitably responsive in treaty rights implementation. This new mechanism for participation was to put decision-making control back into the hands of the Mi'kmaq. The life of the Mi'kmaw Nation depended on it.

Within the assembly, individual chiefs were made responsible for carrying particular portfolios: fisheries, mining, and finance; gaming; governance, Mi'kmaw women and urban Mi'kmaq; education, social, and parks; energy and justice; health; culture, heritage, and archaeology; sport and recreation; and lands, wildlife, and forestry. The portfolio system helped coordinate and organize the diverse matters that came to their attention through the KMKNO's Consultation Department. Along with a technical team, the lead chief would gather and present relevant information to the assembly, who in turn would provide them with instructions. Any major decisions would be ratified by a vote of the Mi'kmaw population.

Today, the KMKNO's board of directors is composed of the chiefs of the assembly, the national Assembly of First Nations' regional vice-chief, the Mi'kmaw grand chief, the kji keptin, and two district chiefs with ex officio status. For now, the Grand Council members have a symbolic role but one that may take on greater political significance as the nation awaits the appointment of the next grand chief following the passing of Benjamin Sylliboy in December 2017. The KMKNO lists its five pillars on its website:

1. To achieve recognition, acceptance and implementation and protection of treaty title and other rights;
2. To develop systems of Mi'kmaw governance and resource management;
3. To revive, promote and protect a healthy Mi'kmaw identity;
4. To obtain the basis for a shared economy and social development;
5. To negotiate toward these goals with community involvement and support.[5]

By consulting and negotiating with the federal and provincial governments, the KMKNO is not giving up any rights claims, nor is it negotiating new treaties. Its representatives position themselves as protecting time immemorial rights, and they understand that it is their collective duty to ensure that Mi'kmaw lands and resources will be enjoyed for generations to come. KMKNO is tackling the thorny questions of membership. By cleaning up the mess made by the Indian Act, they are creating a system in which the Mi'kmaq determine who are the beneficiaries of their rights. Belonging can be determined at the community's discretion following the traditional concepts of *wejikesin* and *ekinawatiken,* meaning "We must go back to our communities and seek their feedback and approval at the outset."

The primary goal is to ensure that all Mi'kmaq enjoy their treaty rights and that federal, provincial, and corporate entities engage with Mi'kmaq in ways that ensure that their rights are foregrounded, respected, and foundational to any development in Mi'kma'ki. KMKNO's slogan is "It Is Time to Make Things Right." They disseminate information about consultations through newsletters, press releases, community notices, and articles in the *Mi'kmaw Maliseet Nations News* and through their website, Facebook, YouTube, and Twitter.

The KMKNO set up working groups to manage natural resources such as moose and fish. In 2009, it conducted extensive community negotiations to establish moose-hunting guidelines for the nation, and it continues to examine how the Mi'kmaq can create a fair and open process for exercising their authority to harvest. Working with Natural Resources Canada and Environment Canada, the Mi'kmaq are developing rights-based, adaptive, collaborative moose-management plans. Holistic rights implementation occurs through Mi'kmaw-controlled harvester identification, a Mi'kmaw-directed reporting mechanism to monitor harvest levels and locations, and a community-controlled Mi'kmaw customary law program to dispense with breaches to Mi'kmaw harvesting guidelines. One of the most successful examples of self-determination, the Moose Management Initiative is operated by the Unama'ki Institute of Natural Resources, with support from KMKNO. It operates on the ethos of sacred resource use, sharing, and responsible harvesting. Their education program is revitalizing Indigenous environmental knowledge and ethical resource management for the next seven generations.

The fisheries working group includes members from the Department of Fisheries and Oceans, Indigenous and Northern Affairs Canada (now Crown-Indigenous Relations and Northern Affairs Canada, and Indigenous Services Canada), the Nova Scotia Department of Fisheries and Aquaculture, and the Office of Aboriginal Affairs. It is currently working on a detailed mandate to negotiate fisheries matters with the goals of supporting the ability to make a moderate livelihood (as per the *Marshall* decision) and establishing Mi'kmaw laws and authorities (pursuant to Mi'kmaw harvest and management plans). These discussions are complex and challenging, particularly as the Crown's position continues to be adversarial rather than conciliatory. Things are changing, though, as government agencies embark on implementing the Truth and Reconciliation Commission's ninety-four calls to action and nation-to-nation mandates as issued by Prime Minister Trudeau.

The Mi'kmaq Rights Initiative is central to the nation-rebuilding process underway in Mi'kma'ki. The Mi'kmaq have successfully litigated for recognition of their treaty rights. As a nation, they decided to not participate in the federal claims commission program but instead established a unique course of action for consultation and negotiation. The KMKNO works diligently to manifest treaty rights in Nova Scotia to the benefit of the members of the Mi'kmaw Nation. It is controversial work that challenges colonial consciousness and pressures governments and private businesses to do things differently and to come to agreements that substantively honour the Peace and Friendship Treaties.

One of the greatest obstacles to reconciliation is the widespread position, held by agents of the Crown such as those in Fisheries and Oceans Canada, that Supreme Court decisions affirming Indigenous treaty rights are losses rather than wins. In litigation, the relationship between the Crown and Indigenous peoples remains adversarial. In response to perceived losses, Crown agents aggressively assert their regulatory power and control. In 2017, an official with Fisheries and Oceans Canada stated: "We've been tested by the courts many, many times on issues relating to fisheries by Indigenous peoples in Canada and I'll put it bluntly to you, in most cases we come out on the losing side of those issues. And we need to be careful moving forward that we don't create another situation that results in another precedent, and that is a possibility. We didn't think we were going to lose the Marshall case, but we did."[6]

Reconciliation requires full recognition of Mi'kmaw rights and title, meaningful consultation, and fulfillment of the fiduciary obligations of the Crown. To facilitate this, the Assembly of Nova Scotia Mi'kmaq Chiefs entered into a memorandum of understanding on treaty education with the province of Nova Scotia on Treaty Day 2018: "Treaty Education is a vehicle for us to begin the long-term, generational journey toward reconciliation." Together, the Mi'kmaq and the province are building programs and services for the education system, the civil service, and the broader public. Four questions guide the work: Who are the Mi'kmaq historically and today? What are the treaties, and why are they important? What happened to the treaty relationship? What are we doing to reconcile our shared history to ensure justice and equity? Treaty education will be integrated in all grade levels, and an awareness campaign based on the phrase "We are all treaty peoples" will generate greater understanding of rights and responsibilities as a way to build better relationships between Nova Scotians and the Mi'kmaw Nation.

ALTHOUGH THE MI'KMAQ Justice Institute closed its doors in 1999, Donald's run-in with the Department of Fisheries and Oceans and the court cases that followed guaranteed that the spirit and intent of the Marshall Inquiry recommendations lived on in Mi'kmaw consciousness and were looked to as a way to facilitate community control over resource disputes. When we went fishing on that fateful day in August 1993, it never crossed our minds that harvesting and selling the innocuous eel would lead to the transformative Supreme Court of Canada decision *R v Marshall*. We were simply trying to keep food on the table and gas in the boat and, hopefully, we'd have a bit left over for beers at the 123 Legion in Whycocomagh. Fortunately, the outcome was a true victory for the Mi'kmaw Nation. Donald's treaty rights legacy is written into the province's treaty education curriculum, which every school student and civil servant will receive.

After decades of exclusion from and marginalization within settler economies, the Mi'kmaq finally had incredible opportunities for nation rebuilding and economic growth. Membertou was transformed. The band leveraged its Marshall agreement seed monies to develop businesses and expand its land base. Its infrastructure now includes a shopping mall, a casino, a convention centre–hotel complex, a world-class hockey arena, a bowling alley and boxing gym, a communications network, a state of the art high school, running trails, health facilities, sidewalks, and street lamps. It is no longer recognizable as the community of Donald's youth. Today, Membertou exemplifies the extraordinary capacity, tenacity, ingenuity, and strength of Mi'kmaw communities.

8

Nijkitekek | That Which Heals
Restorative Justice

BY THE TIME OF the *Marshall* decision, years of imprisonment, heavy smoking, and exposure to noxious chemicals while working as a plumber had damaged Donald's lungs. From the early 1990s onward, he needed medication daily. During our fishing years, his illness progressed. When he had trouble hauling the nets, he took over driving the boat, and we managed. We made many visits to Emergency to combat life-threatening asthma attacks, and Donald stopped smoking.

During this time, Donald travelled around the country, giving speeches, attending conferences, and supporting prisoners. He continued his work with Indigenous youth and flew up to northern Ontario with his nephew Paul Bradley Gould, a constant companion, to set up a cultural exchange program with the Windigo fly-in communities. In May 2000, he was honoured in Ottawa with the Wolf Project Award, established to recognize, honour, and promote activities to improve racial harmony. The event was hosted by William Commanda and attended by Indigenous peoples from around the world and dignitaries such as Governor General Adrienne Clarkson.

Donald Marshall with Governor General Adrienne Clarkson at the ceremony for the Wolf Award, Ottawa Circle of All Nations Gathering, May 2000. *Photographed by L. Jane McMillan*

In October, he was honoured at Treaty Day for his heroic efforts and led a march in support of Indigenous fishers. In December, he received the citizen of the year award in his hometown, Membertou, a recognition that was deeply significant for him. That same year, Donald participated in another historic first – a justice circle to deal with a breach of federal fishing regulations.

Following the *Marshall* decision, the Mi'kmaq recognized that they needed to create a customary law protocol for managing harvesting offences. An incident involving a member of the Pictou Landing First Nation, located on the northeastern coast of Nova Scotia, offered the perfect test case. Pictou Landing is a small fishing community with a registered population of 649. In 2000, the band entered into a fishing agreement with the Department of Fisheries and Oceans to determine lobster quotas and signed a band council resolution to enact a communal licence. Under the licence, communal fishers were required to contribute 15 percent of their profits to the band for various development projects. In return, fishers received a set number of lobster tags, which served to regulate the lobster quota by limiting the number of traps one could fish. During the season, fishers were given twelve tags each to attach to their traps to indicate they were part of the communal agreement. When tags expired, the old ones were traded in for new.

On June 20, 2000, a band member committed an offence contrary to the Fisheries Act by fishing lobster with old tags and with more than the allowable number, violating the community agreement. Fisheries officers caught him by placing a marked lobster in an invalid trap, which they identified at the weighing station. The band member knew the terms of the communal agreement and admitted that he had made a mistake by fishing with too many traps. He decided to plead guilty to the charges.

The chief of Pictou Landing approached the Department of Fisheries and Oceans to see if it would be willing to use Indigenous law to mediate the charge, rather than having the case go to court. Department officials approached the Crown and defence counsel, and a judge sought counsel from the Aboriginal Justice Learning Network, a program of the federal Department of Justice. The judge decided to let the community determine the disposition of the case through a Mi'kmaw justice circle. The Aboriginal Justice Learning Network contacted the Mi'kmaq Young Offenders Project (renamed the Mi'kmaq Youth Option Program),[1] which agreed to facilitate the process.

Following the heartbreaking closure of the Mi'kmaq Justice Institute in 1999, the youth program had been resuscitated to ensure the continuation of access to court workers. The Mi'kmaq also looked to it for inspiration because it was one of the few programs that had successfully drawn upon Mi'kmaw legal principles to manage disputes and fostered their legitimacy within the community by mobilizing grassroots participation. The program tapped into a stream within Mi'kmaw legal consciousness that held that the adversarial justice system (which featured the state as the victim and punishment as the cure, in a narrow adjudication process separated from community) did not work for Indigenous peoples. Community members with strong traditional teachings rather than outsiders were in the best position to help redirect relationships. The program was also fuelled by the energy of the restorative justice movement – in and outside of Indigenous communities – which was sweeping the nation. Restorative justice, its supporters argued, would reduce crime, repair relations, and minimize criminal justice costs through peace building.

Immediately following the collapse of the Mi'kmaq Justice Institute, workers with the youth program found negotiating a Mi'kmaw justice identity a challenge, but they didn't let the province dictate the program's mandate. Members from the major Mi'kmaw political organizations supervised, directed, and administered the program, and chiefs temporarily came on board to negotiate support for the program within the Tripartite Forum, which became even more important for dialogue and mobilization in the wake of the *Marshall* decision. Against the disappointing history of the Mi'kmaq Justice Institute, program workers found themselves in constant battle with the provincial Department of Justice to justify the existence of the program and rationalize their requests for funding. The province in turn used Western-based notions of statistical effectiveness and efficiency to assess their claims and limit funding. However, seeing the benefits of Mi'kmaw justice practices in action, workers resisted state regulations that interfered with the goals of Mi'kmaw self-determination. As Nova Scotia implemented its own restorative justice process, the Department of Justice restricted the types of cases that the Mi'kmaq Youth Option Program could handle. Refusing to be co-opted, the program set its own culturally relevant case criteria and moved in the direction of hearing cases involving adult repeat offenders. Having successfully conducted justice or sentencing circles for a number of serious offences – including sexual offences and domestic violence cases, cases that settler restorative justice claimed were too volatile for Mi'kmaw communities to handle – they were ready to go it alone.

Rooted in Mi'kmaw traditional law, the sentencing circles provided a forum for the victim and the wrongdoer to deal directly with each other, to discover the root causes of the offence, discuss the harmful consequences of the wrongdoer's actions, and work collaboratively with the community to make healing and reintegration plans to restore relationships. The circle did not determine guilt or innocence – the wrongdoer had already accepted responsibility and wanted to make amends in a process of healing relations through the nurturing of apiksiktuaqn. Each case was unique and required a flexible approach, which made the process problematic in the eyes of government officials. A former director of the Mi'kmaq Youth Option Program noted that the province "thinks flexibility equals no accountability, but the accountability is within the community."[2] Responsibility for managing a dispute resided with circle participants, where it was visible to the community. Dispute management was not removed from the community, as it was with state-run institutions. It was believed that disputes are better mediated through the laws of kinship and place and shared knowledge of an individual's family background and the contributing circumstances of the event.

In the Pictou Landing case, the wrongdoer was considered a good candidate for a justice circle since he had accepted responsibility for the offence. The Youth Option model, however, had been designed for criminal offences with a victim. In this case, as per the Mi'kmaw laws for managing disputes and for responsible harvesting and sharing, community members determined that the victim was not the DFO but was the resource – the lobster. A forum of community members was then convened to manage the dispute. To prepare for the circle, the Youth Option staff identified possible participants with the guidance of the chief of Pictou Landing and selected elders. A series of consultation meetings with all parties to the case helped the staff solicit and instruct potential participants. Advanced preparation promoted constructive action to improve opportunities for meaningful outcomes – people knew what they were getting into. Because of hostilities on the water, staff made a special effort to elicit an effective, collaborative working relationship between Pictou Landing First Nation and the Department of Fisheries and Oceans. Fisheries officers, the Crown prosecutor, the wrongdoer, the chief, and community representatives met over the course of several months, and significant concerns came to light. Given the intense conflicts between non-Indigenous and Mi'kmaw fishers and the Department of Fisheries and Oceans after the *Marshall* decision, some feared the case would heighten tensions. The process had to be absolutely transparent and mutually just.

Judge Clyde MacDonald met with the federal Crown prosecutor and the defence counsel to discuss the options. Judge MacDonald decided not to attend the circle and instead chose to await the recommendations from the participants and then make his decision in response to the guidelines delivered through the justice circle facilitators. As per justice circle protocol, the local Grand Council member was invited to attend, but in this case, he identified that he was a relative of the wrongdoer and chose not to take part.

When the circle process opened, the participants included a facilitator and co-facilitator from Youth Option, the chief, the wrongdoer, two elders, a support person for the wrongdoer, Mi'kmaw counsel for the accused, a federal Crown prosecutor, the band fishery liaison, four federal fisheries officers, a representative of the band's fishers, a Pictou Landing community representative, and Donald Marshall. Donald was keen to support alternatives that would keep Indigenous peoples out of the courts and simultaneously honour treaty rights. He was all for restorative processes and was hopeful that this process would demonstrate to Canadians the ability of the Mi'kmaq to regulate their fisheries and administer their own justice system. He also wanted the resolution of the issue to bring peace on the water and restore relationships between fishing communities.

There was a great deal of excitement about the circle's potential to lead the way to community control of regulatory offences. The Mi'kmaq identified the community of harm in ways that fit with their legal consciousness and employed value systems of netukulimk and *apiksituaguan* (a concept framing relational forgiveness and responsibility). By constructing the resource as the victim, they were establishing mechanisms to repair the social, spiritual, and environmental harm. This justice circle provided an excellent opportunity for communicating management strategies and community accountability by validating resource harvesting and sharing practices. It also allowed for the expansion of Mi'kmaw legal infrastructure. Contrary to commonly held fears that fishing and treaty rights cases would infringe on the enjoyment of Mi'kmaw rights, this case had the potential to entrench Mi'kmaw prerogative over the implementation and supervision of those rights. Importantly, the circle created a safe environment for the Mi'kmaq to confront their historical adversary, the government of Canada, face to face in a venue that was Mi'kmaw built and controlled. It was a critical opportunity to have their voices heard rather than silenced, as was regularly the case in the adversarial system.

The justice circle followed several rounds, during which each person had the opportunity to share his or her thoughts and talk it out in the customary way. The first harm examined was not the harm to the lobster but the harm to the relationship between the Department of Fisheries and Oceans and Pictou Landing First Nation. The facilitator later explained the challenges of the circle process, illustrating the complexities of Mi'kmaw legal consciousness when dealing with the issue of rights protection:

> The biggest challenge or fear was that this topic often becomes volatile and is very touchy. I was afraid it would turn into Jerry Springer. Secondly, the community vilified the officers. It was a challenge to have the group stay open-minded and remember that the DFO was also taking a chance to try this, and to keep reminding everyone that DFO supported this. Thirdly, the offender was almost canonized. It was difficult constantly reminding the group that the offender was not the victim and that he knowingly committed this offence.
>
> Even after I repeatedly asked the offender if he accepted responsibility, the group still felt he was wrongly accused. The [offender], to his credit, repeated he accepted responsibility and was wrongful in his actions. I think part of this [challenge] came from [the wrongdoer's] upstanding character, and everyone found it difficult to believe he would knowingly do this; and secondly, the fact that people were looking to blame DFO in some way for everything that has happened in the past. The success was having everyone share their pain in a constructive way and having the opportunity to listen without being attacked. The other success was that [the wrongdoer] and the DFO officer that charged him had an opportunity to rebuild a friendship that was damaged by this incident. That was very powerful.[3]

Although the two parties rebuilt a friendship, the circle did not easily reach a consensus on the sentence plan for the offender. Participants were polarized in their views as to what they considered fair in terms of peace-building reparations, denunciation, and deterrence:

> Generally, participants of the formal legal and enforcement system were in agreement that in order to maintain relationships out on the waters, a

strong message of deterrence should be made. They were careful to mention that there is already much friction between non-Native and Aboriginal fishermen on the waters. To preserve peace and promote fairness, they felt the offender should not be treated any differently due to his Mi'kmaw status. They also expressed that this circle model could be used to promote equality and fairness. Participants of the Aboriginal community viewed the circle process as unique to deal with this matter and asked the circle to consider the mitigating circumstances relating to the [wrongdoer's] persona and reputation. They suggested a less punitive sentence plan.[4]

Instead of submitting a unified sentence plan to the judge, the circle submitted recommendations outlining the various preferences of the participants. The Crown suggested a fine, forfeiture of catch on a specific date, and a one-week prohibition from fishing during the next season. The Department of Fisheries and Oceans articulated concerns regarding conservation and argued that all violations of the federal regulations required equal treatment, without prejudice in the eyes of the law. The officers agreed with the Crown's recommendation but resisted the recommendations of the Mi'kmaw community, reflecting the federal government's inability to embrace the unique circumstances of Indigenous resource use in the face of treaty rights implementation or to let go of control in their handling of regulatory offences.

Because they believed that the offence was out of character, community members asked that the circle take into consideration the wrongdoer's past behaviour and the fact that negative media attention (and the media's tendency to represent Indigenous fishers as criminals) would damage the offender's reputation. They wanted the circle to take into consideration the suffering that all Mi'kmaq had experienced because of federal fisheries regulations, which alienated them from the fishing economy. They agreed that a monetary fine was acceptable, but they argued that the community was also a victim because the community agreement had been breached and relations had to be made right. To make matters right, they argued that the fine should be channelled into the community for the collective benefit of all, rather than making a payment to the government. The Mi'kmaq had long argued for fine payments to be redistributed within their communities rather than going into municipal, provincial, or federal coffers, a situation that remains unresolved. Mi'kmaw participants also took the opportunity to articulate their objection to the confiscation of gear when charges were laid. They argued that taking gear was an unfair punishment for communities struggling to access resources and suffering from economic deprivation.

For similar reasons, the elders did not agree with the Crown's suggestion of a one-week fishing prohibition. Fishing was the wrongdoer's livelihood; it was how he provided for his family, and he directed a percentage of his catch to the community, as per the agreement. A prohibition would thus be harmful to the community in general. Preventing individuals from fulfilling their duty to contribute to the community, they argued, was more harmful than remedial. They agreed with community members that the fine payment should filter inward, and one elder recommended community service as a way to hold the wrongdoer accountable to the collective. As a whole, the community perceived the offence as a violation of trust and wanted to ensure that resource conflicts could be resolved peacefully in ways that respected the lobster and livelihoods and facilitated the restoration of responsible harvesting.

The judge accepted the recommendations. The fisherman was required to give the community the products of an additional week's catch as his sentence. Pictou Landing fishers were reminded of the principles of netukulimk, of their duty to respect the environment in which they work, and instructed to protect the bounty of the resource for the future benefit of the community. Mi'kmaw concepts of justice were upheld, and Mi'kmaw legal practices were validated. Relations between the Department of Fisheries and Oceans and Pictou Landing First Nation improved and were set forth on a healing path.

All parties agreed that the circle process was an opportunity to educate fishers, both Mi'kmaw and non-Mi'kmaw. They described it as a respectfully orchestrated healing and sharing process. In the end, healing extended beyond the fisher and the fisheries officer, who embraced in "reconciliation of their differences" to the applause of the circle participants. There was consensus that the circle had been a positive experience, one that allowed parties with differing positions to enter into an effective dialogue on a controversial issue and set a foundation for future discourses on resource sharing and the prevention of future disputes.

When a similar regulatory offence case came to the Mi'kmaq Youth Option Program several months later, the outcome was much different. Staff approached the judge presiding in the area to see if he would consent to a Mi'kmaw justice circle to manage the dispute. The judge, new to the area, determined that the community of harm was too broad – in other words, he could not wrap his head around the idea of the resource being a victim. Supported by the Crown prosecutor, the judge would not permit a justice circle to manage the harm. Instead, the case went to court. The process was entirely removed from the community once again. In its dealings with the settler justice system, it was difficult for Mi'kmaw regulatory rights to make headway.

After the success of the fishing circle, however, the Mi'kmaq prioritized the criminal justice needs of communities. The Mi'kmaq Youth Option Program was reconfigured as the Mi'kmaw Legal Support Network in 2002. The new organization, really a collection of programs, was intended to fill significant gaps left when the Mi'kmaq Justice Institute ceased to provide services to those Mi'kmaq encountering the Canadian justice system. The network initially had a mandate to manage two main services in need of attention – the Native Court Worker Program and the Mi'kmaw Customary Law Program. As those programs had taken shape, gaps in services to victims had opened a window on faults in the holistic approach to justice. Mi'kmaw legal principles required that everyone in a dispute be equally embraced, so a victim support team was added to the network. To bridge the gap between the Canadian court system and Indigenous peoples, court workers would accompany clients to court, provide information on community resources, facilitate communication between justice officials and clients, assist with accessing legal aid, and help write victim impact statements.

The customary law program facilitated Mi'kmaw ownership and control over justice, with dispute management and sentencing circles as its centrepiece. With the support of Mi'kmaw government and the KMKNO/ Mi'kmaw Rights Initiative, the Mi'kmaw Legal Support Network undertook to devise a customary law process for managing regulatory offences related to harvesting. It took years of bureaucratic wrangling, but finally, in 2011, it announced a customary law pilot project. As in the Pictou Landing case, justice circles would be based on the principles of netukulimk (responsible harvesting) and apiksiktuaqn (mutual forgiveness); the resource would be positioned as the victim or the offended; and remedies would centre on restoring the relationship between the resource, the offender and his or her family, the community, the ancestors, and the nation.

To date, a few moose-hunting cases but no fishing cases have been managed according to customary law. Even though the Indigenous fishing strategy requires community consultation before the laying of charges, Mi'kmaw harvesters continue to be fined or forced to engage in expensive court battles to protect rights already recognized by the Constitution and affirmed by the Supreme Court of Canada. Mi'kmaw lawyer Douglas Brown argues that prosecutors and judges "exhibit a consistent pattern of error and indifference with regard to Mi'kmaw harvesting rights despite the wide-ranging critique of the Nova Scotia justice system made by the Marshall Inquiry twenty-five years earlier."[5]

IN THE SUMMER of 2002, Donald suffered a respiratory failure, and his respirologist told us he was not likely to survive. The world dropped away from me. At the hospital, family and friends lined the corridors. The doctors made it clear that only a double lung transplant would keep him alive. We were scared. We were angry. Why couldn't he get a break? It was hard to process.

To be placed on a transplant list, potential recipients have to undergo a battery of tests to determine their fitness, assess risks, and weigh the probability of a successful surgery. Doctors also need to agree that death will likely occur within two years without surgical intervention. Each candidate requires a support person to share in every step of the journey and help get the patient in the best possible shape to increase the chances of surviving the risky operation. At the time, lung transplants were still largely experimental and infrequent. Donald's condition deteriorated rapidly, but he made it through the arduous candidacy tests. We were hopeful and desper-

The vessel named after Donald Marshall Jr. by the Membertou Band in recognition of his contributions to the Mi'kmaw Nation's treaty rights. *Photographed by Roy Gould*

ate. Everything but his lungs worked well, and he was young. We moved to Toronto, and he was placed on the list on December 20, 2002.

We followed the procedures of the Organ Donor Program at the University Health Network, and we waited, and waited. At times, our courage waned, particularly during the SARS epidemic, which shut down the hospitals and suspended surgeries. As the illness took away his energy, Donald's valour remained intact. The love of his family nurtured him, and his desire to spend more time with his children, Randy Sack and Crystal Nimchuk, compelled him to keep up the fight. Randy was raised in Sipekne'katik and had spent summers with us in Aberdeen from the time he turned five. His daughter, Crystal, raised solely by her mother in Halifax, had become, at the age of seventeen, just months before we left Nova Scotia, a welcome surprise in her father's life. He loved his kids deeply and was bolstered by their visits in Toronto.

While praying for a miracle in Toronto we followed the ongoing fallout from the *Marshall* decision in Atlantic Canada. Membertou named two of the fishing vessels in its fleet *The Donald Marshall Jr.* and *The Grand Chief Donald Marshall Sr.* This buoyed Donald's spirits, and we looked forward to going for a ride on the boat, but Donald continued to be deeply frustrated by the divisiveness that the fishing agreements were causing. He wanted a united Mi'kmaw Nation, and he wanted the Mi'kmaq to be able to fully realize their treaty rights without having to confront racism at every turn.

On May 5, 2003, we got the call and rushed to the hospital. As we waited for the lungs to arrive, we spent the day talking about fishing, craving moose meat pies, making plans for youth camps, and imagining all the adventures he was going to have with his children and, maybe, his future grandchildren. We laughed. We cried. We held each other tightly. We thought of the donor and the donor's family, giving thanks for their courage and generosity. Word spread quickly once it was confirmed that the surgery would take place late in the day. Allies across the country prayed. Donald's mentor, Grandfather William Commanda, conducted a pipe ceremony as Donald underwent the complicated operation.

Etched forever in my memory is his first unencumbered breath. Realizing he was alive, his face lit up, his eyes widened with pure joy, and the most beautiful, grateful smile stretched across his face. We laughed and marvelled at the miracle. He had survived the most perilous step in the transplant journey.

Two days after the surgery, on May 7, 2003, during the Province of Nova Scotia House of Assembly debates and proceedings, a notice of motion was moved by Robert Chisholm, NDP MLA for Halifax, to adopt the following resolution:

Whereas Donald Marshall Jr. has lived a remarkable life, having inspired a 1989 Royal Commission Report that recommended sweeping and fundamental changes to the justice system in Nova Scotia; and

Whereas Donald Marshall Jr. also helped to establish that the Mi'kmaw and Maliseet people have a regulated right to earn a living from hunting, fishing and gathering; and

Whereas Donald Marshall Jr. is currently recovering from a double lung transplant operation this past Monday in Toronto,

Therefore be it resolved this House offer its best wishes for a speedy recovery to Donald Marshall Jr. from his double lung transplant and its appreciation to the family and friends who are providing care and comfort to him during his ordeal.

The early post-transplant years were critical and full of major transitions. Donald had finally caught his breath, and there was no stopping him. As soon as he received medical clearance, he returned to Nova Scotia, to his family and a hero's welcome. His niece Madelaine, a registered nurse, helped Donald adjust. I stayed in Toronto to work. The following year, our intimate relationship ended, and we went on separate paths. After a year of transitory animosity, our friendship was firmly re-established, and I became very concerned for Donald's well-being.

Back home, Donald suffered many deaths of close friends and family members, one after the other, in a short period of time. His brother was viciously assaulted and suffered a brain injury, and his best friend, Arty Paul, had a massive stroke. Acutely aware of his own mortality, Donald adjusted to a potent cocktail of anti-rejection drugs, a new relationship with his teenage daughter, and a renewed desire to see justice done, both in his wrongful conviction case and the fishing decision. At this time, he began a relationship with the soon-to-be former wife of the duty counsel for Roy Ebsary. And his attention turned to accessing the total amount of his remaining compensation, which was locked in an annuity. Understandably, he wanted to live comfortably, travel, and provide for his children. Despite all efforts and appeals to authorities, the annuity remained locked. He was completely frustrated.

Donald's behaviour began to change. Post-transplant anti-rejection drugs are absolutely necessary for survival, but they have side effects. The doctors calculate a formula and prescribe medications that must be taken every day, without fail, in twelve-hour increments. Any change in the schedule, or a failure to take any one of the numerous medications, can trigger a host of problems and may be fatal. In some cases, the immunosuppressant medications can trigger psychiatric reactions. Normally soft-spoken and fairly calm, Donald became extremely erratic and stressed. He was presenting with persecutory delusions and disorganization. His family and friends also noticed a deterioration in his mental health as he began talking, almost non-stop, about complex conspiracies. He became increasingly paranoid about people in the community, and past events consumed him. It was confusing for us because, on the one hand, his complaints were plausible (he had, indeed, experienced horrific injustices), but on the other, the narratives he developed were puzzling and exaggerated.

Unfortunately, we in his community of care did not provide a timely intervention. As 2005 came to an end, an ongoing feud with a Membertou resident escalated into violence. Donald was charged with attempted murder, uttering death threats, and dangerous driving. He was arrested in Halifax after a BOLF alert was issued from Sydney. He had gone to Halifax because he wanted to talk to the attorney general and Judge Felix Cacchione, his former lawyer. It was New Year's Eve. The police transferred him back to Sydney, where he complained of lung problems and was taken to the Cape Breton Regional Hospital. The mental health department requested that Donald undergo psychiatric assessment at the Nova Scotia Hospital.

Donald called me in Toronto from the East Coast Forensic Hospital, and we got Marlys Edwardh, one of his counsels from the inquiry days, on the phone. He needed new legal counsel, as his key legal support, Anne Derrick, had been appointed a judge of the Nova Scotia Provincial Court. Horrified at the thought of him being locked up again, all of us were desperate to get him proper medical care. We retained Duncan Beveridge as defence counsel and did everything we could to get Donald released.

Donald underwent a thirty-day assessment at the East Coast Forensic Unit of the Central Nova Scotia Correctional Facility and was found to be suffering from a psychotic disorder, possibly related to his medical condition and the pharmacological management of it – the anti-rejection drugs. I flew out for the cause hearing in the hope that Donald would be released into my care so he could receive medical attention from the lung transplant experts in Toronto. The attending psychiatrist did not think that Donald was fit to be released. He also said he met the criteria for exemption from criminal responsibility as laid out in section 16(1) of the Criminal Code of

Canada. He recommended that Donald be returned to the East Coast Forensic Unit for ongoing psychiatric treatment and management. Disposition of the case would be left to the Criminal Code Review Board. The court concurred. It was devastating.

After one hundred days and a carefully monitored change in his medications, Donald attended court back in Sydney. On April 12, 2006, the Crown attorney withdrew the attempted murder charge, as there was insufficient evidence and no reasonable prospect of conviction. The other charges, two counts of uttering death threats and dangerous driving, would go to trial on September 25, 2006. A condition of his release was that Donald keep away from Membertou. Greatly relieved to be free and feeling much better, he went fishing. I moved back to Nova Scotia.

DONALD AND THE Membertou resident with whom he had the conflict agreed to settle the charges through a healing circle, and the court agreed to divert the charges to the Mi'kmaw Legal Support Network. A healing circle was held on December 19, 2006, at the Elders' Centre in Membertou. The purpose of the forum was to assemble community members to develop a plan to resolve the conflict between the parties to the dispute. The circle consisted of fourteen members who had the interests and skills needed to develop a sentencing plan that would take the needs of the community, wrongdoer, and victim into consideration. I was asked by the Mi'kmaw Legal Support Network, on behalf of Donald, to support him through the process. All involved participated voluntarily. We understood that by choosing to participate, we would be working to ensure that the common goal of restoring harmony would be achieved. The participants also included Marshall family members, a band councillor, four elders, and a member of the RCMP's Membertou Detachment. The executive director of the Mi'kmaw Legal Support Network and her co-worker facilitated. Prior to the circle, the network's customary law team visited and consulted with each of us and provided instruction on how to make meaningful contributions.

Healing circles are another method of engaging communities and families in dispute resolution. Mi'kmaw elders teach that harmful acts are broader than one person or incident, that crime has consequences that can affect the whole community. They teach that community participation in the outcome helps foster collective responsibility, much like the gestures and displays during the Wi'kupaltimk feast, when community members gather to ask forgiveness of one another for past wrongdoings, both intentional and inadvertent. The non-adversarial process encourages humility and forgiveness, and wrongs between people are not given an opportunity to escalate. By talking it out in a setting deemed appropriate by tradition, the process of nijkitekek (healing) promotes awareness of the seriousness of the offence throughout the community and creates a space to end the dispute and make peace.

At Donald's healing circle, one elder commented that Membertou had its share of squabbles, but it still managed to preserve a feeling of community and family. He hoped the men would resolve their dispute, get on with their lives, and be role models to the children. He said that as a young man he had learned the responsibilities of apiksiktuaqn (mutual forgiveness) and of restoring community through cooperation. He described the work of a healing circle as a responsibility to develop an understanding of one another, to learn to respect one another, and to nurture a sense of belonging. Life, for the elder, was too short to harbour negative feelings.

This circle lasted three hours. Issues relating to the wrongdoer and victim were evaluated, and the discussion focused on their rehabilitative needs. The circle process encouraged talking it out in order to identify patterns of wrongful behaviour, their root causes, and areas of common ground. By doing so, we could develop a plan to correct relations between the parties and bring about positive social change. A talking stick was passed to each of us for a total of five rounds. At first, as the circle progressed, tensions were extremely high, but they noticeably eased, round by round. The manner in which we addressed one another shifted from the formal to the informal to the familiar. I felt my own fear and anger – at myself, at Donald for not taking better care, at the family for not providing an adequate community of care, and at the other party for instigating the whole mess and pressing charges in the first place – dissipate as we talked about what happened.

With community support, both men discussed how the feud had escalated to the point where criminal charges were laid. The facilitators used an interest-based approach to address the underlying hurt caused by the wrongful behaviour and to produce outcomes that would improve the working relationship among participants. An interest-based approach does not seek consensus as its primary objective; rather, by combining a broad range of interests in decision making, the focus is on working together to understand one another, rebuilding relationships, and generating healthy connections. Over the course of the circle, the participants' interests come to reflect the goals of the Mi'kmaw legal method.

One elder reported that it was hard for her to see the two families feuding. She had seen the men grow up and commented on how the tension between them was affecting so many other people. She believed in the healing powers of Mi'kmaw traditions and customs, such as the sweat lodge, and believed returning to these teachings could assist them both in walking a good road. Another elder talked of our responsibility to forgive one another, referring again to the tradition of wi'kupaltimk as a way forward and expressed confidence that the men would overcome this conflict and move on. He, too, had known them since they were boys and hoped they would resolve this matter and forgive each other; it was time for apiksiktuaqn. A common theme in the discussion was letting go of the conflict and focusing on the future in a good way.

At the end of each round, Donald and the other party were given the opportunity to comment on the teachings they had heard. During one round, the two men, who could barely acknowledge each other at first, got up from their chairs, met in the middle of the circle, and embraced. It was profoundly transformational. The circle process treated the two men as equals and, as participants, we felt safe publicly uttering our perspectives on highly sensitive and emotional matters. Focusing on interests and involving everyone to foster a sense of purpose and respectful participation in a creative problem-solving environment made for a powerful and successful circle. Together, we helped the two men recognize the harmful consequences of their actions and address the circumstances that had contributed to the disruption of their affiliation.

Our healing plan focused on repairing relationships rather than on punitive sanctions. We agreed that the families of both men had suffered in the time it took to resolve the matter. We also agreed that their mental health had contributed to the events and that the police response and media reports had caused the incident to escalate. We were happy that the two men had proffered and accepted mutual apologies. We witnessed apiksiktuaqn in action. With elder guidance, we decided that the best way to foster a sense of reintegration would be for both disputants to complete a day of community service as payment for the harm done. Once done, the matter would be considered resolved and no further action would be required. They would work with the Membertou Seniors Group to put together and distribute Christmas baskets for the reserve.

In the closing round of the circle, the injured party said the incident was regrettable and that he hoped for reconciliation between the families. Grand Chief Donald Marshall Sr. had been his godfather, and he did not want to lose his ties to the family. He hoped that he and Donald would be able to joke around again. He said he was happy that Donald was now well and understood the hurt he had caused. Donald said that asking for forgiveness was a "strong thing" and that it took a humble man to do so. Donald recognized that the incident was a large stumbling block, but he felt renewed by the circle process and thanked everyone for their support. To close, an elder said a prayer and asked us to leave in positive spirits, with confidence that we had improved community relations. Everyone shook hands, and then we had a feast, as per custom. They assembled and handed out the Christmas baskets without incident. The Crown withdrew the remaining charges of uttering threats and dangerous driving in February 2007.

FOR THE FIRST TIME since he had been taken away to jail at seventeen years of age, Donald moved back to Membertou and built a house with a picket fence. In mid-2007, he got married and fathered a second son, whom he named after himself. Donald John Marshall or "D.J." D.J. was Donald's pride and joy, but his time with him was too brief. Donald had a turbulent marriage that in 2008 resulted in unsubstantiated charges, estrangement, and separation from his child.

A year later, Donald's body began to suffer complications from the lung transplant. Knowing that his time was running out, he visited with friends

Caroline Marshall (Donald's mother) and L. Jane McMillan at Donald Marshall's funeral, August 10, 2009. *The Canadian Press/Andrew Vaughan*

and family throughout Mi'kma'ki. By summer, he was hospitalized. We had good visits and long drives during his last months and planned to go fishing when he recuperated. On the evening of August 4, we talked on the phone and expressed loving words. I said I'd see him in the morning. Later that night, he was taken to the intensive care unit, where he lost consciousness and did not recover. The next morning, the hospital corridors filled yet again with friends and family – hoping and praying. Donald Marshall Jr. died on August 6, 2009, at about 1:30 a.m. surrounded by family, who lifted him to the next world. He was fifty-five.

John MacIntyre, retired chief of the Sydney City Police, died two months later, on September 30, 2009. He was ninety.

Donald's funeral was well attended. In addition to the local papers, obituaries ran in the *New York Times* and the *Globe and Mail.* The Grand Council, the Assembly of Nova Scotia Mi'kmaq Chiefs, the national chief of the Assembly of First Nations, the lieutenant-governor, the premier of

Nova Scotia, and friends, family, fishers, ex-cons, the wrongly convicted, complete strangers, and Indigenous allies from across the country all paid their respects. Day and night, hundreds of mourners came through the house, where he was waked for the customary two days before burial. The CBC had a live radio feed from the church, and Canadians heard John Gracie, a Nova Scotian singer-songwriter, play the Hollies tune "He Ain't Heavy, He's My Brother" as requested by Junior's brothers. Lester Nepoose, brother of wrongly convicted Wilson Nepoose, came from Sampson Cree Nation to honour Donald, who had helped his family heal from their trauma. He brought a beautiful Pendleton blanket that sat on the casket during the wake and was placed in the grave per Cree funerary tradition.

People waved Mi'kmaw flags off fishing poles as the funeral procession passed by. Hundreds of us walked in an honour march from the church to the graveyard in Membertou, where Donald was drummed into the ground to the accompaniment of the Mi'kmaw Honour Song. A traditional *salite* feast – a celebration of life and communitarianism – brought the family and community together to heal. Members of the community donated items to be auctioned off to raise money to offset funeral costs and to support the grieving family. The items included Mi'kmaw baskets, framed photos of the Membertou boat with Donald's name, and hand-made wooden eagle feathers with the date of his birth and death. Sorrowful, Donald's mother conceded that her son was no longer suffering.

After the funeral, I walked along Pomquet Beach with our friend Freda Ens, who had come from Vancouver to attend the funeral. Near the place where Donald and I had fished for eels, we came upon a small whale. Freda said that, in Haida tradition, it was a sign from the ancestors that Donald had made his journey safely to the spirit world. I welcomed this knowledge.

9

I'l'oqaptmu'k | Revisiting for Renewal
Mi'kmaw Legal Consciousness Today

> Donald Marshall was a catalyst for revolutionary change in the
> justice system – through empowerment of self, we empower the
> community. The legacy of Donald Marshall Jr. is cast within the
> bedrock of the Mi'kmaw nation.
>
> – Chief Paul Prosper, Marshall Inquiry Symposium,
> Membertou, Nova Scotia, January 15, 2015

ON AUGUST 10, 2009, Algonquian elder William Commanda said a prayer for
Donald Marshall Jr. at a special ceremony on the sacred territory of Victoria Island, Ottawa:

Some of you may know that I carry the Sacred Three Figure Welcoming
and Sharing Wampum Belt created by our ancestors in the 1700s, before
our continent was divided, when we agreed to share our grand natural
resources and our values with the newcomers. Sadly, this commitment
was not honoured, and we became the most oppressed and dispossessed
in the land of our ancestors.

Donald Marshall Jr. has been the thunderbird who rose out of the ashes
to shine the light on our ancient values of truth, honour, and fairness and
to fight for our rights, our natural resources, and our visibility.

There was no commonly held phrase like "wrongfully convicted" before
he took on the challenge to speak his truth, and there was no recognition
that we were sovereign peoples who made agreements regarding sharing
our resources till the ancient eel awakened the voice that spoke for Indigenous rights and responsibility. His was also the voice to affirm our right to

dignity and healing, and he went on to experience a few joys of life after the great sacrifices he was called upon to bear, in the spirit of hope and renewal.

I am honoured to have known and shared much with him during the past two decades of his life. I knew his father, the Hereditary Chief, and I acknowledge with gratitude and tears the pain his mother and family have had to carry in the struggle for Indigenous peoples, and I acknowledge also the deep loss to the community in his unavailability to assume traditional responsibilities.

Many now begin to realize that he was not only a warrior fighting for the Indigenous cause, but that because he asserted our right to our place in the centre, his legacy of honour, justice, and self-respect benefits all. He animated the universal quest for racial harmony.

Junior was passionate about his commitment to the vision for the Indigenous Healing and Peace Centre in Ottawa, and while I feel a deep sadness that his unique wisdom and understanding, his passionate cry for the struggle of youth, nature, and endangered species like the ancient eel will no longer be available to us, yet I know his courage, tenacity, humility, love, and vision will continue to inspire the development of the centre, and his presence will be felt by many in the years to come.[1]

It had been twenty years since the Marshall Inquiry and ten years since the *Marshall* decision. A number of commemoration events marked Donald's contributions to social justice and treaty-rights mobilization. The Mi'kmaw Nation held a conference in Halifax, where they expressed their frustrations with the federal and provincial governments over the slow pace of treaty implementation. The Nova Scotia Barristers' Society dedicated an issue of its official publication, *The Society Record,* to the royal commission. The society's Equity Office and Race Relations Committee (established in response to Marshall Inquiry recommendations 9 and 10) hosted a conference at the Mi'kmaw Native Friendship Centre titled "Reflections: 20 Years after the Marshall Inquiry." The Indigenous Blacks and Mi'kmaq Initiative at Dalhousie University, a program pioneered by law professor Archie Kaiser and others in response to recommendation 11, celebrated its twentieth anniversary by inaugurating the Donald Marshall, Jr., Memorial Award.

Inspired by Jarvis Googoo (Donald's cousin and a participant in the program), the award is presented to the graduating student who best demonstrates commitment and involvement in raising awareness and working for Indigenous justice. Rosalie Francis, another Mi'kmaw law graduate, later arranged to have Donald's portrait unveiled in the atrium of the law school's library. On October 28, 2010, the community, family, and friends gathered in Membertou Heritage Park to install a bust of Donald Marshall Jr. Today, it sits beside likenesses of Grand Chief Donald Marshall Sr. and Grand Chief Membertou.

IN THE IMMEDIATE aftermath of the Marshall Inquiry report in 1989, Mi'kmaw communities viewed the inquiry and its recommendations as progressive and hopeful. The royal commission had opened a window on racism in the administration of justice. It acknowledged that Indigenous people had a right to a justice system that respected them and "dispensed justice in a manner consistent with and sensitive to their history, culture, and language." The release of the royal commission's report was an empowering turning point for the Mi'kmaw Nation. Mi'kmaq now asserted a culturally unique application of the principles of fairness and justice. They demanded the right to counter colonization and govern themselves through management of their own adjudicative practices. The Supreme Court's 1999 decision in *R v Marshall* provided further encouragement to push forward to establish community control over justice matters – now reinforced by the recognition of long dormant treaty rights.

Nearly thirty years have passed since the Marshall Inquiry report and nearly twenty since the *Marshall* decision. The Mi'kmaq use their collective wisdom as yardsticks to measure the distance between their legal entitlements and entanglements and the systemic discrimination that led to Donald Marshall Jr.'s wrongful conviction.

The Mi'kmaq have made progress in their quest for justice. There have also been serious setbacks. Indigenous justice programming stagnated in the Harper era, when the settler justice system once more dominated the lives of Mi'kmaw people. In 2012, for instance, the Conservative government's Safe Streets and Communities Act imposed punitive sanctions that ignored the realities of systemic discrimination and rolled back initiatives intended to correct historical inequalities. Mi'kmaw experience with Fisheries and Oceans Canada has been no less frustrating, plagued by the department's insensitive treatment of community members in the exercise of their treaty rights and by Canada's general failure to acknowledge Indigenous sovereignty in resource management. The Assembly of Nova Scotia Mi'kmaq Chiefs contend that Canada has not yet met its legal obligation to accommodate the Mi'kmaw treaty right to a moderate livelihood. These are issues of high priority for many Mi'kmaq, matters they feel must be resolutely addressed in order for justice and substantive reconciliation to be realized. As John Borrows, a professor of law at the University of Victoria, argues, implementing historical treaties is all about finding the right relationship.

Close observers and my own research identify the Marshall Inquiry recommendations and the Supreme Court's *Marshall* decision as principled rationales for Mi'kmaw self-determination and the establishment of an independent justice system. The same observers recognize the perpetuation of historical impediments to implementing the recommendations and the exercise of Mi'kmaw treaty rights. These obstacles include the dominant culture's profound lack of knowledge regarding Indigenous treaty rights, its chronic failure to identify and respect the Mi'kmaq as a nation, and the continuing denial of the legitimacy of Mi'kmaw governance in the management of their lands and resources. Mi'kmaw community members continue to point to evidence of insidious systemic discrimination.

Calls for a thorough review of the Marshall Inquiry recommendations began in earnest in 2008, after a series of tragic events rocked Mi'kma'ki. John Simon died at his home on Wagmatcook Reserve at the hands of the RCMP. Victoria Paul died following an unattended stroke she suffered while in police custody. Tanya Brooks's murder remains unsolved. The apparent indifference of the settler justice system to the fate of individual Mi'kmaw convinced the nation of the need for an accountability review, an empirical audit of the failure to implement the inquiry's recommendations. If the recommendations had been conscientiously implemented, they asked, would these miscarriages of justice have occurred? Had anything been done to erase the entrenched racism detailed in the Marshall Inquiry report? When the Tripartite Officials Committee met in November 2011, those at the table – including representatives of the Assembly of Nova Scotia Mi'kmaq Chiefs, the Nova Scotia Native Women's Association, and the federal and provincial governments – authorized the Tripartite Justice Working Committee to conduct the review.

I was selected as the principal investigator following an open call for proposals to direct the project. Having witnessed first-hand the consequences of Donald's experiences and having closely documented the efforts of justice officials and the Mi'kmaw Nation to remedy the problems experienced by Indigenous peoples as they encountered the Canadian justice system, I was well positioned to carry out the research. We struck an advisory committee, with members of the justice working group, and framed the terms of reference. The advisory committee was chaired by Joan Sack from the Union of Nova Scotia Indians and it guided the community-initiated project at every stage. I spoke with Donald's family, and with their blessings we began the work.

The review tracked initiatives to implement the inquiry's recommendations and their real-world impact and community reception. It began with a brief, general assessment of the recommendations related to visible minorities in the criminal justice system (9–19), the administration of criminal justice (35–45), and police and policing (46–82). It did not include an evaluation of the recommendations pertaining to wrongful convictions and compensation (1–8) or to blacks in the criminal justice system (31–34). We designed research activities to generate meaningful dialogue among sympathetic stakeholders: the Mi'kmaw Legal Support Network, the Nova Scotia Barristers' Society, Nova Scotia Legal Aid, the Legal Information Society of Nova Scotia, and the Indigenous Blacks and Mi'kmaq Initiative at Dalhousie University's Schulich School of Law. We identified the public legal education needs of Mi'kmaw communities in Nova Scotia in order to create productive, sustainable working relationships to address those needs. Communication had deteriorated over the years. There was little collaboration with or engagement by provincial and federal justice workers or officials. The isolation reflected top-down rejection of Indigenous community-based justice programs and the imposition of Ottawa's tough-on-crime agenda in an era of extreme fiscal restraint. Fearing more funding cuts and layoffs, people were afraid to speak out in support of Indigenous autonomy or legal pluralism and focused instead on saving themselves.

The Mi'kmaq wanted to know how their own people were feeling about justice issues, what their experiences were, and what changes they wanted to see. To tap community perspectives and directly engage their members in our research, we established collaborative community forums. We created a short documentary film outlining the context and significance of the forums and screened it in each community to stimulate discussion. Over the course of eight months in 2012–13, Mi'kmaw court worker and film-maker Barry Bernard, myself, and the research support team travelled across the province and held forums in Membertou, Potlotek, We'koqma'q, Millbrook, Sipekne'katik, Acadia (Bear River), Annapolis, Glooscap, Pictou Landing, Paq'tnkek, Eskasoni, and Halifax (at the Mi'kmaw Native Friendship Centre). In Wagmatcook, we only held a focus group at the annual assembly of the Nova Scotia Native Women's Association. The chief and council thought a community forum and discussions on justice could set back the fragile healing underway after John Simon's death.

We also held focus groups with students of the Indigenous Blacks and Mi'kmaw Initiative at Dalhousie University; Nova Scotia Legal Aid; the Racial Equity Committee of the Nova Scotia Barristers' Society; Indigenous members of the RCMP; and members of the Mi'kmaw Legal Support Network. We conducted interviews with staff of the Nova Scotia Office of the Police Complaints Commissioner, the Office of the Ombudsman, the Aboriginal Policing Analyst "H" Division, and the Commissioner's Aboriginal Advisory Board for the RCMP. Finally, we observed a number of events, including RCMP Aboriginal Perceptions Course training and the advent of the Idle No More movement.

Each community forum opened with ceremony and Mi'kmaw prayer. We gave participants a list of the Marshall recommendations pertaining to visible minorities in the criminal justice system, and we paid particular attention to recommendations dealing with the Mi'kmaq and the criminal justice system. We used the talking circle format so everyone had the opportunity to speak and share their thoughts and experiences. We encouraged participants to share their stories of involvement and views of the Canadian justice system. What did they think of service quality, access to programs, and treatment by the police, the courts, victims' services, and corrections services? Forum participants rated the implementation of the recommendations and provided their opinions on what they saw as priority areas for improving access to justice and mobilizing Mi'kmaw legal traditions.

Within the forums, everyone from chiefs, elders, and members of band councils to the youngest participants were keen to discuss their justice experiences and ideas. Over three hundred people participated, their ages ranging from eighteen to eighty-five. Participants reflected the political, spiritual, educational, health, and employment histories of the communities in which they lived. Many had personal narratives of encounters with the police, the courts, and corrections. Those who didn't knew a family member who had. Most said they lived in poverty. They often identified social problems such as violence and substance misuse as negatively impacting their quality of life and the safety of their communities.

With alarming regularity, those sharing intimate accounts of their encounters with the justice system said they felt they had been mistreated and misunderstood by police, lawyers, judges, and service providers. They saw the Marshall Inquiry recommendations as foundational to establishing a Mi'kmaw justice system and imperative for self-determination. They also recognized that there were serious structural obstacles impeding their implementation – the most pressing being a profound lack of knowledge and respect for Indigenous rights and legal principles among non-Indigenous Canadians. They framed this ignorance as a product of colonialism and systemic racism.

Although somewhat tangential to the immediate inquiry, many who came to the community forums wanted to discuss fishing and the problems they had experienced exercising their treaty rights. They also frequently talked about community cultural capacity and the need to return to Indigenous legal principles in daily life through the reinvigoration of Mi'kmaw language, elder knowledge, customary leadership, a reorienting of nationhood away from the Indian Act, and the eradication of poverty and addiction. Collectively, the participants expressed a desire to work in a co-learning relationship with non-Indigenous Canadians, to help them understand the need for accountability, to resist policies that expunge Indigenous peoples' treaty rights and rights to self-determination, and to put Canada on the path to substantive reconciliation. Mi'kmaw people get that settlers are here to stay, but their voices made clear that they would not tolerate the oppression of their rights as Indigenous peoples, including stewardship over their ancestral territories.

Those who had accessed Indigenous justice initiatives such as the Mi'kmaq Justice Institute or the Mi'kmaw Legal Support Network said they valued them highly. They felt these initiatives had been instrumental in building capacity within Mi'kmaw communities and had laid a substantial foundation for people working together to improve access to justice. However, they fell short of the community's expectations for self-determination and employment. The majority of participants, and particularly those working in Mi'kmaw organizations, were disheartened by the patent inadequacies of funding arrangements, typified by a pilot-project approach to Indigenous justice that fostered a dependency relationship with the funder while depriving community initiatives of the capacity for sustainability, stability, and forward planning. Repeating the oft-expressed sentiment that the Mi'kmaq were set up to fail, they noted that paternalism continued to characterize Indigenous justice relations rather than a commitment to empowering Mi'kmaq "to succeed, be sustainable, and assure control over decision-making and program direction."[2] The Marshall Inquiry recommendations would remain unfulfilled so long as Mi'kmaw-operated courts remained a dream and the federal and provincial governments withheld adequate funding for the Mi'kmaw Legal Support Network. As had been the case with the Mi'kmaq Justice Institute, the network's funding was precarious – a year-to-year crapshoot that afforded little room for innovation, advancement, or the incubation of meaningful proceedings. Paula Marshall, the network's executive director, had to work miracles to keep the staff employed and the doors to Mi'kmaw justice open, even if just a crack.

For most Mi'kmaq, the Canadian justice system was not an ally but an opponent with whom they were always fighting to protect their rights and freedoms. Forum participants interpreted the Marshall Inquiry recommendations as resolutions that defined their justice goals. If fully implemented, the Mi'kmaq would have "a system of justice that understands and respects" Indigenous realities. A Mi'kmaw system would "focus on community responsibility for restoring relations" and could include "traditional and cultural practices in rehabilitation and reintegration." A Mi'kmaw justice system would "have ceremony," "practice prevention," and "help family healing." In the settler system, "criminals' rights are protected more than victims' rights," whereas a Mi'kmaw system would "instill a sense of purpose" and "help all people through their trauma." "The Canadian justice system allows people to avoid responsibility, and they hide behind confidentiality." "Here, we know everyone; we know what they did, and we know if they will do it again." Many resented external interference in dispositions: "I don't want some white judge judging me. They don't know me, and they don't know my life."[3]

In all community forums – large, small, rural, and urban – people said racism informed the development of their legal consciousness. The message was clear: racism remains a significant, systemic problem in Canadian society. Jim (Jake) Maloney, long-time advocate for Indigenous justice and policing services and Donald's head of security during the royal commission hearings, gave the following summary of his experiences of oppression:

I don't like the Mounties. I don't think they should be here. I think they are a racist group. They deal with racist lawyers who deal with racist judges. They deal with racist social services and people in health care, fisheries, all people with self-interests that don't want the Aboriginal rights and Aboriginal title and Aboriginal ways brought up. If the recommendations on the Marshall Inquiry came to be, and I was at the Donald Marshall Inquiry, and now I certainly don't see no changes. Marshall didn't get a good deal. It killed him. So, the recommendations: I certainly don't know very many that made any difference. I wish I had a better story to tell you, but I am disappointed that the Marshall recommendations were never honoured, and the only way I suppose that is the case is because racism is alive and well. We tried it all. We fought in your wars, we joined your churches, we spoke your language and gave up our lands and just tried to be friends, signed treaties. What else can we give you? I know our people are generous, but come on now, it is time to give back. Thank you.[4]

Respondents pointed to the Canadian justice system as a colonial institution that would always present problems for Indigenous peoples. They believed autonomous Indigenous justice systems that reflect cultural values would best remedy the problems faced by Mi'kmaq, but the disappointment of witnessing programs fail, combined with the intergenerational trauma associated with colonization, residential schools, and chronic poverty, left them little reason to hope:

> I strongly believe that justice will never happen in Canada as long as the colonial mindset is still in place. We have to decolonize, not just ourselves but the colonizers, the people that came to this country because they think their truth is the only truth. The two fundamental lies of Canada are Crown title and Crown sovereignty. They believe that they own it, but it is not true, even within their own laws. We need to have our treaty education within the whole entire school system. They are setting up systems that don't work ... We do have First Nations people that have been colonized in their own minds because they have to in order to survive the system, so sometimes they become the worst part of the system because they have to survive the system. A First Nation person working in the non-Aboriginal system has to go the extra mile to show they are not Aboriginal, so we need to decolonize that whole system. We need to decolonize everything so that we can have a chance at justice.[5]

Despite these significant challenges, expressions of resilience and resolve emerged in the participants' narratives of survival and accommodation. There was a shared belief that the Marshall Inquiry recommendations, particularly those relating to Mi'kmaw-run organizations and services, could turn the tide. They recognized the Mi'kmaw Legal Support Network as the institution best positioned to support the creation of Indigenous courts, facilitate community justice committees, and expand the scope of customary law processes. But they were aware that the network's programs were underfunded and understaffed and unable to reach all Indigenous peoples who came before the courts, let alone build capacity to take on the role of creating and delivering a community-based justice system. The participants were less aware of Mi'kmaw Victim Support Services (which required the victim to apply to the province's general program to secure a referral to the Mi'kmaw program) than they were of the network's Mi'kmaw Customary Law Program. The latter program was gaining positive attention for fostering a tradition-based model grounded in holistic approaches to justice, including offering opportunities for victim-offender reconciliation and healing through ceremony. Only those who found themselves in court and happened to encounter an Indigenous court worker were aware of Mi'kmaw Victim Support Services. Everyone recognized a desperate need for better coordination among programs and the expansion of services to stop people from falling through the gaps. There was a strong desire for community intervention before matters got to the courts. Most said they continued to manage problems on their own.

Justice issues are not neatly compartmentalized in the lived experience of the Mi'kmaw Nation. Rather than looking at the recommendations as boxes to be ticked off and shelved, many consider the Marshall Inquiry recommendations a living document, something to be read wider than the words on the page, something that captures the chance for the attainment of fairness, equity, and the just treatment of Indigenous peoples in Nova Scotia:

> I look at this list of Marshall recommendation, and I think L'nu law. I think of policing our own and taking care of our own and ensuring our own are rehabilitated enough to come into the community after committing an offence. How we get there – it is important to understand the issues that are preventing us from getting there. All these things are going to require us to come together as a community and to put faith in whatever system is going to be established. We need to put faith in an L'nu system. We have established the gaps.[6]

Our review made clear that many Mi'kmaw people ultimately regard the Marshall Inquiry recommendations as transformative and transforming. They help map the state of justice in Mi'kma'ki today. Wed to the political will to support the needs and address the concerns of the Mi'kmaw Nation, they can serve as a guide towards a better, more just tomorrow. Success will depend on non-Indigenous Canadians understanding that Mi'kmaw justice is not adversarial or rule-based but rather administrated through traditional practices that reflect deeply entrenched values indispensable to the meaning of Mi'kmaw culture and identity.

A DECOLONIZING ARTICULATION of Mi'kmaw legal consciousness emerged through the community forums. Based on the communities' concerns, we developed priority areas for executing the recommendations and work-shopped them at a meeting of the Tripartite Forum. This exercise helped shape and define the many ideas, directives, and challenges expressed by community members. In the end, four priorities or pathways to self-determination were identified.

First, the Mi'kmaq wanted to create an autonomous legal system using principles framed in their customary law and restorative justice practices. They were in the process of fully embracing the role of circles, ceremony, and talking it out as pathways to resolve conflict and restore relationships. The shame associated with customary practices and beliefs – shame indoctrinated through settler law, residential schools, and Catholicism – was being repudiated in favour of honouring traditional knowledge. People who were once pro-incarceration and thought of restorative justice and healing ceremonies as "hocus pocus" were now embracing ideologies such as self-determination and community-based justice as being "just us." Realizing that a separate system would require a rights reconciliation agreement for the Mi'kmaw Nation and the relocation of justice services, community members were generally supportive of an expanded, restructured, holistic, and culturally informed Mi'kmaw Legal Support Network to carry out the work.

Second, to help members facing the Canadian justice system, research participants stressed that education should be prioritized to overcome racism and systemic discrimination. All justice personnel should receive safety, treaty, and cultural competency training to ensure they have the disposition, behaviours, and skills needed to work successfully in cross-cultural settings, and they should commit to the journey of co-learning.

Third, communities felt that kinship and family law procedures should be developed to better reflect Mi'kmaw values and to protect children and families from the current system, which was seen as tearing families apart.

Finally, participants felt community-based policing should be reinforced to improve public safety and reduce conflicts driven by cross-cultural misunderstandings, racism, and ignorance. As is the experience of Indigenous communities across Canada, the Mi'kmaq rightly feel both over-policed and under-protected.

The Mi'kmaq made clear that they did not want to dispense entirely with the Canadian justice system. They wanted it to be more responsive to their lived realities and respectful of their unique rights and cultural practices. They also wanted choice, the freedom to access the most meaningful pathway to justice, rather than being coerced participants in a legal system resonant with centuries of colonial oppression. That choice is a necessary first step in decolonizing justice.

After hearing from the community members, the advisory committee asked Tripartite Forum officials to create a venue for their voices to be heard. Dan Christmas – senior adviser for Membertou, a highly respected and longtime advocate of Indigenous self-determination, one of the original architects of the Mi'kmaq Justice Institute, and now a member of the Senate – agreed to facilitate a series of consultative focus groups that, in time, generated the agenda for a high-level symposium on the Marshall Inquiry recommendations.

In 2014, Christmas chaired focus group discussions with a broad range of community-concerned organizations and interest groups: the Assembly of Nova Scotia Mi'kmaq Chiefs and the executive directors of the Union of Nova Scotia Indians and the Confederacy of Mainland Mi'kmaq; the Mi'kmaw Legal Support Network; federal and provincial government justice officials; Nova Scotia Legal Aid and Dalhousie Legal Aid; the RCMP and municipal police services; federal and provincial Crown prosecutors; Mi'kmaw Victim Support Services and Dalhousie University's Indigenous Blacks and Mi'kmaw Initiative; and the Nova Scotia Status of Women and the Nova Scotia Native Women's Association. Each group discussed a series of ten questions grouped into three categories: "The Past: The Eleven Marshall

Inquiry Recommendations," "The Present: Current Events or Challenges," and "The Future: The Four Priority Pathways Identified in the Evaluation."

Like the community forum participants, those in the focus groups agreed that there had been many positive changes resulting from the Marshall Inquiry. However, the eleven recommendations pertaining to the Mi'kmaq and the criminal justice system had not been satisfactorily implemented. There were no Indigenous criminal courts or Indigenous justice committees assisting the courts. The Mi'kmaw Legal Support Network was but a shadow of what had been envisaged for the Mi'kmaq Justice Institute. The provincial court presided in only one of the thirteen reserves in Nova Scotia. Interpreters existed but were too few in number. Participants noted that court workers provided vital services but were woefully inadequate to meet demand. Despite recognition of their vital importance, there was funding for only four full-time Mi'kmaw court workers and one part-time staff for the entire province. In addition, their presence was limited to criminal courts at a time when there was a dire need for their services in family courts. Finally, probation and aftercare services did not facilitate reintegration because they were understaffed and culturally unprepared to serve Mi'kmaw communities. Programs such as the Seven Sparks Healing Path suffered from the same pilot-project funding syndrome that plagued other innovative services.

Participants agreed that three issues lay at the heart of the problem: insufficient funding, lack of political will, and barriers to community capacity building. Existing programs helped Mi'kmaw people be processed through the criminal justice system but did not allow them to fully develop their own agencies and programs to prevent crime and resolve disputes. Speaking to the administration of justice in their communities, chiefs expressed their frustration in endeavouring to define their roles and responsibilities in the face of the federal and provincial governments' persistent lack of engagement and indifference to Indigenous sovereignty or self-determination. One chief noted:

> If they want real change, right – and I don't really know if the government wants real change – because there are lots of people relying on the existing system, and let's face it, Mi'kmaw people keep a lot of people employed

within the criminal justice system. If they want real change, they have to engage communities, not on the basis of "This is our system, this is our process, and we're just gonna make it a little easier for you guys to engage and interact within this criminal justice system." *Trust* is a key word. They have to trust us to know what is best for our own people and to develop mechanisms to help resolve disputes, you know, to allow some kind of community restorative process to put things back into balance. Until you get that sort of willingness to sort of delve into those areas where we can develop our own systems and processes to address the real issues, then it's always going to be an outside process. It's going to be a process that is geared toward their system and their processes. We'll never have that opportunity to really try to work on the innovative sort of opportunities to address the real issues within our community because it is a mindset of them knowing what's best. Them knowing what's best is what got us into this mess, so it's obvious that it's time to turn the table around and give us a chance to do it. Let us make our own foolish mistakes, or whatever.[7]

For their part, federal and provincial representatives said they were satisfied with what had been done already vis-à-vis the Marshall Inquiry recommendations. Their boxes were checked.

Despite differences of opinion, everyone agreed that the Mi'kmaw Legal Support Network needed more, better-paid case workers. Individual project funding rather than core funding had resulted in unsustainable caseloads and staff-retention problems. The project-funding model had brought down the Mi'kmaq Justice Institute. Participants of every stripe agreed that multi-year funding agreements would improve retention and innovation by enhancing job security, long-term planning, and case management. Consistent and predictable service provision would, in turn, increase community buy-in and help build capacity for the development and application of Indigenous legal principles. The focus groups feared that the story of the institute was repeating itself, and dangerously so. Absent adequate funding and support, the future of the network was uncertain. It risked being simply another relic of bad policy decisions for which the Mi'kmaq were not responsible but for which, once again, they would be blamed.

Discussions directed to the second group of questions, "The Present: Current Events or Challenges," linked the root causes of crime in Mi'kmaw communities to the historical legacy of colonialism – from physical displacement and residential schools to contemporary racism, poverty, unemployment, lack of housing, substance abuse (particularly opiates and alcohol), paternalistic decision making by government agencies, reliance on social assistance, and frequent incursions by children's services. Inadequate federal transfer funding, by failing to keep pace with inflation or population increases, had only compounded the sense of indignity, dependence, and frustration. With diminished community capacity for prevention, intervention, and resolution, every community faced systemic trauma and social health crises. Ignorance of Mi'kmaw legal rights among justice and government workers and a tendency to pathologize institutionally generated problems only made matters worse.

Frustrated with escalating crime rates, some community members had been taking matters into their own hands. Parents Against Drugs campaigns had led to successful police intelligence and intervention that reduced community fears and upset distribution networks. Some communities instituted band council resolutions to remove drug dealers from band-owned homes, with the police serving as peacekeepers in these situations. Participants agreed that relations with police services had improved in all communities. However, profound and debilitating confusion about jurisdiction continued to be a problem, as did a perceived reluctance among police to enforce band bylaws made under the authority of the Indian Act. Many communities called for the return of tribal police services.

Chiefs expressed some concern about whether sentencing circles reduced recidivism or enhanced victim satisfaction in the process or outcome. Nonetheless, they did not believe that the Canadian justice system, which focuses on the offender, provided an ideal alternative. Victims and their families shared dissatisfaction with sentencing with their leaders, particularly when they saw what they perceived as lenient sentences being imposed on recidivist offenders. Sentencing and justice circles, as participatory processes, were lauded for affording a voice to victims and the broader community, but the benefits of the process would be lost in the absence of support services such as local detox programs, shelters, and well-being counselling. The application of Mi'kmaw legal principles for collective healing and reintegration was central to Mi'kmaw legal consciousness and fuelled the demands for a transfer of jurisdiction and adequate resources for its implementation.

As in the community forums, the focus groups identified legal education as a priority. Cultural competency is key, but it had not been achieved across all justice sectors. They noted that lawyers and law students received little training in Aboriginal or Indigenous law and that the laws pertaining to taxes, wills, estates, and family differ for reserve residents. They feared that lawyers unfamiliar with the rules would negligently give bad advice that would prejudice their clients' interests and access to justice. The recent inclusion of a section on Aboriginal law in the Nova Scotia bar exam was a welcome first step, but everyone understood that awareness and recognition of Aboriginal law had yet to permeate the profession and that there were tensions within the law school about Indigenous content and courses.

Finally, participants noted that Dalhousie University's Indigenous Blacks and Mi'kmaq Initiative faced grave challenges. Due to fiscal restraints, the university had not fulfilled its commitment to cover tuition costs. In order to continue, the program had been forced to seek support from the province and the Ontario Law Foundation. Agreeing that the lawyers who had graduated from the program had become vital catalysts for change in the Mi'kmaw Nation, the focus groups were worried that progress would halt if Indigenous students could no longer afford tuition costs and if the curriculum at the only law school in Nova Scotia did not include Mi'kmaw law.

ARMED WITH FEEDBACK from the focus groups, we held a two-day symposium in Membertou in January 2015. Approximately one hundred senior federal, provincial, and Mi'kmaw justice representatives attended, including people from the justice departments, corrections, the RCMP, court services, public prosecution, legal aid, the Nova Scotia bar, and educational programs and initiatives.

The event began with the Sons of Membertou singing the Honour Song, followed by a prayer from Kji Keptin Antle Denny of the Mi'kmaw Grand Council. Chief Terry Paul gave the opening remarks and asked for a moment of silence in memory of Caroline Marshall, Donald's mother and the chief's own godmother, who had passed away on Christmas Eve. Chief Paul had been a very close friend of Donald's. He stated, "There is quite a bit of racism still happening, and we need to inform the public more about who we are, that it is much better to try and work things out together." He further noted that the number of Mi'kmaw people in conflict with the law had increased and that the Mi'kmaw Legal Support Network needed more funding.

The provincial premier, Stephen McNeil, delivered brief welcoming remarks. He referred to Donald Marshall's wrongful conviction as a "shameful chapter in Nova Scotia history." His government had called on Ottawa to hold an inquiry into missing and murdered Aboriginal women. The "most important piece," he said "is that the Mi'kmaw community, the provincial and federal governments have come together to build on what we know was a system that was failing Aboriginal communities across the province."[8] Like his federal counterparts, the premier tried to steer the dialogue away from funding: "I think we need to ensure that the system is open and welcoming, people feel that they are treated fairly – and that's not money, that's attitude." Peter MacKay, the federal minister of justice, was expected to attend. He did not. The minister of Indigenous affairs and northern development was expected to attend. He, too, did not. Various deputy ministers were present, but they contributed little of substance to the discussion and committed to even less.

The symposium included a series of panels on the criminal court system, legal services, policing, and aftercare and correctional services. Each panel included a question-and-answer session in which federal and provincial justice service providers reflected on what they had done to implement the Marshall recommendations. The panelists' presentations consisted largely of self-congratulatory assessments of rather modest achievements. In contrast, the Mi'kmaw participants – including a community-based lawyer, an RCMP officer, and representatives from the Mi'kmaw Legal Support Network and Nova Scotia Legal Aid – addressed in great and passionate detail the many challenges they faced in delivering adequate, culturally oriented justice services for their expanding client base.

In addition to the panels, in a World Café exercise, the attendees workshopped the four priority pathways for decolonizing justice. Assigned to groups, participants were asked to identify areas where they felt they could bring something to the table and indicate priorities for action under each rubric. Forty-one themes emerged from these discussions. The federal and provincial justice providers, the change makers and power holders, limited their talking points to facets of prevention. However, the few judges in attendance expressed a willingness to do whatever they could to facilitate culturally respectful dispute-management processes. Regardless of the resistance and reluctance of policy makers to commit to a new future, the organizers of the symposium and the Tripartite Forum were resolute in charting a course for the next twenty-five years. Mi'kmaw priorities were immediately incorporated into the justice committee's work plans.

In her keynote remarks to the symposium, Justice Anne Derrick succinctly and eloquently summarized the findings of the many reports, commissions, and judicial decisions concerned with Indigenous injustice in Canada and the impact of colonization on Indigenous peoples – Indigenous peoples must be empowered and allowed to do justice for themselves:

> The work being done by the Tripartite Forum Justice Committee and this symposium is located within the broad and authoritative consensus about the criminal justice system and Aboriginal people. This consensus casts any efforts at reform under a daunting shadow, but it should also serve to inspire, challenge, and focus what must be done to realize the visions of justice that have emerged from tragic events, such as Donald Marshall's wrongful conviction and imprisonment. These visions of justice must be as resilient as Junior was: their promoters must be as resolute. Building justice models delivered by Mi'kmaw people that are community-based and culturally relevant is an aspiration that echoes through the Tripartite Forum Justice Committee's Report. And while reflecting on the description in the Report of a generalized view that "Most lawyers and judges ... do not comprehend the state of poverty, the consequences of colonization or

the experiences of systemic racism and discrimination that Mi'kmaw people face," it is legitimate to ask at the same time whether recent legislated changes to the criminal law and the policy directions that underpin them comprehend these realities or ignore them.

I was so heartened to read in the Tripartite Forum Justice Committee Report that "the Marshall Inquiry Recommendations are considered as a living document ..." This speaks to the resilience of Junior's spirit and his legacy: that although so much was taken away from him, he left so much behind. It tells us that his struggle continues to inform us, guide us, and inspire us to be better. It strengthens our resolve to know that the light he shone on the justice system will always burn brightly into the shadows cast by the challenges that must be confronted and overcome.

THE RESULTS OF the federal election in November 2015 signalled a dramatic shift in Ottawa's approach to Indigenous justice. As put by the newly elected prime minister, Justin Trudeau, in his mandate letter to the minister of justice, "No relationship is more important to me and to Canada than the one with Indigenous peoples. It is time for a renewed, nation-to-nation relationship with Indigenous peoples, based on recognition of rights, respect, co-operation, and partnership."[9] The work of the Tripartite Forum's justice committee immediately received fresh impetus. Change was in the air.

Mi'kmaw chiefs, for instance, had long raised concerns about the lack of services and support for families. Too many children were going into care, and families were being treated in ways inconsistent with custom. Spearheaded by Lawrence O'Neil, associate chief justice of the Nova Scotia Supreme Court, and Michael MacDonald, the chief justice of Nova Scotia, a meeting took place between Nova Scotia judges and Mi'kmaw chiefs at the Membertou Reserve on June 9, 2016. It was the first such meeting in the province, and the judges had elected to be part of the solution. Together, the chiefs and judges identified barriers to judicial action in family group conferencing and committed to training the bench to deliver holistic, community-oriented remedies. It was a very different judiciary from the one that had locked up Donald Marshall and then blamed him for his wrongful conviction.

A few months later, in October, the federal minister of justice, Jody Wilson-Raybould, sat down for a candid exchange with the Tripartite Forum's justice committee. The Department of Justice sought direction on how to support implementation of Indigenous legal principles. The Mi'kmaq are currently developing a comprehensive Indigenous justice strategy for criminal, family, civil, and regulatory matters, employing community-based processes intended to unsettle the colonial underpinnings of the Canadian justice system. In this renewed era of justice reform, the Marshall Inquiry recommendations and the Marshall symposium's policy directives are also helping to drive change within the provincial department of justice, victims' services, and Dalhousie's Schulich School of Law. They have informed the drafting of Indigenous justice strategies at Nova Scotia Legal Aid and within the Racial Equity Committee of the Nova Scotia Barristers' Society. The law school responded to some of the challenges by establishing the Chancellor's Chair in Aboriginal Law and Policy and by hiring Listuguj Mi'gmaq legal scholar Naiomi Metallic to take the lead in using law as a tool for reconciliation.

In March 2017, Nova Scotia changed the law to permit justices of the peace and family and provincial court judges to issue emergency orders under the federal Family Homes on Reserves and Matrimonial Interests or Rights Act. The amendments will enhance protection from domestic violence by facilitating access to the justice system. Parallel amendments to the provincial Children and Family Services Act mandated consideration of Mi'kmaw laws and customs. As a result, Mi'kmaw families in crisis now have access to expanded family group conferencing services, and bands now receive notice when children from their communities are placed by the court. The amendments also extend legal recognition to Mi'kmaw customary care services and customary adoption. The Mi'kmaq had to fight to be included in the amendment process. The negotiations were contentious. In the end, they prevailed: Mi'kmaw laws of kinship and place are now, perhaps for the first time in centuries, part of the general law of Nova Scotia.

These outcomes closely align with the federal Truth and Reconciliation Commission's ninety-four calls to action, which are grouped into four intersecting categories: child welfare, education, language and culture, and health and justice. Importantly, action 28 calls upon "the Federation of Law Societies of Canada to ensure that lawyers receive appropriate cultural competency training, which includes the history and legacy of residential schools, the United Nations Declaration on the Rights of Indigenous Peoples, Treaties and Aboriginal rights, Indigenous law, and Aboriginal–Crown relations."[10] Recommendation 50 states: "In keeping with the *United Nations Declaration on the Rights of Indigenous Peoples,* we call upon the federal government, in collaboration with Aboriginal organizations, to fund the establishment of Indigenous law institutes for the development, use, and understanding of Indigenous laws and access to justice in accordance with the unique cultures of Aboriginal peoples in Canada."[11]

The federal government vowed to take immediate action on all ninety-four calls of action. It has without qualification accepted the United Nations Declaration on the Rights of Indigenous Peoples in the hope that meaningful implementation of the declaration will reinvigorate section 35 of the Constitution and the recognition of Indigenous rights. At the provincial level, the chief justice of Nova Scotia and other members of the judiciary are actively working with the Mi'kmaw Legal Support Network and the Department of Justice to realize the intent of the Marshall Inquiry recommendations and to affirm Mi'kmaw legal principles in ways that recognize that we are all treaty peoples. The Mi'kmaw Legal Support Network continues to be innovative in responding to community needs. Its persistent efforts to revitalize Mi'kmaw legal principles have found traction and legitimacy even among settler society. The team works hard to maintain sentencing-circle protocols, carry culture into prisons, educate legal professionals, and be accountable to Mi'kmaw citizens. That said, the inadequacies of its funding model have not been addressed, and its focus remains largely on a deficit model of correction.

Assessing the distribution of jurisdictions and the adequacy of interface between Canadian and Indigenous legal systems is more important than ever in this era of aspirational reconciliation. The Mi'kmaq still struggle to decolonize their legal traditions, an exercise fraught with both external and internal pressures. They rely on culturally available narratives of law to interpret their lives and their relationships. These interpretations define their legal consciousness, which in turn determines which approaches are deemed legitimate by local communities. The Mi'kmaw Nation continues to define and redefine key principles as it works to correct the legal poverty created by the settler system. Determining who has decision-making authority and what practices should be recognized as legal are being shaped by multiple variables: age, gender, class or status, family, employment, community membership, spiritual belief, language abilities, residential school attendance, and, of course, personal or family exposure to the Canadian justice system.

The good news is that there is now a critical mass of legal experts in the Mi'kmaw Nation, people who are navigating the Canadian landscape, demanding self-determination, and living the sacredness of treaty relations by working to fulfill the rights and responsibilities codified in those agreements. More than fifty L'nu have been trained as lawyers in the settler system and are increasingly weaving elder knowledge into all aspects of their shared lives. Mi'kmaw spirituality and law are reinvigorating the building of Indigenous institutions. In the spirit of *etuaptmumk,* a two-eyed seeing approach that combines Indigenous legal wisdom with salvageable elements of settler law on a journey of co-learning, many have come to see the value of creating an institute of L'nu law.

There are points of crisis, solidarity, conflict, and contradiction within communities regarding what Mi'kmaw justice was in the past and what it should be in the present. They are productive if often volatile encounters. The underlying premises of Mi'kmaw justice remain both spiritual and practical, focusing mainly on the well-being of family and community members. Justice for the Mi'kmaq is about relationships and practices that reflect the interconnectedness of the environmental, physical, social, and spiritual realms. The teachings and principles of Mi'kmaw law are at the heart of Mi'kmaw rights reconciliation. They form the scaffolding for co-management, livelihood, leadership, ceremony, and governance, for today and for tomorrow, just as they have for the past fourteen thousand years. Mi'kmaw elder Albert Marshall tells us to "revisit the teachings for renewal. I'l'oqaptmu'k."[12] The time for Wi'kupaltimk – the ceremony of reconciliation – is coming.

THERE HAVE BEEN many changes and challenges since Donald Marshall's wrongful conviction. What remains constant is the understanding that when Mi'kmaw legal concepts are foregrounded, honoured, and respected, the parties – individuals and communities – have more satisfactory and transformative experiences than when Mi'kmaw identity, culture, and practices are denied or ignored.

Community-based, decolonized justice, as opposed to mere indigenized settler justice, is the most effective way to reduce criminal activity, facilitate reintegration, and assist in family healing. If we, as settlers, are to truly honour our commitment to righting relations with Indigenous nations, we must tear down the edifices of ignorance, apathy, and feigned benevolence. Reconciliation cannot simply be about helping hands, expressions of regret, and an invitation for inclusion in settler institutions. We, settlers all, must come to understand that what is needed is a practical, sustainable, and generative paradigm shift in relationships – person to person, nation to nation, and knowledge system to knowledge system. Deconstructing 500 years of institutional scaffolding and correcting 150 years of willful blindness will take some work.

Without rights education and the implementation of Mi'kmaw treaties, systemic discrimination and poverty will continue to contribute to intergenerational impacts, generate conflicts with the law and limit opportunities for justice to be lived and felt. The authority of Indigenous legal principles and practices needs to be recognized and supported and these systems need to be decolonized through incorporation and use of Indigenous laws through ceremony, knowledge translation, collaboration, respect and education. The ideologies justifying the apparatuses of control must shift if reconciliation is to be substantive.

"We have our own laws" and "We should have our own courts" were common refrains throughout the review process. Support for Marshall Inquiry recommendation 20 – to create an Indigenous criminal court – was near universal. Often envisaged as full or holistic services, the remedies available to such courts include community-based alternatives to fines or incarceration. Deterrence and denunciation would be served through the court's visibility and through community input on sentencing. Whether styled as a centre, an institute, or a courthouse, the Mi'kmaq wanted a public venue for the administration of Mi'kmaw law, a court administered by Indigenous people working together to craft remedies by drawing from shared, culturally meaningful legal principles.

At the time that Mi'kmaw people were expressing this dream, the provincial Department of Justice was closing a number of satellite courts – several of which served Indigenous communities – without warning. Wagmatcook and We'koqma'q First Nations particularly suffered when the provincial court in Baddeck shut down. Failures to appear increased, and tensions flared as police served more and more bench warrants. Getting to the more distant courts was close to impossible for people who barely survived on social income assistance and had no access to public transportation. A one-way trip could cost as much as forty dollars – more than a quarter of a ration cheque. One resourceful individual hitchhiked eighty kilometres in a snowstorm to attend his hearing at the Wellness Court in Port Hawkesbury. He arrived wearing flip-flops. The presiding judge, Laurel Halfpenny MacQuarrie, bought him a pair of winter boots over recess.

Judge Halfpenny MacQuarrie reached out to Chief Norman Bernard and Chief Roderick Googoo. A circle was convened with officials from the Department of Justice, Mi'kmaw leaders, representatives of the Mi'kmaw Legal Support Network, and several judges. It took a great deal of convincing, but the Department of Justice finally acknowledged the harm of closing down the courts. A change of policy – collaborative, communitarian, and consultative – followed. Plans were vetted, a site was selected, and construction on a new courthouse began. The idea for a place of Mi'kmaw justice – a courtroom or *etli-ilsutekemk* – took shape in the basement of the Wagmatcook Culture and Heritage Centre.

Nova Scotia's first "Gladue" court – a court to support the cultural needs of Indigenous peoples in conflict with the law – opened on April 4, 2018, in Wagmatcook Mi'kmaw Nation in Cape Breton. The press release proclaimed: "Establishing Nova Scotia's first Gladue and Aboriginal Wellness court in one of our Mi'kmaq communities is a welcomed step to implementing the Truth and Reconciliation Commission Calls to Action and recommendations of the Marshall Inquiry."[13] The combination of a Gladue and wellness court reflected the broader issues facing Indigenous peoples, allowing communities and workers to identify and address the root causes

Chief Norman Bernard, Chief Rod Googoo, Judge Halfpenny MacQuarrie, and Wagmatcook Elder Mary Catherine (Molly) Pierro repatriating Donald Marshall's eagle feather at the Donald Marshall Junior Centre for Justice and Reconciliation, June 21, 2018. *Province of Nova Scotia. Photographed by Len Wagg*

of offending behaviour and develop recovery support plans to link people to services. The project partners – which included Wagmatcook and We'koqma'q First Nations, the Mi'kmaw Legal Support Network, Nova Scotia Legal Aid, the Public Prosecution Service, Victoria County, the RCMP, and the Nova Scotia Barristers' Society – were inspired by the vision of the Provincial Court Bench of Nova Scotia and, in particular, the leadership and commitment of Laurel Halfpenny MacQuarrie. Guided by a circle of community elders and chiefs, it is the second court to sit on a reserve in Nova Scotia and the first to be open to Indigenous and non-Indigenous residents of Victoria County. It is also the first Nova Scotia court dedicated to applying the principles set down by the Supreme Court in *R v Gladue* in 1999. There is no doubt the court will invigorate laws of ceremony through a'tukwaqan (stories) and nijkitekek (healing).

Opening day began with a smudging ceremony, welcoming prayers, and the honour song performed by the Wagmatcook Indian Bay drummers. Wekoqmaqewiskaq, the lady singers, sang a healing song, and Chief

Donald Marshall's legal team from the Royal Commission reunited to participate in the feather repatriation and naming ceremony for the Donald Marshall Junior Centre. *L to R:* Hon. Felix Cacchione, Marlys Edwardh, Hon. Anne Derrick, and Stephen Aronson. *Province of Nova Scotia. Photographed by Len Wagg*

Googoo, Chief Bernard, Judge Halfpenny MacQuarrie, and Paula Marshall, the executive director of the Mi'kmaw Legal Support Network, shared emotional stories about how the court came to be. The air was electric and purposeful. Judge Warren Zimmer was gifted with an eagle feather. The community elders presented the judges with sashes embroidered with Mi'kmaw clan symbols in beadwork. As the ceremony concluded, court got underway. Chief Bernard with compassion and pride turned to me and said, "This is all because of Donald Marshall Junior and his inquiry. Those recommendations made this."

This court serves local Mi'kmaw communities and residents of Victoria County. The court has offices for crown attorneys, legal aid, victim services, probation, and the Mi'kmaw Legal Support Network court workers, as well as two holding cells, video-conferencing capabilities, and administration areas. It is identified as a response to Marshall Inquiry recommendation 20 that "a community-controlled Native Criminal Court be established in Nova Scotia." The court sits three Wednesdays per month, which includes days for arraignments, a trial day, and, on the third Wednesday, a Wellness Court in the morning and a Gladue Court in the afternoon. There is one judge who sits regularly in the criminal court. The court also hears Supreme Court (Family Division) child protection matters. The court has no restrictions on the types of cases it hears, including in-custody matters.

The room is stunning. The walls are appointed with colourful pictures painted by local artists and, most impressive, the dais is round – a place where judges, lawyers, and community members can meet each other equally in a circle. On June 21, 2018, National Aboriginal Day, the court was officially named the Donald Marshall Junior Centre: A Centre for Reconciliation and Justice. In Mi'kmaw it is Donald Marshall Etli-Mawita'mk: Etli-Mawita'mk Wukjit Apiksiktuaqn Aqq Kokwaja'taqn. The naming ceremony brought together Donald's family; his former legal team, including Anne Derrick, Stephen Aronson, Felix Cacchione, and Marlys Edwardh; and a host of chiefs, judges, and other dignitaries to witness and honour his life and legacy. The Chiefs, Premier Stephen McNeil, Justice Minister Mark Furey, Lieutentant Governor Arthur LeBlanc, and the Chief Justices of the Nova Scotia courts gave moving remarks, acknowledged the harms done to the Marshall family and pledged "never again."

Donald's brother David Marshall gave a poignant speech recounting the profound challenges his family had faced:

> It is hard to put into words the harm done to our family, my parents, my brothers and sisters, our children, our community of Membertou and our Mi'kmaw Nation through the wrongful conviction and life sentence of Junior. It is horrible to have someone you love locked up, but it is beyond tragic when you know they are innocent. We suffered the crimes committed against him by the Canadian justice system greatly.
>
> It changed all of our lives in uncountable ways. We felt hurt, hopeless, and helpless. We were shamed. Our self-worth was challenged every day because people thought our brother was a murderer. It generated fear and mistrust of everyone, but especially the police, lawyers, judges, and jails. We lived mired in racism and our hearts were broken.
>
> My brother was a remarkable man to endure his wrongful conviction, to maintain his innocence, and to relentlessly pursue justice. We all learned

from his example, from his tremendous courage and his deep belief in his rights as a Mi'kmaw person, as an L'nu. We are very grateful for his strengths. He is a hero to us and we want to honour him. We do not want people to forget what happened to us. I wish my parents could be here to witness this.

Once the speeches concluded, an eagle feather that had belonged to Donald Marshall was repatriated to the court with the help of a jingle dancer and drummer in a powerful ceremony. It sits today in a special case in the centre of the dais in the Donald Marshall Junior Centre for Justice and Reconciliation. It was a fitting tribute to a champion of Indigenous justice, and a step forward for the Mi'kmaw Nation.

Kepmite'tmnej Donald Marshall Jr. "Legends don't die."

Mi' walatl | Thankful For

DONALD MARSHALL JR., or "J.R.," was a wonder, and my profound gratitude for all that he brought to my world is deep in my bones. Our time together transformed my life. I carry the memories of our love and adventures in my heart and feel his absence in my work daily. J.R. has a strong, courageous, and close-knit family whose kindness made this incredible journey possible. I am forever grateful to J.R.'s mother, the late Mrs. Caroline Marshall (Googoo), his siblings (Donna, Roseanne, Pius, Bernice, David, Terry, Josephine, Laura, John, Simon, Stephen, little Donna, and Virginia), and their spouses (Joe, Doreen, Terry Lynn, Lee Marie, Chris, Wade, Adrianne, and Sheila) for welcoming me into their lives, for their unwavering perseverance against tremendous adversity, and for their love of their brother. Your ongoing support means the world to me. J.R.'s children and grandchildren are sweet inspiration. J.R. had many very special nieces, nephews, and godchildren who gave him such joy and took great care of him on his healing journey. I honour you all. Thank you to Paul Bradley Gould and Jocelyn Mas'l for carrying J.R. in your hearts, to Glen Gould and Darren Sylvester for sober driving, and to Mud and Kelly for years of excellent home care. The family gatherings in Aberdeen were the best and happiest times. To the umpteen cousins, aunts, uncles, and loyal friends who shared their teachings, triumphs, and tragedies, I appreciate your warmth and generosity. *Kesalul.*

J.R.'s formidable extended kinship networks linked me to many who helped me in my study of Mi'kmaw legal consciousness and Mi'kmaw legal traditions and principles. We travelled throughout Mi'kma'ki and spoke with justice warriors in Membertou, Eskasoni, Wagmatcook, We'koqma'q, Potlotek, Paq'tnkek, Millbrook, Pictou Landing, Glooscap, Annapolis Valley, L'sitkuk (Bear River), Acadia, Sipekne'katik, Listuguj, Miawpukek, Tobique, Elsipogtog, Esgenoopetitj, Kingsclear, and Eel River Bar. Many thanks for the *pitewey* (tea), *kastio'mi*, *lusknikn*, and teachings. Over the years, dear friends, mentors, and family members have left this world, but their philosophies and instructions are not forgotten. Thank you for *katawapul* (eel stew) Grand Chief Sylliboy, for the *plamu* Gordon Julian, and for the survivor stories Albert Doucette, Arty Paul, and Charlie Marble.

Wela'lioq to the past and present members of the Grand Council, the many incredible Elders, and the Assembly of Nova Scotia Mi'kmaq Chiefs, particularly Chief Terry Paul. This book would not have been possible without the help of many grassroots people, water warriors, and notably the eel fishers of Malagawatch (Seven, Lunch, and Chuckie Bernard) and Paq'tnkek (Kerry Prosper, John Prosper, and Billy Googoo), who taught me to consider Mi'kmaw rights, laws, treaties, nationhood, and ways of being from their points of view. Everyone was so bighearted with sharing wisdom and good tips for cleaning eel slime.

Our years in We'koqma'q and this book were made stronger by the expansive generosity and great storytelling of the extended families of Terry and Rara Gould, Gina and Maynard Poulette, Junior and Belinda Bernard, Teresa and Noel Bernard, Ducy and Bob, Rose and Gordon, and all of the Goulds, Googoos, and Bernards. Here's to all the goonie googoos and the strong Shubie women.

Numerous amazing people profusely imparted their deep knowledge of culture and custom, of historical and contemporary justice realities, and the problems of racism and colonization, including all those associated with the Mi'kmaw Legal Support Network, especially Paula Marshall and Barry Bernard; the CLIF Demonstration Project; Unama'ki Tribal Police

Services; Indigenous members of the RCMP; the Tripartite Forum Justice Working Committee; the Nova Scotia Barristers' Society Racial Equity Committee; the Indigenous Blacks and Mi'kmaw Law Initiative; the Unama'ki Institute of Natural Resources; the Union of Nova Scotia Indians; the Confederacy of Mainland Mi'kmaq; the Native Council of Nova Scotia; the Atlantic Policy Congress of First Nations Chiefs Secretariat; the Mi'kmaw Native Friendship Centre; the Mi'kmaw Rights Initiative team; and the Nova Scotia Native Women's Association. Your experiences of justice and injustice taught me about hope and survival and the necessity of revitalizing Indigenous legal principles. The late Kji Keptin Alex Denny and now his son Kji Keptin Antle, Senator Dan Christmas, Murdena and Albert Marshall, Dale Sylliboy, Dwight Dorey, Reg Maloney, Rosalie Francis, the former board of directors, and all those people responsible for the Mi'kmaq Justice Institute were key voices in shaping this research and continue to ignite the spirit of activism needed to overcome ongoing oppression and firmly establish a Mi'kmaw-centred justice system.

Powerful and heartfelt stories of Mi'kmaw legal consciousness, ancestor beliefs, and the quest for Mi'kmaw justice were shared over the years by members of the Abram, Augustine, Barnaby, Battiste, Bernard, Brooks, Christmas, Condo, Cope, Cremo, Dedam, Dennis, Denny, Dorey, Doucette, Evans, Francis, Ginnish, Gloade, Googoo, Gould, Herney, Isaac, Jadis, Jeddore, Joe, Johnson, Julian, Julien, Kabatay, Knockwood, LaBillois, Lafford, LaPorte, Levi, Lewis, MacDonald, Maloney, Marble, Marshall, Martin, Matthews, Michael, Metallic, Milliea, Moore, Morris, Nevin, Nicholas, Oakley, Palmater, Patles, Paul, Peck, Perley, Peters, Phillips, Pictou, Pierro, Polchies, Poulette, Prosper, Robinson, Sack, Sacobie, Sanipass, Sappier, Sark, Simon, Sock, Stephens, Stevens, Sylliboy, Sylvester, Tony, Ward, Wells, Wilmot, Wysote, and Young families. With deepest respect, I name each and all of the hundreds of people who shared their teachings and legal insights, which I hold with the highest esteem, in my prayers of gratitude for all that you have contributed to this book. Wela'lioq.

Sukwis Josephine Peck; Tuma Young; Ann Denny; Helen Sylliboy; Roseanne, Laurianne, Barb and Devann Sylvester; John R. Sylliboy; Bernie Francis; Jarvis Googoo; and Alwyn Jeddore guided my linguistic choices. Any errors in interpretation are mine.

Anne Derrick and Archie Kaiser embraced J.R. with unconditional love, loyalty, compassion, and perseverance. Words cannot express how grateful I am for their remarkable humanity, enduring friendship, and safe port in many storms. Marlys Edwardh and Graham Turrall were beacons of hope throughout the royal commission, the lung transplant, and beyond. Thank you for everything.

Freda Ens, Romola Trebilcock, and the late Elder William Commanda are heroes who held J.R.'s innocence profoundly in their hearts and helped shape his legacy in their struggles for justice. I am blessed with their friendship.

Win Wahrer of Innocence Canada (formerly AIDWYC) and the family of wrongfully convicted allies gave much succor to J.R. Thank you for including us in your healing efforts.

I am indebted to my academic family – Anthony Davis (StFX and MSVU), Virginia P. Miller, and Don Clairmont (Dalhousie) – who, with their prodigious wisdom, taught me the foundations and intersections of community-engaged political anthropology, ethnohistory, and transitional justice. In British Columbia, Bruce G. Miller (UBC) fertilized my mind, introducing me to the theories and methodologies of legal anthropology, the legal traditions of the Stó:lō Nation and to the extended family networks of the law and society associations. Bruce is a fierce ally and a wonderful mentor with a consequential sense of social justice. Thank you for the encouragement, education, and kindness. Julie Cruikshank, Janice Graham, Wes Pue, and Charles Menzies fortified me with their sustaining guidance, and my dearest comrade Gerald Sider cultivates challenging dialogues and nurtures the fruits as my academic zade. This very smart and generous team of advisers helped me acquire research support from the Killam Fellowships Program, the Canada Research Chairs Program, and the SSHRC Aboriginal Research grants program. Bruce Miller and Gerald Sider were instrumental in bringing this book to life.

I am abundantly appreciative for the friendship, legal scholarship, and conversations with colleagues Trish Monture; Val Napoleon; Annie Bunting; Sákéj Henderson; Marie and Jaime Battiste; Rose Prosper; John Sam; Cindy Marshall; Marie Francis; the Hon. Harry and Janice LaForme; Judge Laurel Halfpenny MacQuarrie; Tuma Young; Don Julien; John G. Paul;

Joe B. Marshall; Viola Robinson; Jennifer Cox; Naoimi Metallic; Heather McNeill; Shelly Martin; Sherry Pictou; Clifford Paul; Keith Christmas; Gerald Gloade; Gerald Bernard; Jim Maloney; Louis Joe Bernard; Walter Denny; Pauline MacIntosh; Juliana, Lish, and Judy Julian; Deborah Ginnish; Joey and Carol Sylvester; Marcella Marshall; Carol Metallic; Harry and John Lafford; Marie Sack; Doreen Bernard; Judy Peters; Krista Hanscomb; Jane Meader; Curtis Michael; Darlene Paul; Blair and Mary Ellen Paul; Joanne Lewis; Tom Sylliboy; Caroline Gould; Roy Gould; Diane Christmas; Laurianne Julian; Heidi Marshall; Patty Bedwell-Doyle; PJ Prosper; Angelina Amaral; Alan Sylliboy; Hon. Cathy Benton; Trevor Bernard; Trevor Sanipass; Kiera Ladner; Fred Metallic; Jane Abram; John Borrows; Jean Teillet; Senator Murray Sinclair; Ron Niezen; Kent McNeil; Michael Asch; Jonathan Rudin; Craig Proulx; Eve Darian Smith; Damein Bell; Lynette Russell; Jennifer Llewellyn; Jane Moseley; Denise, Carla, and Sister Dorothy Moore; TJ and Catherine Martin; Cheryl Bartlett; Fred Wien; and the folks at AAHRP and IMN. Many hours were spent discussing the limits and potentials of the Canadian justice system with Alex Christmas; Doug Brown; Janice Maloney; Cheryl Maloney; Jean Knockwood; Brian Arbuthnot; Diana Lewis; Ken Paul; Pam Glode Desrochers; Michael Stephens; the late Anthony Morris and all of the court workers and customary law staff of MLSN; De-Anne Sack and Debbie Maloney, as well as the Gladue court judges at Old City Hall, College Park, and 311 Jarvis. Thanks to Janelle Young and the team who provided excellent research assistance and to all those who participated in the evaluation of the Mi'kmaq Justice Institute and the Tripartite Forum review of the Marshall Inquiry. *Wela'lioq.*

I marvel at the tenacity and deep belief in Mi'kmaw treaty rights held by Bruce Wildsmith, Eric Zscheile, and former TARR Centre researchers, who argued the *Marshall* fishing case with expert witnesses Bill Wicken and John Reid. Thank you all for your convictions.

Many thanks to Randy Schmidt, senior editor at UBC Press, for the enthusiastic encouragement, professionalism, and creativity that made this book a reality. I deeply value the time, energy, and insights of the reviewers and the sage advice of Holly Keller and the editorial team at UBC Press and the superlative wordsmithing of Lesley Erickson.

Finally, thank you to my family. Melvyn Green, my wonderful husband, provided exceptional counsel as a brilliant jurist and literary prestidigitator. My dad, Michael, and my siblings – Martha, Brenda, and David – and their spouses Rick and Don and kids, Eva, Callum, Liam, and Olivia are the best champions. This one is for Mom.

NOTES

Introduction

1 Kepmite'tmnej (The Mi'kmaw Honour Song) was received in a sweat lodge ceremony by George Paul of the Metepenagiag First Nation in the 1980s. Kepmite'tmnej translates as "let us greatly respect." The Mi'kmaq sing this song to honour their ancestors and their teachings. See http://www.beatoninstitutemusic.ca/mikmaq/mikmaq-honour -song-video.html.

2 Dianne L. Martin, "Lessons about Justice from the 'Laboratory' of Wrongful Convictions: Tunnel Vision, the Construction of Guilt, and Informer Evidence," *University of Missouri–Kansas City Law Review* 70, 4 (2004): 847–64.

3 *Settler society,* as a conceptual term, is used by academics to differentiate between Indigenous peoples (people who, as the ancestors of the original inhabitants of the territories, have distinct rights of temporal priority) and all other people who came to inhabit their territories. Very few people in Canada today would identify themselves as settlers. This speaks to the dominance of settler society. Unless you live on the receiving end of daily systemic oppression, the Canadian state and all its institutions are settler society writ so large and ascendant that their cultural and ideological roots are virtually invisible. This erasure contributes to the distancing and denial of settler responsibility in the colonization of Indigenous peoples, their lands, and their laws.

4 Grand Chief Donald Marshall reinvigorated Treaty Day celebrations in 1986 after the Supreme Court's *Simon* decision affirmed the validity of the 1752 Peace and Friendship Treaty. The Mi'kmaq, the Crown, and the province come together to exchange gifts,

feast, and make exhortations about their relationships, and acknowledge the achievements of members of the nation in awards ceremonies. The event is held annually on October 1.

Chapter 1: The Wrongful Conviction

1 "Marshall Denies Stabbing Seale," *Cape Breton Post,* November 4, 1971; Gregory T. Evans, *Commission of Inquiry Concerning the Adequacy of Compensation Paid to Donald Marshall, Jr.* (Halifax: The Commission, 1990), 9.
2 Interview transcript no. 88 (JM), Membertou, Nova Scotia, April 1, 2000. On file with author.
3 Tord Larsen, "Negotiating Identity: The Micmac of Nova Scotia," in *The Politics of Indianness: Case Studies of Native Ethnopolitics in Canada,* ed. Adrian Tanner (St. John's: Institute of Social and Economic Research Memorial University, 1983), 52.
4 Interview transcript no. 53 (RG), Membertou, Nova Scotia, June 9, 1996. On file with the author.
5 Interviews that I conducted with Membertou residents between 1995 and 2016 revealed that relations between members of the town of Sydney and the community of Membertou were very tense in the 1970s.
6 Héléna Katz, *Justice Miscarried: Inside Wrongful Convictions in Canada* (Toronto: Dundurn, 2011), 42, and Michael Harris, *Justice Denied: The Law versus Donald Marshall* (Toronto: Totem Books, 1986), 104.
7 Donald's eldest sister, Roseanne, recalled, "No one in the court believed my father. Everyone thought he threatened that boy. I bet if he was white, they would have believed him." Personal communication, April 18, 2018.
8 Clifford Paul, "Police Not after Truth, Just Indians" *Micmac News,* November 1987.
9 T.A. Hickman, L.A. Poitras, and G.T. Evans, *Royal Commission on the Donald Marshall Jr., Prosecution,* vol. 1, *Commissioner's Report: Findings and Recommendations* (Nova Scotia: The Commission, 1989) [hereafter "Royal Commission"].
10 Bruce Wildsmith, "Reflections: 20 Years after the Marshall Inquiry," *Society Record* 24, 4 (2009): 22–23.
11 "Jury Out for Four Hours" *Cape Breton Post,* November 6, 1971.

Chapter 2: Prison and Freedom

1 Mr. Stewart, direct exam by Ms. Derrick, April 4, 1990, *In the Matter of the Donald Marshall, Jr., Compensation Hearing,* transcript, vol. 3, 420.
2 *Micmac News,* June 1973.
3 Letter from Donald Marshall Jr. to S., December 24, 1973. On file with author.
4 Letters from Donald Marshall Jr. to Hazel. On file with author.

5   "Escaped," RCMP news release, September 24, 1979; "Recaptured," RCMP news release, September 27, 1979. On file with author.

6   Quoted in Harris, *Justice Denied*, 292–93.

7   Ibid., 305.

8   Mr. Stewart, direct exam by Ms. Derrick, April 4, 1990, *In the Matter of the Donald Marshall, Jr., Compensation Hearing*, transcript, vol. 3, 443.

9   *R v Marshall*, (1983) 57 NSR (2d) 286.

10   Royal Commission, 1:95.

11   Alexander Hickman, Lawrence A. Poitras, and Gregory T. Evans, *Royal Commission on the Donald Marshall, Jr., Prosecution: Digest of Findings and Recommendations* (Halifax: The Royal Commission, 1989), 1, 13 [hereafter "Royal Commission, *Digest of Findings*"].

12   Anne Derrick and Archibald Kaiser, "Submissions on Behalf of Mr. Donald Marshall, Jr., *In the Matter of an Inquiry Pursuant to Section 63 of the Judges Act* 1990," tab 7. On file with author.

13   Mary-Ellen Turpel/Aki-Kwe, "Further Travails of Canada's Human Rights Record: The Marshall Case," in *Elusive Justice: Beyond the Marshall Inquiry*, ed. Joy Manette (Halifax: Fernwood Publishing, 1992), 90.

14   "Jury to Be Charged Today in Ebsary Trial," *Chronicle Herald*, September 13, 1985.

15   Bob Wall, "Analyzing the Marshall Commission: Why It Was Established and How It Functioned" in Mannette, *Elusive Justice*, 19.

Chapter 3: The Royal Commission

1   See Wall, "Analyzing the Marshall Commission," 13–34.

2   Terms of reference, Order-in-Council appointing the royal commission, given by the Honourable Alan Abraham, C.D., Lieutenant-Governor of Nova Scotia, October 28, 1986.

3   Royal Commission, 1:xii.

4   Peter Kavanagh, "Nova Scotia's $7 Million Man," *Canadian Lawyer* 12, 6 (1988): 18. Joy Mannette gives a figure of $8 million in *Elusive Justice*.

5   See, for example, Marcus Gee and Peter Kavanagh, "Exploring an Injustice," *MacLean's*, October 19, 1987, 23.

6   Royal Commission, 1:28.

7   Ibid., 1:34.

8   Ibid., 1:41.

9   Ibid.

10   Sákéj Henderson, "The Marshall Inquiry: A View of the Legal Consciousness" in Mannette, *Elusive Justice*, 48.

11   Royal Commission, 1:34.

12 Ibid., 1:41.

13 Ibid., 1:50.

14 Ibid., 1:51.

15 Ibid., 1:65.

16 Ibid., 1:74–75.

17 Ibid., 1:77.

18 Ibid., 1:85.

19 Ibid., 1:82.

20 Ibid., 1:116.

21 Ibid., 1:118.

22 Ibid., 1:126. When Junior testified before the commission, he accused Justice Pace of being drunk during two days of the Reference hearings. Pace threatened a defamation suit.

23 Royal Commission, 1:126.

24 Ibid., 1:130.

25 Wall, "Analyzing the Marshall Decision," 25.

26 Joy Mannette, "The Social Construction of Ethnic Containment: The Royal Commission on the Donald Marshall Jr. Prosecution," in Manette, *Elusive Justice,* 65.

27 Wall, "Analyzing the Marshall Decision," 30n20.

28 Kavanagh, "Nova Scotia's $7 Million Man," 20.

29 Parker Barss Donham, "An Open Letter to the Marshall Inquiry," *Sunday Daily News,* October 30, 1988.

30 Kavanagh, "Nova Scotia's $7 Million Man," 20.

31 Henderson, "The Marshall Inquiry," 59.

32 Royal Commission, 1:165; Scott Clark, *The Mi'kmaq and Criminal Justice in Nova Scotia: Research Study/Prepared for the Royal Commission on the Donald Marshall, Jr., Prosecution* (Halifax: The Commission, 1989), 105.

33 Clifford Paul, "MacIntyre: 'Couldn't Solve a Jigsaw Puzzle,'" *Micmac News,* November 1987, 19.

34 Royal Commission, 1:166.

35 Ibid., 1:167.

36 Ibid., 1:171.

37 See Turpel, "Further Travails," and Manette, "The Social Construction of Ethnic Containment," in Manette, *Elusive Justice.*

38 Royal Commission, 1:162.

Chapter 4: Recommendations and Outcomes

1 Royal Commission, *Digest of Findings,* 1.

2 Anne Derrick, "Reflections on the Royal Commission," *Society Record* 27, 4 (2008): 18.

3 Royal Commission, *Digest of Findings*, 1.

4 Personal communication.

5 Personal communication.

6 Royal Commission, 1:162–63.

7 Clayton Ruby, Donald's counsel at the inquiry, made a personal complaint to the Canadian Judicial Council on February 8, 1988, suggesting the conduct was racist and inconsistent with the values required by a judge. Correspondence on file with author.

8 Henderson, "The Marshall Inquiry," 42.

9 Scott Clark, Royal Commission, vol. 3, *The Mi'kmaw and Criminal Justice in Nova Scotia: A Research Study*, 69–70.

10 Royal Commission, *Digest of Findings*, 28.

11 Donald Clairmont and L. Jane McMillan, *Directions in Mi'kmaw Justice: Notes on the Assessment of the Mi'kmaw Legal Support Network* (Halifax: Atlantic Criminology Institute, 2006), 140.

12 Report to the Canadian Judicial Council of the Inquiry Committee Established Pursuant to Subsection 63(1) of the Judges Act at the Request of the Attorney General of Nova Scotia, August 1990. On file with author.

13 Interview, Office of the Police Complaints Commissioner, Bedford, Nova Scotia, April 9, 2013. On file with author.

14 *R v Stinchcombe*, [1991] 3 SCR 326.

15 Don Clairmont and Rick Linden, *Developing and Evaluating Justice Projects in Aboriginal Communities: A Review of the Literature* (Ottawa: Solicitor General of Canada, 1998), 4–5.

16 Ibid., 5.

17 Union of Nova Scotia Indians, *Mi'kmaq Response to the Report of the Royal Commission of the Donald Marshall, Jr., Prosecution* (Sydney: Union of Nova Scotia Indians, 1990), 1.

18 Ibid., 2–3.

19 Ibid., 3.

20 Union of Nova Scotia Indians, *Treaty Federalism and the Covenant Chain: Presentation by the UNSI to the Royal Commission on Aboriginal Peoples* (Sydney: Union of Nova Scotia Indians, 1992), 12.

Chapter 5: Mi'kmaw Legal Principles

1 *In the Matter of the Donald Marshall, Jr., Compensation Hearing*, transcript, vols. 3 and 4.

2 Evans, *Commission of Inquiry Concerning the Adequacy of Compensation*, 20.

3 Ibid., 8.

4 Ibid., 22–23.

5   Elder Murdena Marshall's Mi'kmaw Sacred Teachings describe the seven stages of life and the seven sacred gifts. She teaches that the personal connection all people share with one another is animated through our actions.

6   Stephen Augustine, "Negotiating for Life and Survival," in *Living Treaties: Narrating Mi'kmaw Treaty Relations,* ed. Marie Battiste (Sydney: Cape Breton University Press, 2016), 17.

7   Alexander Denny, Jigap'ten Santeoi Mawa'iomi, original communication to Mr. Theo C. Van Boven, Secretary, Human Rights Committee (*Denny v Canada,* 1980). On file with author.

8   Sákéj Henderson "L'nu Humanities," in *Visioning a Mi'kmaw Humanities: Indigenizing the Academy* (Sydney: Cape Breton University Press, 2016), 49.

9   Chrestien Le Clercq, *New Relation of Gaspesia,* ed. William F. Ganong (Toronto: Champlain Society, 1910), 237.

10 Quoted in Bernard Hoffman, "The Historical Ethnography of the Micmac of the Sixteenth and Seventeenth Centuries" (PhD diss., University of California, Berkeley, 1955), 512.

11 *Mi'kmaw Resource Guide* (Truro: Mi'kmawey Debert Cultural Centre, n.d.), 6. http://www.mikmaweydebert.ca/home/wp-content/uploads/2015/06/Pg_94_DOC_MikmawResourceGuide.pdf.

12 Le Clercq, *New Relation of Gaspesia,* 261.

13 Augustine "Negotiating for Life and Survival," 16–23.

14 Patrick Augustine sketches Mi'kmaw concepts of law in terms of relationships with land, water, animals, and ecology in "Mi'kmaw Relations" in Battiste, *Living Treaties,* 55. The Unama'ki Institute of Natural Resources defines netukulimk as "the use of the natural bounty provided by the Creator for the self-support and well-being of the individual and the community. Netukulimk is achieving adequate standards of community nutrition and economic well-being without jeopardizing the integrity, diversity, or productivity of the environment." www.uinr.ca.

15 Tuma Young, "L'nuwita'simk: A Foundational Worldview for a L'nuwey Justice System," *Indigenous Law Journal* 13, 1 (2016): 75–102.

16 Denny, communication with Van Boven.

17 Michael Runningwolf and Patricia Smith, *On the Trail of Elder Brother: Glous'gap Stories of the Micmac Indians* (New York: Persea Books, 2000), 72. See also Silas Rand, *Legends of the Micmacs* (New York: Longmans, Green and Co., 1894; reprint, Johnson Reprint Corporation, 1971).

18 Eleanor Johnson, "Mi'kmaw Tribal Consciousness in the 20th Century," in *Paqtatek,* vol. 1, *Policy and Consciousness in Mi'kmaw Life,* ed. Stephanie Inglis, Joy Mannette, and Stacey Sulewski (Halifax: Garamond Press, 1991), 27.

19 Nicolas Denys, *The Description and Natural History of the Coasts of North America (Acadia)* (Toronto: Champlain Society, 1908), 416–17.

20 Hoffman, "The Historical Ethnography," 309.

21 William Wicken, *Mi'kmaw Treaties on Trial: History, Land, and Donald Marshall Junior* (Toronto: University of Toronto Press, 2002), 35.

22 Hoffman, "The Historical Ethnography," 513.

23 Robert Redfield, "Primitive Law," in *Law and Warfare,* ed. Paul Bohannan (Austin: University of Texas Press, 1967), 12.

24 Abbé Maillard, *An Account of the Customs and Manners of the Mickmakis and Maricheets Now Dependent on the Government of Cape Breton* (London: S. Hooper and A. Morley, 1758), 19–30.

25 Hoffman, "The Historical Ethnography," 91–97.

26 Ibid., 509.

27 Ruth Holmes Whitehead, *The Old Man Told Us: Excerpts from Micmac History, 1500–1950* (Halifax: Nimbus Publishing, 1991), 154; Wicken, *Mi'kmaw Treaties on Trial,* 216.

28 Hoffman, "The Historical Ethnography," 599.

29 Le Clercq, *New Relation of Gaspesia,* 238–46.

30 Ibid., 255–56.

31 Joe B. Marshall and Jaime Battiste, "Treaty Advocacy and Treaty Imperative through Mi'kmaw Leadership: Remembering with Joe B. Marshall," in Battiste, *Living Treaties,* 138–65.

32 "Treaty Texts–1752 Peace and Friendship Treaty," Government of Canada, Indigenous and Northern Affairs Canada, https://www.aadnc-aandc.gc.ca/eng/1100100029040/1100100029041.

33 Sidney L. Harring, *White Man's Law: Native People in Nineteenth-Century Canadian Jurisprudence* (Toronto: Osgoode Society for Canadian Legal History, 1998), 178.

34 Ibid., 181.

35 There are approximately 750 survivors alive today. Many of them came together in a class action suit led heroically by the late Nora Bernard of Millbrook in the early 1990s. The action against the Canadian government and the Catholic Church sought reparations for harms inflicted by the school personnel. The outcome of the Indian Residential School Settlement Agreement undoubtedly influenced Mi'kmaw legal consciousness and litigiousness. Shubenacadie Indian Residential School triggered transgenerational trauma in thousands and was supplanted by insidious and ruinous child welfare apprehension policies.

36 Interview transcript no. 11 (CG), We'koqma'q, May 4, 2001. On file with author.

37 Ibid.

38 Henderson, "The Marshall Inquiry," 46.

Chapter 6: Mi'kmaw Justice Initiatives

1 "Innocence behind Bars," Rubin Carter to Donald Marshall, 1993. On file with author.

2 Evans, *Commission of Inquiry Concerning the Adequacy of Compensation,* 24.

3 Ibid., 25.

4 Interview transcript (JM), Unama'ki Tribal Police, Eskasoni, February 15, 2000. On file with author.

5 Interview transcript (MI), Unama'ki Tribal Police, Eskasoni, February 7, 2000. On file with author.

6 Interview with chief of Unama'ki Tribal Police Services, Eskasoni, February 7, 2000. On file with author.

7 Nova Scotia Aboriginal Affairs to Dan Christmas, Executive Director, Union of Nova Scotia Indians, July 15, 1994, in "Report of the Mi'kmaq–Nova Scotia–Canada Tripartite Forum Sub-Committee on Justice," Halifax, October 12, 1994.

8 Executive director, Native Council, to Deputy Minister for Intergovernmental Affairs, Nova Scotia, and Tripartite Forum, September 27, 1994. On file with author.

9 Interview transcript no. 77a (AD), Eskasoni, Nova Scotia, March 14, 2000. On file with author.

10 Interview transcript no. 114 (DC), Membertou, April 28, 2006. On file with author.

11 *R v Gladue,* [1999] 1 SCR 688.

12 Interview transcript no. 86 (DC), Membertou, May 11, 2006. On file with author.

13 Interview transcript no. 61 (RH/LC), Millbrook, June 5, 2000. On file with author.

14 Personal communications.

Chapter 7: In Search of Livelihood

1 Agreed Statement of Facts, *Province of Nova Scotia and Her Majesty the Queen v. Joseph Peter Martin, Donald John Marshall, Jr. and Leslie Jane McMillan* (1993); *R v Marshall (No. 1)* [1999], 3 SCR 456. Peter Martin's charges were dismissed early on by Judge Embree at the Provincial Court in Antigonish.

2 Michael Paré, Crown Counsel, Department of Fisheries and Oceans, to Judge John Embree, April 19, 1994. Letter on file with author.

3 *R v Marshall (No. 1),* [1999] 3 SCR 456, 3.

4 *R v Marshall (No. 2),* [1999] 3 SCR 533.

5 See http://mikmaqrights.com/about-us/the-five-5-pillars/.

6 Tina Comeau "DFO Vows to Enforce Lobster Regulations in Southwestern N.S.," *Chronicle Herald,* September 20, 2017.

Chapter 8: Restorative Justice

1 The name change was an effort to better reflect the non-adversarial principles of Mi'kmaw justice.

2 Interview with director of the Mi'kmaq Youth Option Program, Eskasoni, June 16, 2000. On file with author.

3   Interview transcript, "On the Fishing Circle" (PM), Halifax, June 27, 2001. On file with author.

4   Sentencing proposal, May 30, 2001, submitted by Paula Marshall to Justice Clyde MacDonald. On file with author.

5   Douglas Brown, "Litigating Section 35 Aboriginal and Treaty Rights in Nova Scotia," in Battiste, *Living Treaties,* 219.

Chapter 9: Mi'kmaw Legal Consciousness Today

1   William Commanda, "A Prayer for Donald Marshall Junior," August 10, 2009, unpublished. On file with author.

2   Community forum interview transcripts, We'koqma'q, November 27, 2012; Mi'kmaw Native Friendship Centre, January 22, 2013; and Eskasoni, April 13, 2013. On file with author.

3   Excerpts from my report, *An Evaluation of the Implementation and Efficacy of the Marshall Inquiry Recommendations in Nova Scotia* (Halifax: Tripartite Forum Justice Committee, 2014).

4   Community forum interview transcripts, Sipekene'katik, February 5, 2013. On file with author.

5   Community forum transcript, Sipekene'katik, February 5, 2013. On file with author.

6   Community forum transcript, Millbrook, February 13, 2013. On file with author.

7   Marshall Inquiry Review Focus Group, October 6, 2014. On file with author.

8   Nancy King, "Membertou Chief: There's Quite a Bit of Racism Still Happening in Cape Breton," *Cape Breton Post,* January 14, 2015.

9   Minister of justice and attorney general of Canada mandate letter, November 12, 2015, http://pm.gc.ca/eng/minister-justice-and-attorney-general-canada-mandate-letter.

10   Truth and Reconciliation Commission of Canada, "Truth and Reconciliation Commission: Calls to Action." http://www.trc.ca/websites/trcinstitution/File/2015/Findings/Calls_to_Action_English2.pdf.

11   Ibid.

12   Elder Albert Marshall, Membertou, October 7, 2016.

13   "Aboriginal Wellness/Gladue Court and Provincial Court Services Established at Wagmatcook," Nova Scotia Department of Justice, press release, April 24, 2017, https://novascotia.ca/news/release/?id=20170424002.

REFERENCES AND FURTHER READING

The events of Donald Marshall Jr's wrongful conviction, life imprisonment, release, and acquittal have been described in various forms, ranging from journal and newspaper articles and chapters in textbooks to documentaries and a movie, the National Film Board's *Justice Denied*, based on Michael Harris's popular account *Justice Denied: The Law versus Donald Marshall* (Toronto: Totem Books, 1986). *Justice Denied* offers a detailed account of the murder of Sandy Seale, the police investigation and trial that led to Donald Marshall's wrongful conviction, and his subsequent life sentence.

In preparation for this book, I thoroughly examined the historical events of Mi'kmaw justice production, searching and selecting archival and oral tradition communications to provide a framework for understanding historical and contemporary issues. Much of the narrative is based on stories that Donald shared with me and my own research and writing as a legal anthropologist and a Canada Research Chair for Indigenous Peoples and Sustainable Communities. I have conducted formal interviews with Mi'kmaw people who shared their expertise on justice, and I have engaged many more people through informal interviews; focus groups; and conferences and workshops on legal principles, family violence, resource management, policing and crime prevention, economic development, social income assistance, and treaty rights. My master's and doctoral theses focused on the changing role of the Mi'kmaw Grand Council and on Mi'kmaw legal consciousness. See "Mi'kmawey Mawio'mi: Changing Roles of the Mi'kmaq Grand Council from the Early Seventeenth to the Present" (master's thesis, Dalhousie University, 1996) and "Koqqwaja'ltimk: Mi'kmaq

Legal Consciousness" (PhD diss., University of British Columbia, 2002). See also "Still Seeking Justice: The Marshall Inquiry Narratives," *UBC Law Review* 47, 3 (2014): 927–90; "Colonial Traditions, Cooptations, and Mi'kmaq Legal Consciousness," *Law and Social Inquiry* 36, 1 (2011): 171–200; "Living Legal Traditions: Mi'kmaw Justice in Nova Scotia," *University of New Brunswick Journal of Law* 67 (2016): 187–210; and, with Kerry Prosper, "Remobilizing Netukulimk: Indigenous Cultural and Spiritual Connections with Resource Stewardship and Fisheries Management in Atlantic Canada," *Reviews in Fish Biology and Fisheries* 26, 4 (2016): 629–47.

For more on Donald Marshall's wrongful conviction and wrongful convictions in general, see Joy Mannette, ed., *Elusive Justice: Beyond the Marshall Inquiry* (Halifax: Fernwood, 1992); Dianne L. Martin, "Lessons about Justice from the 'Laboratory' of Wrongful Convictions: Tunnel Vision, the Construction of Guilt and Informer Evidence," *University of Missouri–Kansas City Law Review* 70, 4 (2004): 847–64; and Kent Roach, "The Protection of Innocence under Section 7 of the Charter," *Supreme Court Law Review* 34 (2006): 249–303; and "Wrongful Convictions in Canada," *University of Cincinnati Law Review* 80, 4 (2012): 1465–526.

On shows of remorse and the parole system, see Richard Weisman, "Showing Remorse: Reflections on the Gap between Expression and Attribution in Cases of Wrongful Conviction," *Canadian Journal of Criminology and Criminal Justice* 46, 2 (2004): 121–38. See also Weisman's award-winning book, *Showing Remorse: Law and the Social Control of Emotion* (Burlington, VA: Ashgate, 2014).

For more on the concept and academic study of legal consciousness, see Ronald Niezen, *Public Justice and the Anthropology of Law* (Cambridge: Cambridge University Press, 2010), and *The Origins of Indigenism: Human Rights and the Politics of Identity* (Berkeley: University of California Press, 2003); John L. Comaroff and Jean Comaroff, *Of Revelation and Revolution: The Dialectics of Modernity on a South African Frontier* (Chicago: University of Chicago Press, 1981); John M. Conley and William M. O'Barr, *Rules versus Relationships: The Ethnography of Legal Discourse* (Chicago: University of Chicago Press, 1990), and *Just Words: Law, Language, and Power* (Chicago: University of Chicago Press, 1998); Sally Engle Merry, *Getting Justice and Getting Even: Legal Consciousness among Working-Class Americans* (Chicago: University of Chicago Press, 1990), and "Culture, Power and the Discourse of Law," *New York Law School Review* 37 (1992): 209–25; John M. Conley and William M. O'Barr, *Rules versus Relationships: The Ethnography of Legal Discourse* (Chicago: University of Chicago Press, 1990); June Starr and Jane Collier, eds., *History and Power in the Study of Law: New Directions in Legal Anthropology* (Ithaca: Cornell University Press, 1989); and Eric Wolf, *Envisioning Power: Ideologies of Dominance and Crisis* (Berkeley: University of California Press, 1999).

On legal pluralism, see Giselle Corradi, Eva Brems, and Mark Goodale, eds., *Human Rights Encounter Legal Pluralism: Normative and Empirical Approaches* (Oxford: Hart Publishing, 2017); Sally Engle Merry, "Legal Pluralism," *Law and Society Review* 22

(1988): 869–96; and Kirsten Anker, *Declarations of Interdependence: A Legal Pluralist Approaches to Indigenous Rights* (Aldershot: Ashgate, 2014).

On Canadian society and institutions as settler society, see Michael Asch, *On Being Here to Stay: Treaties and Aboriginal Rights in Canada* (Toronto: University of Toronto Press, 2014); Chris Benjamin, *Indian School Road: Legacies of the Shubenacadie Residential School* (Halifax: Nimbus, 2014); and Paulette Regan, *Unsettling the Settler Within: Indian Residential Schools, Truth Telling, and Reconciliation in Canada* (Vancouver: UBC Press, 2010); Kiera L. Ladner and Myra J. Tait, eds., *Surviving Canada: Indigenous Peoples Celebrate 150 Years of Betrayal* (Winnipeg: ARP Books, 2017); and Martin J. Cannon and Lina Sunseri, eds., *Racism, Colonialism, and Indigenity in Canada: A Reader* (Don Mills, ON: Oxford University Press, 2018).

To read more about ethnographic approaches to the study of law, see Eve Darian-Smith, *Ethnography and Law* (London: Routledge, 2017); Lawrence Rosen, *Law as Culture* (Princeton: Princeton University Press, 2006); Bruce G. Miller, *The Problem of Justice: Tradition and Law in the Coast Salish World* (Lincoln: University of Nebraska Press, 2001); and Wayne Warry, *Ending Denial: Understanding Aboriginal Issues* (Toronto: University of Toronto Press, 1998). All explore the naive primordialism that romanticizes Indigenous cultures as homogenous. For studies that explore conflict and contradictions within Indigenous communities using historically situated theories of power, see Mindie Lazarus-Black and Susan Hirsch, eds., *Contested States: Law, Hegemony and Resistance* (New York: Routledge, 1994); Peter Just, *Dou Donggo Justice: Conflict and Morality in an Indonesian Society* (Lanham: Rowman and Littlefield, 2001), and "History, Power, Ideology, and Culture: Current Directions in the Anthropology of Law," *Law and Society Review* 26 (1992): 373–412; and Sally Falk Moore, "Systematic Judicial and Extra-Judicial Injustice: Preparations for Future Accountability," in *Memory and the Postcolonial: African Anthropology and the Critique of Power*, edited by Richard Werbner (Chicago: University of Chicago Press, 1998). See also Clifford Geertz, *Local Knowledge: Further Essays in Interpretive Anthropology* (New York: Basic Books, 1983); Elizabeth Povinelli, *The Cunning of Recognition: Indigenous Alterities and the Making of Australian Multiculturalism* (Durham, NC: Duke University Press, 2002); Gerald Sider, *Skin for Skin: Death and Life for Inuit and Innu* (Durham, NC: Duke University Press, 2014); and Gavin Smith, *Confronting the Present: Towards a Politically Engaged Anthropology* (Oxford: Berg, 1999).

Many have long advocated for the decolonization of the Canadian legal system to resolve the tensions between settler and Indigenous approaches to justice. See, for example, Val Napoleon, "Ayook: Gitksan Legal Order, Law, and Legal Theory" (PhD diss., University of Victoria, 2001); Larry Chartrand and Kanatase Horn, *A Report on the Relationship between Restorative Justice and Indigenous Legal Traditions in Canada* (Ottawa: Department of Justice, 2016); Alfred Taiaiake, *Wasáse: Indigenous Pathways of Action and Freedom* (Toronto: University of Toronto Press, 2005); Michael Asch, ed., *Aboriginal and Treaty Rights in Canada* (Vancouver: UBC Press, 1997); John

Borrows, *Freedom and Indigenous Constitutionalism* (Toronto: University of Toronto Press, 2016), and *Canada's Indigenous Constitution* (Toronto: University of Toronto Press, 2010); John Borrows and Michael Coyle, *The Right Relationship: Reimagining the Implementation of Historical Treaties* (Toronto: University of Toronto Press, 2017); Glen Coulthard, *Red Skin, White Masks: Rejecting the Colonial Politics of Recognition* (Minneapolis: University of Minnesota Press, 2014); Alan Cairns, *Citizen Plus: Aboriginal Peoples and the Canadian State* (Vancouver: UBC Press, 2000); Carol LaPrairie, *The New Justice: Some Implications for Aboriginal Communities* (Ottawa: Department of Justice, 1995); Arthur Manuel and Ronald Derrickson, *Unsettling Canada: A National Wake-up Call* (Toronto: Between the Lines, 2015); Bruce Miller, *Oral History on Trial: Recognizing Aboriginal Narratives in the Courts* (Vancouver: UBC Press, 2011); David Milward, *Aboriginal Justice and the Charter: Realizing a Culturally Sensitive Interpretation of Legal Rights* (Vancouver: UBC Press, 2012); Patricia Monture, *Journeying Forward: Dreaming First Nation's Independence* (Halifax: Fernwood, 1999); Craig Proulx, *Reclaiming Aboriginal Justice, Identity, and Community* (Saskatoon: Purich Publishing, 2003); Rupert Ross, *Returning to the Teachings: Exploring Aboriginal Justice* (Toronto: Penguin Books, 1996); and James Waldam, *The Way of the Pipe: Aboriginal Spirituality and Symbolic Healing in Canadian Prisons* (Toronto: University of Toronto Press, 1979).

On Mi'kmaw humanities, see Marie Battiste, ed., *Visioning a Mi'kmaw Humanities: Indigenizing the Academy* (Sydney: Cape Breton University Press, 2016), and *Living Treaties: Narrating Mi'kmaw Treaty Relations* (Sydney: Cape Breton University Press, 2016).

For more on population and resources, see Virginia P. Miller, "Aboriginal Micmac Population: A Review of the Evidence," *Ethnohistory* 23 (1976): 117–27, and "The Micmac: A Maritime Woodland Group," in *Native Peoples: The Canadian Experience*, edited by Bruce Morrison and Roderick Wilson (Don Mills, ON: Oxford University Press, 2004), 248–67; and Tord Larsen, "Negotiating Identity: The Micmac of Nova Scotia," in *The Politics of Indianness: Case Studies of Native Ethnopolitics in Canada*, edited by Adrian Tanner (St. John's: Institute of Social and Economic Research, Memorial University, 1983), 37–136.

For early anthropological analyses of rule making and rule breaking in cultures without Western legal characteristics, see Bronisław Malinowski, *Crime and Custom in Savage Society* (New Jersey: Littlefield, Adams and Company; reprinted 1966); and E. Adamson Hoebel and Karl Llewellyn, *The Cheyenne Way: Conflict and Case Law in Primitive Jurisprudence* (Norman: University of Oklahoma, 1941). Raymond D. Austin explores similar issues in his excellent work on the architecture of Navajo common law in *Navajo Courts and Navajo Common Law: A Tradition of Tribal Self-Governance* (Minneapolis: University of Minnesota Press, 2009). See also, on Indigenous law, John Borrows, *Recovering Canada: The Resurgence of Indigenous Law* (Toronto: University of Toronto Press, 2002); Joan Ryan, *Doing Things the Right Way: Dene Traditional*

Justice in Lac La Martre, N.W.T. (Calgary: University of Calgary Press, 1995); and Russell Barsh, "Indian Law, Indians' Law, and Legalism in American Indian Policy: An Essay on Historical Origins," in *American Indians: Social Justice and Public Policy,* edited by Donald Green and Thomas Tonnesen (Madison: University of Wisconsin Press, 1991), 8–43; and Justin B. Richland and Sarah Deer, *Introduction to Tribal Legal Studies* (Lanham: Rowman and Littlefield, 2016). On Indigenous identities, see Audra Simpson, *Mohawk Interruptus: Political Life across the Borders of Settler States* (Durham, NC: Duke University Press, 2014); and Pamela Palmater, *Beyond Blood: Rethinking Indigenous Identity* (Saskatoon: Purich, 2011).

On netukulimk (responsible harvesting) and resource management, see Trudy Sable and Bernie Francis, *The Language of This Land, Mi'kma'ki* (Sydney: Cape Breton University Press, 2012); Kerry Prosper, L. Jane McMillan, Anthony A. Davis, and Morgan Moffitt. "Returning to Netukulimk: Mi'kmaw Cultural and Spiritual Connections with Resource Stewardship and Self-Governance," *International Indigenous Policy Journal* 2, 4 (2011): 1–17; Russel Barsh, "Netukulimk, Past and Present: Mi'kmaw Ethics and the Atlantic Fishery," *Journal of Canadian Studies* 37, 1 (2002): 15–42; Anne-Christine Hornborg, *Mi'kmaw Landscape: From Animism to Sacred Ecology* (Hampshire: Ashgate, 2008); McMillan and Prosper, "Remobilizing Netukulimk"; and Native Council of Nova Scotia, *Netukulimk* (Truro: Native Council of Nova Scotia, 1993), and *Mi'kmaw Fisheries: Netukulimk: Towards a Better Understanding* (Truro: Native Council of Nova Scotia, 1993).

On Mi'kmaw social organization and leadership, in addition to my master's thesis, see William C. Wicken, *Mi'kmaw Treaties on Trial: History, Land, and Donald Marshall Junior* (Toronto: University of Toronto Press, 2002), and *The Colonization of Mi'kmaw Memory and History, 1794–1928: The King v. Gabriel Sylliboy* (Toronto: University of Toronto Press, 2012); Bernard Hoffman, "The Historical Ethnography of the Micmac of the Sixteenth and Seventeenth Centuries" (PhD diss., University of California, Berkeley, 1955); L.F.S Upton, *Micmacs and Colonists: Indian-White Relations in the Maritimes, 1713–1867* (Vancouver: UBC Press, 1979); Nicolas Denys, *The Description and Natural History of the Coasts of North America (Acadia)* (Toronto: Champlain Society, 1908); Janet Chute, "Frank Speck: Contributions to the Understanding of Mi'kmaw Land Use, Leadership, and Land Management," *Ethnohistory* 46, 3 (1999): 481–540; Angela Robinson, *T'an Teli-ktlamsitasit (Ways of Believing): Mi'kmaw Religion in Eskasoni, Nova Scotia* (Toronto: Pearson, 2005); Jennifer Reid, *Myth, Symbol, and Colonial Encounter: British and Mi'kmaq in Acadia, 1700–1867* (Ottawa: University of Ottawa Press, 1995); Simone Poliandri, *First Nations, Identity, and Reserve Life: The Mi'kmaq of Nova Scotia* (Lincoln: University of Nebraska Press, 2011); and Kevin Leonard, "Mi'kmaw Culture during the Late Woodlands and Early Historic Periods" (PhD diss., University of Toronto, 1996). On puoinaq, see Vincent Erickson, "The Micmac Bouin: Three Centuries of Cultural and Semantic Change," *Man in the Northeast* 15–16 (1978): 3–21.

On oral tradition and Indigenous knowledge, see Julie Cruikshank's *The Social Life of Stories: Narrative and Knowledge in the Yukon Territory* (Lincoln: University of Nebraska Press, 1998). On law and the Mi'kmaw language, see Tuma Young, "L'nuwita'smik: A Foundational Worldview for a L'nuwey Justice System," *Indigenous Journal of Law* 13, 1 (2016): 75–102. On legends, see Daniel N. Paul, *First Nations History: We Were Not the Savages*, 3rd ed. (Halifax: Fernwood, 2006); Silas Rand, *Legends of the Micmacs* (New York: Longmans, Green and Co., 1894; reprint, Johnson Reprint Corporation, 1971); Ruth Holmes Whitehead, *Stories from the Six Worlds: Micmac Legends* (Halifax: Nimbus, 1988), and *The Old Man Told Us: Excerpts from Micmac History, 1500–1950* (Halifax: Nimbus, 1991); and Elizabeth Paul, Peter Sanger, and Alan Syliboy, *The Stone Canoe: Two Lost Mi'kmaq Texts* (Kentville: Gaspereau Press, 2007).

On war, revenge killings, and the concept of hapenkuituik, see James (Sákéj) Youngblood Henderson, *The Mi'kmaw Concordant* (Halifax: Fernwood, 1997); Harald Prins, *The Mi'kmaw: Resistance, Accommodation and Cultural Survival* (Fort Worth: Harcourt Brace, 1996); Robert Redfield, "Primitive Law," in *Law and Warfare*, edited by Paul Bohannan (Austin: University of Texas Press, 1967), 3–24; and Abbé Maillard, *An Account of the Customs and Manners of the Mickmakis and Maricheets Now Dependent on the Government of Cape Breton* (London: S. Hooper and A. Morley, 1758).

On the complicated nature of contact zones and the concept of the middle ground, see Richard White, *The Middle Ground: Indians, Empires, and Republics in the Great Lakes Region* (Cambridge: Cambridge University Press, 1991). For Eurocentric notions of colonialism, see Stephen Cornell, *The Return of the Native: American Indian Political Resurgence* (New York: Oxford University Press, 1988); Elizabeth Furniss, *The Burden of History: Colonialism and the Frontier Myth in a Rural Canadian Community* (Vancouver: UBC Press, 1999); and Paul, *We Were Not the Savages*. Eric Wolf, *Europe and the People without History* (Berkeley: University of California Press, 1982), and Bruce Trigger, *Natives and Newcomers: Canada's "Heroic" Age Reconsidered* (Montreal/ Kingston: McGill-Queen's University Press, 1985) provide detailed examples of Indigenous encounters with foreigners during contact and colonization.

The criminalization of Indigenous peoples and culture and their overrepresentation in jails and the courts is discussed in Lisa Monchalin, *The Colonial Problem: An Indigenous Perspective on Crime and Injustice in Canada* (Toronto: University of Toronto Press, 2016); Susanne Karstedt and Kai-D Bussmann, eds., *Social Dynamics of Crime and Control: New Theories for a World in Transition* (Oxford: Hart, 2000); Chris Cunneen and Juan Tauri, *Indigenous Criminology* (Bristol: Policy Press 2016); Melvyn Green, "The Challenge of Gladue Courts," *Criminal Reports* 6th Series, 89, 2 (April 2012): 362–420; Thomas King, *The Inconvenient Indian: A Curious Account of Native People in North America* (Toronto: Doubleday, 2012); and the Royal Commission on Aboriginal Peoples, *Bridging the Cultural Divide: A Report on Aboriginal People and Criminal Justice in Canada* (Ottawa: Minister of Supply and Services, 1996). For a helpful guide to working with Indigenous clients, see Jonathan Rudin's *Indigenous People and the Criminal Justice System: A Practitioner's Handbook* (Toronto: Emond, 2019).

On community-based justice, see Wayne Warry, *Unfinished Dreams: Community Healing and the Reality of Aboriginal Self-Government* (Toronto: University of Toronto Press, 1998), and Ross, *Returning to the Teachings*. On Indigenous policing, its goals and problems, see Don Clairmont, *Community Perceptions of Policing and Justice Issues: A Survey Conducted on Behalf of the Unama'ki Tribal Police* (Halifax: Atlantic Institute of Criminology, 1999). For more on the Mi'kmaq Justice Institute, see my PhD dissertation, and Don Clairmont and L. Jane McMillan, *Directions in Mi'kmaw Justice: An Evaluation of the Mi'kmaq Justice Institute and Its Aftermath* (Truro: Mi'kmaq–Nova Scotia–Canada Tripartite Forum, 2001).

On eel fishing, see L. Jane McMillan, "*Mu kisi maqumawkik pasik kataq*: We Can't Only Eat Eels – Mi'kmaw Contested Histories and Uncontested Silences," *Canadian Journal of Native Studies* 32, 2 (2012): 199–242; and Anthony Davis, John Wagner, Kerry Prosper, and Mary Jane Paulette, "The Paqtnkek Mi'kmaw and Ka't (American Eel): A Case Study of Cultural Relations, Meanings, and Prospects," *Canadian Journal of Native Studies* 24, 2 (2004): 357–88.

See William Wicken, "R. v Donald Marshall Jr., 1993–1996," *Acadiensis* 17, 1 (1998): 1–7, for a summary of the eel fishing case before the provincial court and for the perspective of an expert witness. For a deep analysis of the treaty testimony in this case, see also Wicken, *Mi'kmaw Treaties on Trial*, and Paul, *We Were Not the Savages*. Thomas Isaac discusses the reconsideration in *Aboriginal Law* (Saskatoon: Purich Press, 2004). On treaties and tradition in other jurisdictions see Carwyn Jones, *New Treaty, New Tradition: Reconciling New Zealand and Maori Law* (Vancouver: UBC Press, 2017).

On contests over fishing after the *Marshall* decision, see Sarah King, *Fishing in Contested Waters: Place and Community in Burnt Church/Esgenoopetitj* (Toronto: University of Toronto Press, 2014). See also Anthony Davis and Svein Jentoft, "The Challenge and the Promise of Indigenous Peoples' Fishing Rights: From Dependency to Agency," *Marine Policy* 25 (2001): 223–37; and Ken Coates, *The Marshall Decision and Native Rights: The Marshall Decision and Mi'kmaq Rights in the Maritimes* (Montreal/Kingston: McGill-Queen's University Press, 2000).

On Department of Oceans and Fisheries policy after *Marshall*, see Jacquelyn Thayer Scott, *An Atlantic Fishing Tale, 1999–2011: A Policy "Rags-to-Riches" Story That's Good News for Aboriginals and for Canada* (Ottawa: Macdonald-Laurier Institute, 2012).

On restorative justice, see Michael Jackson, "In Search of Pathways to Justice: Alternative Dispute Resolution in Aboriginal Communities," *University of British Columbia Law Review* 26 (1992): 147–238; J. Llewellyn and D. Philpott, eds., *Restorative Justice, Reconciliation, and Peacebuilding* (Oxford: Oxford University Press, 2014); J. Braithwaite and H. Strang, eds., *Restorative Justice and Civil Society* (Cambridge:

Cambridge University Press, 2001); and Donald Clairmont, *The Shubenacadie Band Diversion Program: An Evaluation of the Final Year and an Overall Assessment* (Halifax: Atlantic Institute of Criminology, 1996). On its goals, see my essay "Living Legal Traditions" and Don Clairmont's "The Development of an Aboriginal Criminal Justice System: The Case of Elsipogtog" (Dalhousie University, 2013).

For more on the progress made since the Marshall Inquiry and the *Marshall* decision, see L. Jane McMillan and Tripartite Forum Justice Committee, *An Evaluation of the Implementation and Efficacy of the Marshall Inquiry Recommendations in Nova Scotia* (Halifax: Tripartite Forum Justice Committee, 2014).

On the enforcement of bylaws in Mi'kmaw communities, see Naiomi Metallic, "*Indian Act* By-Laws: A Viable Means for First Nations to (Re)Assert Control over Local Matters Now and Not Later," *University of New Brunswick Law Journal* 67 (2016): 211–34.

On internal conflicts in Indigenous communities, see Bruce Miller's work *The Problem of Justice*. Miller argues that the challenges of managing internal diversity in First Nations are often overlooked because communities must first meet state criteria for justifying community-controlled justice programs. These criteria, narrow in scope and homogenizing, then become the narrow framework in which justice programs operate, and they are incapable of addressing power dynamics and the intricacies of Aboriginal cultures in practise. Miller's work significantly influenced my analysis, as has Borrows and Coyle's edited volume, *The Right Relationship*.

On legality and what constitutes a "legal" approach, see Patricia Ewick and Susan Sibley's *The Commonplace of Law: Stories from the Everyday* (Chicago: University of Chicago Press, 1998).

INDEX

Gould, Paul Bradley, 128
Gould, Roy, 28, 48–49
Gould, Steven and Donna, 90
Gracie, John, 147–48
The Grand Chief Donald Marshall Sr.
    (ship), 140
Grand Council of Mi'kmaw Nation:
    about, 67–68; colonization's im-
    pacts, 85–86, 88; dispute resolution,
    68; executive council, 67; grand
    chief, 67, 68; inquiry submissions
    from, 48; inquiry's recommenda-
    tions adopted by, 4; inquiry's re-
    port, response, 53–54; justice and
    leadership historical connections,
    99; KMKNO role, 124; loss of au-
    thority under Indian Act, 88; or-
    ganization levels (national, district,
    local), 67; treaties, 68

Halfpenny MacQuarrie, Laurel, 173–75,
    174(f)
Hamilton, Alvin C., 50
hapenkuituik (vengeance), 78–79, 196.
    See also Mi'kmaw legal principles
Harper, Stephen: setbacks in justice
    reforms, 59, 151–52, 154
Harris, Michael, 191
Harriss, Patricia, 15–17, 29–30, 40–41
harvesting, responsible. *See* responsible
    harvesting (*netukulimk*)
healing circles: about, 143–46; DM's
    circle for conflict (2006), 9, 143–46;
    healing plans, 145–46; interest-
    based approach, 144–45; young
    offenders program, 105. *See also*
    forgiveness; justice and sentencing
    circles; restorative justice
healing processes (*nijkitekek*), 78, 144,
    174
Hickman, T. Alexander, 37

honour and respect (*kepmite'tmnej*),
    67, 184*n*1. *See also* Mi'kmaw legal
    principles
honour songs, 2, 4, 6, 148, 165, 184*n*1
honours for DM. *See* Marshall, Donald
    John, Jr., awards and honours
human rights: historical background,
    87–88; response to inquiry's report,
    59–62; UNDRIP acceptance, 170.
    See also Mi'kmaw legal conscious-
    ness; Mi'kmaw rights

ilsutekek (to make right), 78. *See also*
    restorative justice
independent justice system. *See*
    Mi'kmaw separate justice system
Indian Act: about, 85–89; alcohol
    use, 85–86; amendments, 87–88;
    assimilation, 85; further reading,
    200; legal systems, 85–87; mem-
    bership determination, 85, 103–4,
    124; reserves, 85–89; residential
    schools, 87, 89, 190*n*35. *See also*
    colonialism; Mi'kmaw reserves;
    racism
Indian Advancement Act (1884), 86
Indian Brotherhood, 22–23, 58
Indigenous Blacks and Mi'kmaq
    Initiative, 115, 150–51, 153, 154,
    161, 165
Indigenous Healing and Peace Centre,
    Ottawa, 150
Innocence Canada, 91–92
Inquiry, Marshall. *See* Marshall Inquiry
Island Alternative Measures Society,
    105

Jackson, Michael, 50
JM. *See* McMillan, Leslie Jane
Julian, Gordon, 111
Junior. *See* Marshall, Donald John, Jr.

fines to community, not government, 135–36; KMKNO's framework agreement, 123–26; media coverage, 125; reconciliation, 126–27; right to trade for "necessaries," 116, 118, 152; treaty education, 126–27. *See also* human rights; Marshall, Donald John, Jr., community leadership; *Marshall* case on fishing rights (1994–99); treaties

Mi'kmaw separate justice system: call for decolonized system, 60–62, 156–58; inquiry's conference (1988), 50; inquiry's report, no recommendation for, 59–60; priority area, 160; rationale in inquiry report and *Marshall* decision, 152, 155; vision of MJI role, 101. *See also* courts, decolonized; decolonized, community-based justice

Mi'kmaw Customary Law Program, 137–38, 143, 159

Mi'kmaw Legal Support Network: about, 137, 170; community trust in, 158, 163, 170; court workers, 137; customary law program, 137–38, 143, 159; DM's justice circle (2006), 143; DM's support for, 92; funding, 156, 158, 163, 170; mandate of Mi'kmaq Justice Institute, 55; Marshall Centre for Justice, 173–76; priority of separate system, 160; recent reforms, 170; review of implementation of inquiry's recommendations, 153–54, 156, 158, 161–63; symposium participant (2015), 166; victim support services, 137, 143, 158–59; youth option restructured as (2002), 137

Mi'kmaw Native Friendship Centre, Halifax: DM's safe space, 63; inquiry's report, response, 60–62; MJI participation, 101

Mi'kmawey Mawio'mi. *See* Grand Council of Mi'kmaw Nation

Milgaard, David, 91

Miller, Bruce, 198

missionaries, 76–82

MJI. *See* Mi'kmaq Justice Institute

moose harvests, 122, 125, 138

Mroz, Constable, 12

msit no'kmaq (all my relations), 67. *See also* Mi'kmaw legal principles

murder and customary law, 78–79

murder charges against DM. *See* Marshall, Donald John, Jr., murder charges and wrongful conviction

murder of Sandy Seale. *See* Ebsary, Roy; Seale, Sandy (murder victim)

National Indian Brotherhood, 22–23, 58

Native Council of Nova Scotia: inquiry submission on Mi'kmaw rights, 48; inquiry's report, response, 53–54, 60–62; MJI participation, 97, 98–99, 101; non-Status and off-reserve members, 98

Native Justice in Nova Scotia (Clairmont) (1992), 61

Nepoose, Lester and Wilson, 148

netukulimk. See responsible harvesting (*netukulimk*)

nijkitekek (that which heals), 78, 144, 174. *See also* healing circles; restorative justice

Nimchuk, Crystal (DM's daughter), 139, 141

non-adversarial processes. *See* healing circles; justice and sentencing circles; restorative justice

non-Status Mi'kmaq, 98. *See also* Native Council of Nova Scotia

prison life, DM's. *See* Marshall, Donald John, Jr., prison life (1971–82)

probation and aftercare: inquiry's recommendation (30), 54, 162

The Problem of Justice (Miller), 200

Prosper, Kerry, 113

Prosper, Paul, 149

provincial government: apology to DM (1990), 55; calls for inquiry (1982–86), 34–35; jurisdictional disputes over compensation (1984), 32–33; recent reforms, 169–76; resolution on DM's transplant recovery (2003), 140; response to inquiry's recommendations, 55–56, 57; review of implementation of inquiry's recommendations, 154, 161, 163. *See also* Attorney General, Dept. of; Tripartite Forum

racism: call for inquiry due to, 34–35; colonialism, 154–55; Crown prosecutor's statements, 17; documentation in inquiry's report, 4–5; R. Ebsary's statements, 11; education of settler justice personnel, 160; Indian Act provisions, 85; inquiry's conference (1988), 50; inquiry's findings and research, 39, 46–48; judicial racism, 188n7; racial tensions in Membertou, 14–15; reports on racism in community forums, 157–58; settler justice system, 49–50, 157–58. *See also* colonialism

RCMP, 154, 161, 174. *See also* police

RCMP, DM's murder charges and wrongful conviction: DM as murder suspect, 13; errors in investigation, 19–20, 29, 31; inquiry's findings, 41–42; lack of disclosure to DM's defense counsel, 20; reinvestigation and appeal (1982), 28–30, 42; standing at inquiry, 36. *See also* Marshall, Donald John, Jr., murder charges and wrongful conviction

reconciliation, 9, 170–72. *See also* decolonized, community-based justice; Truth and Reconciliation Commission (TRC)

Reid, John, 115

relations, all my (*msit no'kmaq*), 67. *See also* Mi'kmaw legal principles

reserves, Mi'kmaw. *See* Mi'kmaw reserves

residential schools, 87, 89, 190n35

resource management: co-management programs, 121, 125–26; conservation regulations, 119–20; customary law program, 137–38; dispute resolution, 78–79; further reading, 197; goal of community-based management, 121–22; Indian Act provisions, 86; justice circles with resource as victim, 132–33, 137; KMKNO's framework agreement, 123–26; moose, 122, 125, 138; post-*Marshall* initiatives and resistance, 119–23; spiritual protocols, 78; territorial law, 78, 82, 83; trespass laws, 78. *See also* fishing; justice and sentencing circles; *Marshall* case on fishing rights (1994–99); responsible harvesting (*netukulimk*)

responsible harvesting (*netukulimk*): about, 72; colonization's impacts, 82; customary law projects, 137–38; further reading, 197; justice circles, 133, 136, 137; moose, 125; oral tradition, 73; resurgence after *Marshall*, 118–19; spirituality, 72. *See also* jus-

Law and Society Series

W. Wesley Pue, General Editor

The Law and Society Series explores law as a socially embedded phenomenon. It is premised on the understanding that the conventional division of law from society creates false dichotomies in thinking, scholarship, educational practice, and social life. Books in the series treat law and society as mutually constitutive and seek to bridge scholarship emerging from interdisciplinary engagement of law with disciplines such as politics, social theory, history, political economy, and gender studies.

Recent books in the series include:

Jennifer Tunnicliffe, *Resisting Rights, Canada and the International Bill of Rights, 1947–76* (2019)

L. Jane McMillan, *Truth and Conviction: Donald Marshall Jr. and the Mi'kmaw Quest for Justice* (2018)

Sarah Grayce Marsden, *Enforcing Exclusion: Precarious Migrants and the Law in Canada* (2018)

Jasminka Kalajdzic, *Class Actions in Canada: The Promise and Reality of Access to Justice* (2018)

David Moffette, *Governing Irregular Migration: Bordering Culture, Labour, and Security in Spain* (2018)

Constance Backhouse, *Claire L'Heureux-Dubé: A Life* (2017)

Christopher P. Manfredi and Antonia Maioni, *Health Care and the Charter: Legal Mobilization and Policy Change in Canada* (2017)

Julie Macfarlane, *The New Lawyer: How Clients Are Transforming the Practice of Law*, 2nd ed. (2017)

Annie Bunting and Joel Quirk, eds., *Contemporary Slavery: Popular Rhetoric and Political Practice* (2017)

Larry Savage and Charles W. Smith, *Unions in Court: Organized Labour and the Charter of Rights and Freedoms* (2017)

Allyson M. Lunny, *Debating Hate Crime: Language, Legislatures, and the Law in Canada* (2017)

W. Wesley Pue, *Lawyers' Empire: Legal Professionals and Cultural Authority, 1780–1950* (2016)

For a complete list of the titles in the series, see http://www.ubcpress.ca/law-and-society.